CONFESSIONS OF A
BOOKSELLER

ALSO BY SHAUN BYTHELL

The Diary of a Bookseller

Seven Kinds of People You Find in Bookshops

Remainders of the Day

CONFESSIONS OF A BOOKSELLER

SHAUN BYTHELL

GODINE : Boston

First published in 2020 by
GODINE
Boston, Massachusetts
godine.com

Originally published in Great Britain in 2019 by
Profile Books Ltd

LIBRARY OF CONGRESS CATALOGING-IN-PUBLICATION DATA
Names: Bythell, Shaun, author.
Title: Confessions of a bookseller / Shaun Bythell.
Description: Boston : David R. Godine, Publisher, 2020.
Identifiers: LCCN 2019051062 | ISBN 9781567926644 (hardcover)
| ISBN 978-1-56792-667-5 (ebook)
Subjects: LCSH: Bythell, Shaun. | Book Shop (Wigtown, Scotland) |
Antiquarian booksellers--Scotland--Wigtown--Biography.
| Booksellers and bookselling--Scotland.
Classification: LCC Z325.B97 B968 2020 | DDC 381/.45002092 [B]--dc23
LC record available at https://lccn.loc.gov/2019051062

ISBN 9781567927221 (paperback)

SECOND PRINTING IN PAPERBACK, 2023
Printed in the United States of America

JANUARY 2015

He handled the books with the reverence of a minister opening
the pulpit bible. I had polished the leather that morning till it
gleamed like silk, and Mr Pumpherston's finger-tips rested upon it
as if they were butterflies alighting on a choice flower. He seemed
to purr with pleasure at the contact. The visitor adjusted his
spectacles before he turned over the pages and one could see that Mr
Pumpherston's delight was infectious.

Augustus Muir, *The Intimate Thoughts of John Baxter, Bookseller*
(Methuen & Co., London, 1942)

When Augustus Muir wrote his spoof diary of John Baxter, I
wonder if he was truly aware that this is undoubtedly the best part
of the second-hand book trade, and probably of book-collecting
too: finding and handling something rare and important. I once
had a two-volume set of Francis Grose's *Antiquities of Scotland*,
which, to the person who bought it, was the most important
book imaginable. Grose and Robert Burns met in 1789 and
became friends. Grose asked Burns to write a supernatural tale
to accompany an illustration of Auld Alloway Kirk in *Antiquities
of Scotland*, which he was researching at the time, and thus was
born perhaps Burns's finest poem, 'Tam o' Shanter.' Although
it appeared in two other publications first, Grose's *Antiquities
of Scotland* was the first book in which the poem appeared, and
while it is not of enormous financial worth (the last set I had I
sold for £340), it is an important book to devotees of Burns, in part
owing to the fact that Burns might well never have written 'Tam
o' Shanter' had it not been for Grose's commission. The customer
to whom I sold my copy had travelled down from Ayr when he'd
heard from one of his friends that we had a copy. It was only after
he'd paid that he told me of the Robert Burns connection, and had
he not, I would probably still be ignorant of the fact to this day.

It is an irony of my position that—although I'm surrounded by books every day—most of what I know about them is imparted by customers, the self-same customers whom my first instinct is to discourage from talking.

Muir's description of the way Mr Pumpherston handles the book also resonates: people who deal with rare books regularly visibly handle them differently, making sure to support the boards when opening them so that the hinges don't split, making sure that when the book is removed from the shelf there isn't too much pressure on the headband. Once you've been around rare books for a while, you become acutely aware of people mishandling them.

The pleasure derived from handling books that have introduced something of cultural or scientific significance to the world is undeniably the greatest luxury that this business affords, and few other walks of life—if any—provide such a wealth of opportunity to indulge in this. This is why, every morning, getting out of bed is not in anticipation of a repetitive drudge but in expectation that I may have the chance to hold in my hands a copy of something that first brought to humanity an idea that changed the course of history, whether it be a 1791 copy of *The Rights of Man*, the 1887 English translation of *Das Kapital* or an early edition of Darwin's 1859 *On the Origin of Species by Means of Natural Selection*. This is what it's all about.

THURSDAY, 1 JANUARY

Online orders:
Orders found:

Closed for New Year's Day.

After a lie-in, I cycled to my friend Callum's for his annual New Year party at lunchtime. Left at about 3 p.m. to get back in daylight, lit the fire in the snug and began reading *Miss Lonelyhearts*, by Nathanael West, which had been suggested a couple of weeks ago by a customer who had bought several books that I had also read and enjoyed.

FRIDAY, 2 JANUARY

Online orders: Closed
Orders found:

Spent the morning tidying up, then went for a short walk along the beach at Rigg Bay in the wind and rain with Callum and his partner, Petra, just before dusk. Petra is Austrian, with twin girls who are about ten. She always seems in such a ridiculously happy/hippy mood that it's almost impossible to imagine how she manages it without the assistance of hallucinogenic drugs, but she's wildly eccentric too, so she fits into the human landscape of Wigtown perfectly. As I walked from the van to the shop, the geese were flying over Wigtown to overnight on the salt marsh at the foot of the hill on which the town sits. It's a sight and a sound that never fails to impress, as thousands of them form an almost perfect V-formation as they fly in the thickening darkness in the cold, damp midwinter.

SATURDAY, 3 JANUARY

Online orders: 10
Orders found: 10

Back to normal hours, after a week of opening at 10 a.m. rather than the usual 9 a.m. A grey day, but at least the wind and rain have gone. The end of the festive period is always marked by a sharp fall in the number of customers, but today that feeling of emptiness in the shop was ameliorated by the fact that the first customer was Jeff Mead. Jeff is the Church of Scotland minister for the nearby parish of Kirkinner, and his public persona is probably best summed up by my friend Finn, who once told me that 'Jeff is more comfortable doing funerals than weddings.' This, though, belies his true character, which is mischievous, witty and remarkably intelligent, with a formal theological education. He's close to retirement, and is a large, imposing man. Shortly after I'd bought the shop, back in 2001, he came in for a browse. I'd bought a life-size skeleton which I'd planned to suspend from the ceiling

(I have no idea why, but it's still there, playing a violin) and which I had temporarily placed sitting in one of the armchairs by the fire, with a copy of Richard Dawkins's *The God Delusion* in its bony fingers. I heard a howl of laughter from the depths of the shop, and shortly afterwards Jeff appeared and announced, 'That's how I want to be found when my time comes.'

Telephone call at 11 a.m. from a woman in Ayr. She has books that she wants me to come and look at next week.

On the news this morning was a story about four men who have been abducted from a bookshop in Hong Kong for disseminating literature critical of the Chinese regime. Bookselling can be a perilous business, but mercifully only financially so in Wigtown.

Amazingly, I found all ten of today's orders, which is something of a miracle. Most of them were recently listed and came from the collection of a man who brought in four boxes just before Christmas.

My friend Mary, an antique dealer, brought in a box of fishing prints, and a stuffed badger, which I've put in the shop with a price tag of £100.

Callum and Petra appeared at lunchtime and asked if I was going to the whisky tasting at 4 p.m. in Beltie Books. I told them that I would see how busy the shop was. At 3:30 the shop had been quiet for an hour, and just as I was considering closing early and going to Andrew's whisky tasting, about a dozen people in their twenties and thirties came in. They all bought books.

Till Total £136.50
10 Customers

MONDAY, 5 JANUARY

Online orders: 7
Orders found: 7

Another grey day, and miraculously, another on which I managed to find all the orders.

Patrick from Historic Newspapers dropped in to pick up the pile of overseas orders that had accumulated over the Christmas period. Our domestic mail goes out via Royal Mail, but international orders are cheaper using the courier that Historic Newspapers has a contract with, so we piggy-back on that.

Petra dropped in to ask if she could start a belly-dancing class in the big room upstairs. I'm not sure what sort of uptake she'll have, but I told her that she's welcome to use the room on Friday mornings.

A customer asked for my business card, but I couldn't find one. It must be over a year since I was last asked for a business card. The idea seems charmingly old-fashioned in a world of hyper-connectivity. When I first bought the shop, customers—particularly other book dealers—would regularly leave them, but it just doesn't happen any more, much like the calling cards of Georgian and Victorian times.

A German couple in their fifties browsed for an hour. The woman bought a copy of David Cecil's biography of Jane Austen. As she was paying, she said, 'Very nice to meet you at last,' which seemed a little odd until she explained that the reason they'd come to Wigtown was because she'd read my partner Anna's book, which is—in part—about Wigtown (and me). Shortly after they'd left, a man in an orange boiler suit who'd bought a copy of her *Three Things You Need to Know About Rockets* last week came back in and, inspired by Anna's references to *Moby Dick*, bought a copy of that too.

Tom came round to discuss the project that Anna devised—the Writers' House idea. She wants to set up a company to buy and convert a property on the square and run it as a creative space, with courses on writing, reading and art, in conjunction with Spring Fling (an arts festival in the area which happens every June). He wants to have a brainstorming meeting here in the shop and was looking for suggested names to invite, so I gave him a few. The meeting will be here in the big room where we host the Writers' Retreat during the festival. It's next Friday evening, and he's organised food and wine.

Till Total £87.50
13 Customers

TUESDAY, 6 JANUARY

Online orders: 3
Orders found: 3

All three orders today were for books about railways.

Yet another utterly foul day, though the rain abated in the afternoon. The winter so far seems to have been nothing but heavy rain, driven by strong winds. I don't think we've had a single frost.

In today's inbox:

From: xxxxxxxxxxxx

Subject: the world needs my book

Message Body:

id love to advertise my book with u.
I have written a book that ensures the person you find becomes your life partner, this also removes the need for lying, manipulation and game playing. prevents emotional damage and removes the risk to human life through suicide. by arming people with knowledge about personalities.

The first customer of the day was an elderly woman who wanted to use the shop's telephone to call her daughter-in-law, who had failed to pick her up from the doctor's. The second customer was a balding man with a ponytail who tutted at the price of every single book he picked up.

I found an old blackboard in the cellar and made a frame for it out of an old picture frame. It looks rather nice. I've decided to try to write something amusing on it every day, an endeavour that is doomed to failure as weeks—sometimes months—may pass before a witty thought enters my head. To make it simpler, I picked a quotation from Noël Coward, taken from a book called *Famous Last Words*: 'Goodnight my darlings, I'll see you tomorrow.'

My mother dropped round at about 4 p.m. and talked without interruption for half an hour. Topics covered were the Writers' House idea and a source of potential funding that she's found (she repeated this at least six times), her friends' friends who have a castle in Deeside which is about to fall into the river because of the floods (repeated four times) and the tenants of The Open Book* who left the place in a bit of a mess ('despicable'). It wasn't the most recent occupants, two Spanish women, but another couple (repeated four times).

About twenty minutes after she'd left (with a breezy 'Must dash, goodbye lovey') I looked out of the window and saw her bashed-up VW badly parked in the bus stop, while she busily chatted to someone. When I closed the shop half an hour later she was still there, bending the ear of whoever had the good fortune to bump into her.

Till Total £125.49
11 Customers

WEDNESDAY, 7 JANUARY

Online orders: 1
Orders found: 0

Opened the curtains this morning to see the first sign of the sun in what feels like months.

I spent the first hour of the working day being slowly asphyxiated by a customer's perfume, which I can only assume was manufactured as a particularly unpleasant neurotoxin by a North Korean biochemist in a secret bunker. Kim Jong extremely ill.

Another order came in for a book from the Railway Room. These are always the hardest to find. Railway enthusiasts must not care much for order on their bookshelves.

A woman slightly older than me, I'd guess, came in around 11 a.m. I vaguely recognised her, so when she came to pay for a pile

---

* The Open Book was Anna's idea. Realising she couldn't be the only person who daydreamed about running their own bookshop, she persuaded my parents to buy a shop in the middle of Wigtown, which is run as an Airbnb which anyone can rent in order to experience running a bookshop for a week. It is booked solid for the next three years and attracts visitors from all over the world.

of novels—all of which I'd read and enjoyed—I asked her why she seemed familiar. It turns out that she used to go to the same auction house in Dumfries that I occasionally attend, so we reminisced about all the various characters and questionable activity that inevitably seem to surround auctions. It then emerged that she has a tea room in Rockcliffe (about 35 miles away), so we moaned about customers, and particularly about running a business on your own, and one that people expect to be open when it suits them rather than when it suits you. We have a shared loathing of the tyranny of social obligation in rural communities. She hates having anything planned as much as I do, it appears. And she's just finished reading *Any Human Heart*, one of my favourite books.

I started sorting through the two remaining boxes from the deal before Christmas. Not good shop stock, but all barcoded and in pristine condition—perfect for FBA,* so I processed them and boxed them up ready for 'uplift.' Some surprisingly high prices for paperbacks, but that's the way things have gone since online selling—it is harder to predict the value of a book than it once was.

In the afternoon I had a massive row with a customer over whether Maigret was a fictional French detective (me) or a Belgian surrealist painter (them), after which I telephoned the woman in Ayr whose books I'm supposed to be looking at tomorrow to postpone. She sounded enormously relieved and clearly has yet to go through them and sort the books she wants to keep from those she wants to dispose of.

Till Total £65.49
3 Customers

---

* FBA (Fulfilled by Amazon) is a service Amazon provides where booksellers can store their stock in one of Amazon's warehouses (euphemistically named 'fulfilment centres'). When orders come in for the books, they will package and send them out to customers. Although it solves the problem of not having enough space for books in the shop—as with almost every service that Amazon provides to third-party sellers, it comes at a cost which always leaves you on the brink of wondering whether it is worthwhile. Inevitably their 'charges' will multiply and keep creeping up to the point at which your margin is so tight that it's almost suffocating. But not quite. Parasites prefer to keep their hosts alive.

THURSDAY, 8 JANUARY

Online orders: 3
Orders found: 2

Another sunny day. Two in a row feels like some sort of record, given the weather so far this winter. One of today's orders was for a book called *Minorities in the Arab World*, which will be shipped to a priest in Lebanon.

My mother appeared this afternoon and talked for about half an hour about the door knocker on The Open Book, which apparently has a film of white mould over it. Why this matters, or why she thinks that I need to know, baffles me. She disappeared for five minutes, then returned with Alicia, the Taiwanese woman who is running The Open Book for a week. We arranged to go to the pub for a pint after work. Alicia, it transpires, is not her real name, but she's chosen it because it's simpler while she's in Europe. She's studying in Spain at the moment, and decided that Wigtown would provide her with a welcome break from the warmth and fine food of Spain.

Till Total £42
3 Customers

FRIDAY, 9 JANUARY

Online orders: 5
Orders found: 5

Torrential rain once again. Nicky arrived fashionably late as always. Even her black ski suit couldn't repel the rain—she looked like an angry seal as she pushed the door shut against the wind and rain. Nicky is the sole remaining member of what was once a staff of two full-time and one part-time employees. She is a good friend, although our opinions differ wildly on many things. She is a Jehovah's Witness. I am not religious. She's in her late forties, with two grown-up sons, and is endlessly entertaining. She's also devoted to the shop, and enormously capable. She considers me as an impediment to the success of the business, and consistently ignores my instructions, choosing instead to deal with things as though the shop was her own.

At 9.30 a.m. I put the space heater on in the big room and moved the stereo for Petra's belly-dancing class. I've agreed to let her use the big room above the shop which the elderly ladies use for their art class on Tuesdays. Astonishingly, two people turned up. Once the rhythmic thumping of the activity upstairs had begun, I took the mail to the post office (just across the road), where the counter was manned by William, whose disposition was pretty fairly matched by today's weather. He greeted me as he does everyone, by completely ignoring me and muttering about how much he despises Wigtown and almost everything about it.

At about 10.30, as Petra and her dancers were in full flow, Isabel (who takes care of the shop's finances once a week) came in to do the accounts, and as soon as she heard the banging she stopped in her tracks and looked horrified. When I explained that it was a dance class, and not an orgy, she was visibly relieved. She also offered to take the cash from the till to the bank for me, since I've been stuck alone in the shop for three weeks and unable to get there.

With all the rain, the leaking shop window is dripping incessantly onto the Christmas window display (which was a pretty dismal show at its best) and now looks like a dreary and damp winter flower arrangement.

Three wildfowlers came in. One of them spotted a large, framed Victorian print, *Fishing in Connemara*, which was priced at £40, and said, 'I don't mean to be cheeky, but what's your best price on that?,' so I told him that he could have it for £35. He bought it, and three Robin Ade signed prints which I'd bought from Mary, my antique dealer friend. Nobody has shown any interest in the stuffed badger that I also bought from her, sadly, other than children, who are fascinated by it.

In the evening I went to the pub with Alicia (Taiwan), Gina (New Zealand), Elouise (Australia) and Petra (Austria). I was the only Scot at the table. They're all here working in various pubs and cafés.

Till Total £132.99
5 Customers

SATURDAY, 10 JANUARY

Online orders: 4
Orders found: 3

Cold, grey day. Nicky appeared at 9.08 a.m., blaming the weather for her late arrival. The rain came on again at 10 a.m. and the sound of water dripping into buckets in the shop window began its usual symphony.

As I was filling the log basket, I heard a frog croak in the pond—the first one I've heard since last autumn.

On the way to the post office, I spotted Eric, the Wigtown Buddhist, in his orange robes—a welcome splash of colour on an otherwise grey day. I'm not sure when he moved here, but Wigtown has absorbed him with the amiable indifference it shows to everyone, no matter how incongruous they may appear in a small rural Scottish town.

Nicky spent the day re-arranging things that didn't need to be re-arranged.

After lunch I took down the Christmas decorations from the window displays. The left-hand window was still full of little puddles in places.

Today's blackboard:

> Avoid social interaction: always carry a book.

Very few customers today, and most of them left before lunch. A family appeared at 2 p.m., and I had high hopes that at least one of them would buy something, but they left after ten minutes, empty-handed. No more customers between then and closing.

Till Total £34.49
4 Customers

MONDAY, 12 JANUARY

Online orders: 10
Orders found: 10

Grey, cold day, but dry.

Pleasingly, I found all of the orders this morning. One of them was for a German-language copy of *Mein Kampf*, published when Hitler was still alive. Inside, it was inscribed and contained a postcard—lacking any knowledge of German, I have no idea what any of it means. Still, it sold for £90, to a customer in Germany.

Five customers by 10 a.m., and all bought books. One bought three of Sandy the tattooed pagan's walking sticks. He is one of just a handful of regular customers. He lives near Stranraer and claims to be the most tattooed man in Scotland. He's also a keen (and talented) stick-maker. We have a barter system whereby he gives me sticks in exchange for books, and I sell the sticks in the shop. Must get in touch with Sandy and tell him we need more.

As I was taking today's orders to the post office, William was emerging from its dark recesses for a cigarette. In an unprecedented display of politeness and decency he not only held the door open for me but went as far as to say 'Good morning, Shaun.' Either he's ill or I am.

Till Total £72.50
5 Customers

TUESDAY, 13 JANUARY

Online orders: 2
Orders found: 2

Grey, cold day. The rain began at 10 a.m.

A group of people in their seventies appeared at noon looking for books by Eric Ambler, Geoffrey Household and Eric Linklater. One of them approached the counter and asked me, 'Do you respond to questions?' He bought a biography of Wilfred Thesiger which came from a house in the Borders whose library I bought last year. They were all very flattering about the shop, but disappointed that I didn't have any of the authors they were looking for. The reason isn't that I don't come across them; it's that nobody—until today—has ever asked for them, so I don't buy them when I find them in collections.

As I was on my way to the post office I bumped into the French wildfowlers who used to come and stay in my parents' holiday cottages. We had a brief conversation on the pavement outside the shop. My French is pretty rusty, but we managed to talk for about five minutes. They shot three geese yesterday morning on the saltmarsh. At least, I think that's what they said.

Till Total £17.30
3 Customers

WEDNESDAY, 14 JANUARY

Online orders: 1
Orders found: 1

Clear, cold morning. Ice on the windows for the first time this year.

Andy (window cleaner) appeared at 9.30 a.m. for his cash. Tony, who used to clean the windows once a week, sold the business to Andy a couple of years ago. Andy is slightly less regular with his round. The woman who worked in the shop before I took over—Joyce—had an acerbic wit which seemed to offend everyone but me. She used to refer to Tony as the 'window-smearer,' which, as with most of her observations on life, was unfair.

Joyce—a vocal atheist—once told me that she was convinced the house had a resident ghost, whose presence she had felt on the bottom landing of the stairs on a number of occasions. She assured me that he was benign, and she had even given him a name: George. I have yet to encounter any evidence of this spectre, and suspect that she was trying to wind me up.

The sole order was for a large, heavy book called *Shackleton's Voyages*, a recent title in pristine condition. It sold for £3, and the postage was £13, but it was an Amazon order, so we had to take the hit.

Isabel came in at 11.30 to do the accounts.

The old man with the cowboy hat who huffs and puffs in the erotica section turned up at noon. He is about 6 foot tall, wears black nylon trousers with an inbuilt crease, a husky jacket and—today—a flat cap in place of his beloved cowboy hat. He always makes the unconvincing pretence of being interested in the antiquarian books in front of the counter for the first ten minutes of his visit, and inevitably ends up spending at least an hour in the erotica section. Every few seconds he punctuates the passage of time with a heavy exhalation, a grunt, a sniff or some tuneless whistling. He also drums his fingers on the covers of the books he picks up. Today he told me that he'd had to abandon his car 'on the top' because of the weather and had managed to get a lift to Wigtown. He was supposed to be visiting Christian, the bookbinder (4 miles away), but obviously couldn't without his car. As he rambled at considerable length about this, it transpired that what he was really asking was for the use of the phone so that he could call Christian and let him know he couldn't make it. He hasn't worked out how to use his new mobile phone yet, so I lent him the landline, on which he spent at least twenty minutes chatting to Christian, all the while clicking his pen. Just as I was thinking that this litany of staggering incompetence had run its course, he dropped the phone on the floor, before heading off for a cup of coffee, leaving his bags on the counter behind him. He has a slightly arrogant disposition mixed with a false chumminess, which, when combined, gives the impression that he thinks I want to be his friend and am very lucky that he's considering it.

When he returned from his coffee, he started noisily mauling the books in the antiquarian section then asked for some paper so that he could write down one of the titles to take home with him, presumably to buy it online. He left without buying anything.

Telephone call at 2.15:

> Caller: Have you any books concerning the First World War?
> Me: Yes, we have a few hundred.
> Caller: Are they a fair size?

Till Total £46.50
5 Customers

THURSDAY, 15 JANUARY

Online orders: 4
Orders found: 4

Clear, crisp winter's day, with ice on the pond.

One of today's orders was for a book called *Scottish Castles*. I'd bought it originally as a new book and it had remained on the shelf, unsold, for years. The cover price was £35. The supply of new copies must have dried up, so second-hand ones—now more scarce than ever—have shot up in value. The copy we sold today went for £75.

Alicia from The Open Book appeared at 9.30 a.m. and asked to borrow a bike to cycle to Finn's, so I adjusted one to fit her. It took her an hour and a half to cycle the 8 miles to get there, going into the wind.

Sandy the tattooed pagan appeared at eleven o'clock and asked me to order a copy of Mactaggart's *Scottish Gallovidian Encyclopedia* for his friend Lizzy, whose birthday is on Tuesday. Mactaggart is one of the essential components of every Galloway book collection. The first edition of it was published in 1824, but it was almost immediately withdrawn from sale by the publisher because Mactaggart, the son of a Galloway farmer, had libelled a local dignitary. I've never seen a copy of the first edition, but thankfully enough of them survived for a publisher to reprint it, first in 1876 and again in 1981. It is a valuable record of the Galloway tongue, saved from oblivion by two far-sighted publishers. It is full of utterly wonderful local words and expressions from the Georgian era, many of which survive to this day. Here is one that I had never come across before, but which was clearly in common usage at the time of publication:

> **Cutty-Glies**—a little squat-made female, extremely fond of the male creation, and good at winking or *glying*, hence the name cutty-glies. Poor girl, she frequently suffers much by her natural disposition: to be short and plain, it seems this is the class of females destined by some infernal law to become prostitutes.

In the afternoon I drove to Ayr to look at a book collection. I made the mistake of driving over the hills, which were covered in snow. I now see why the wheezing porn enthusiast from yesterday left his car 'on the top.' I arrived twenty minutes late, to be met by an elderly widow who showed me up four flights of stairs to her flat. The collection consisted largely of modern hardbacks in mint condition, but very little of interest. I took about 10 per cent of it, including one or two interesting antiquarian things and another copy of *Scottish Castles*, the title I sold this morning on Amazon for £75. Wrote her a cheque for £400.

Returned to find Alicia sitting silently in the kitchen while Eliot—the artistic director of the Wigtown Festival, and a good friend—conducted a telephone conversation with his wife and children on speakerphone in front of her. When he eventually finished talking to them, I cooked a Spanish chicken dish and he made patatas bravas. I used one tray. He used three frying pans, two saucepans and almost every herb and spice I had, and failed to wash up a single dish or put anything back where he found it. In fact, after we'd eaten, he sat and watched as Alicia and I tidied up.

Till Total £13.50
2 Customers

FRIDAY, 16 JANUARY

Online orders: 4
Orders found: 3

There was a light dusting of snow on the ground this morning, which Nicky blamed for her late arrival.

The bathroom was occupied until 10 a.m., when Petra's belly-dancing class began. The rhythmic pounding seemed to startle the only customer to darken the doorstep before eleven. She left fairly abruptly upon hearing it. Petra and Alicia had a cup of tea in the sun on the bench in front of the shop afterwards.

In the afternoon I wrote up the AWB (our local booksellers' association) minutes and emailed them to Andrew (treasurer) and Laura (chair) for approval.

Much of the afternoon was occupied with setting up the house for tonight's Writers' House meeting. Tom and Willeke arrived at 4.30 with ten bottles of wine and baskets of snacks. Tom is English and Willeke is Dutch. They moved to a cottage just outside Wigtown a few years ago and being bright, funny and under fifty, they are a welcome addition to the community. I lit the fire in the drawing room and the snug. By six o'clock there were about twenty-five people in the sitting room, drinking and chatting. The meeting lasted until nine, after which Ben and Katie (a French man and German woman who are about to open a gourmet burger business in Wigtown), Tom and Willeke, Eliot, Alicia and I stayed up drinking and chatting in the kitchen. Tom and Willeke stayed overnight.

Nicky promised to open the shop in the morning, knowing full well that tonight would be a late night.

Bed at 2 a.m.

Till Total £17
2 Customers

SATURDAY, 17 JANUARY

Online orders: 1
Orders found: 0

Nicky opened the shop at 8.55 a.m., and I shuffled down shortly afterwards. She spent the morning going through the books in the antiquarian section that we'd listed online and checking prices against books which had been listed subsequently by other people to make sure our prices were competitive. Without exception, we had been undercut on the eighty or so books she checked.

Clear, cold morning. Tom and Willeke appeared at about 9.15 and tidied up the kitchen. Alicia came down about ten minutes later, and Eliot followed shortly after that. Tom and Willeke left at about 10.30, Eliot at 11.15.

Today's bookshop imbroglio:

Customer: Did I leave my tide timetable here?
Me: I've never seen you before.

Customer: Never mind that. Do you sell tide timetables?
Me: No.

Sandy's copy of *The Scottish Gallovidian Encyclopedia* arrived, so I called and left a message on his answerphone.

Captain (the cat) is already nudging the borderline of morbid obesity and is the size of a small child. He now has the bonus of the full thickness of his winter coat upon him, and frequently startles customers who, on feeling what they imagine is a svelte kitten rubbing against their legs in the shop, look down to find something more akin to a fat puma instead.

Till Total £35.50
4 Customers

MONDAY, 19 JANUARY

Online orders: 5
Orders found: 4

Cold, overcast day. One of the orders today was for a book called *Underground Adventures*. There was a scrap of paper—a packing list scribbled by a previous owner—inserted in the first few pages which read:

> Beer
> Tent
> Sleeping bag
> Airbed
> Blankets

The missing book in the orders today was for *Patagonia,* which I sold to one of our few regular local customers, Bum-Bag Dave, last week. I'm not sure why it is still showing as available on Monsoon: I clearly remember delisting it. Another of today's orders was for a biography of Robert Adam, which I listed yesterday. It sold for £100. The next-cheapest copy on Amazon was £400.

Sandy the tattooed pagan turned up to collect his copy of Mactaggart's *Scottish Gallovidian Encyclopedia*, and gave it to Lizzy, who seemed singularly underwhelmed by it. He brought in a box of books to sell which included a copy of *The Fifteenth (Scottish) Division* (1926 edition). Gave him £50 credit.

My mother appeared at 11.30 and talked incessantly on a variety of subjects, ranging from wild speculation about the sexuality of the residents of The Open Book (whom she's having to lunch on Wednesday) to her reasons for clearing the loft ('so that when we're dead and buried, you and your sisters won't have to do all that'). She was here for half an hour, and punctuated every five minutes by saying 'I'll fly off now,' before embarking on another lengthy, rambling aside.

As is often the case in winter, the total paid out today significantly outweighed the day's takings. Today was Blue Monday, supposedly the most depressing day of the year. The till total certainly isn't much to smile about.

Till Total £18
3 Customers

TUESDAY, 20 JANUARY

Online orders: 5
Orders found: 5

Cold, clear day. One of today's orders was for a copy of Putnam's *Blackburn Aircraft since 1909*, which came from a bewigged widow in Leeds over a year ago. Since then we've listed 5,000 books, which makes an average of 16 books listed per day. Not a huge quantity but sufficient, considering all the other jobs which drain time every day.

My father dropped in for a chat. We discussed *Any Human Heart*, which he'd finished on Sunday. He seemed to like it, although he criticised the title for containing the word 'heart,' as it might be off-putting to men. While we were discussing it, an old man came into the shop with a leather bag slung over his shoulder, full of books that he wanted to sell. I picked out a few, mainly erotica and devil-worship, and gave him £25. My father looked less than impressed that I was buying such sordid material.

At 2.30 a woman brought in what she described as 'antique and collectable' books. I understood this to mean books about antiques and collectables, but instead it was a plastic crate full of shabby mid-Victorian era fiction—a genre that is almost unsellable in the shop unless it is by someone well known (Rider Haggard, Oscar Wilde, the Brontës etc.). I bought two purely because they appealed to my puerile sense of humour: *The Sauciest Boy in the Service* and *The Cock-House at Fellgarth*.

A customer came to the counter and asked if we had any miniature books so I directed him to the cabinet labelled 'Miniature Books.' He looked at it, then back at me and said, 'Yes, I've already looked through that.' This often happens—people appear to imagine that we have a secret stash of 'the good stuff' that we don't really want to sell.

Telephone call from a woman in Portpatrick who has books to sell, so I suggested that she bring them over in the morning.

Till Total £32
4 Customers

WEDNESDAY, 21 JANUARY

Online orders: 3
Orders found: 1

Another cold day.

At 1.30 p.m. Emily, the young artist who leases the warehouse at the back of the shop, turned up with the rent for her studio. Nice to have someone finally giving me money, rather than vice versa.

Found a book teaching Germans how to speak English, *Der perfecte Englander*, which included the following:

> 'Well, Sir, if you have done supping, please to stay yet a little and favour us with some anecdotes.' [*You would NEVER invite a stranger to bore you with anecdotes after you've worked in a bookshop for a while.*]
> 'You must observe a strict diet and perspire a good deal. Take, therefore, some cups of elder-tea.'

'My stock of stuffs for pantaloons is well assorted this season.'
'You are very punctual. I wish to be measured for an overcoat.'
'Tell her to wash my shirt and stockings better than the last
time.'

Drove to Newton Stewart for a 3.30 p.m. appointment with
Peter, a solicitor, to write my will. As soon as I left, I felt an abrupt
sense of my own mortality—and wondered whether not having
written a formal will with a solicitor was contributing towards
keeping me alive.

Lit the fire and finished reading *Miss Lonelyhearts*. Brilliantly
funny, dark and tragic, and, for a book published in 1933, surprisingly modern. I don't think I've laughed out loud at a book quite
as much as when I read the letters that Miss Lonelyhearts (a disil-
lusioned, hard-drinking male journalist) receives from his readers.

Till Total £33
2 Customers

THURSDAY, 22 JANUARY

Online orders: 3
Orders found: 1

Sorting through some boxes of books that have piled up in the shop
today, I found a piece of paper in a copy of *Catriona,* Stevenson's
sequel to *Kidnapped*, published by Cassell in 1895. On the paper
was a pencil caricature of a woman. On the back—also in pencil—
was a message saying that the sketch was of Queen Victoria, and
was executed by Lawrence Alma-Tadema in 1900, the year before
Victoria's death. Knowing nothing about Alma-Tadema, I found
a book about Victorian artists among the art section and looked
him up. He was Dutch but settled in England in 1870. He was a
fine painter, mainly of scenes of classical subjects, and I'm rather
embarrassed not to have heard of him. In any case, the date of the
book, the quality of the paper and the subsequent deterioration
in condition appear to confirm the message's veracity. I've put it
on eBay.

Busy day in the shop: two French couples—none of whom appeared to speak a word of English—bought £40 worth of books, all in English.

Till Total £235
4 Customers

FRIDAY, 23 JANUARY

Online orders: 0
Orders found: 0

Sunny morning, but I fired up the gas heater in the big room anyway and moved the stereo in for Petra's dance class. Five people turned up, including Gina, the Kiwi woman who's working in one of the cafés.

Nicky arrived on time, with a wide-eyed look of excitement on her face—'You won't believe what I've got for you.' In nervous terror I guessed that it might be a 'Foodie Friday' treat. (Every Thursday night, after her Jehovah's Witness meeting at Kingdom Hall, Nicky scavenges the supermarket discount shelves in Stranraer.) With undisguised delight she replied, 'You're RIGHT,' before pulling from the pockets of the brown overcoat that she occasionally wears over her ski suit—like a Midwestern gunslinger—two bottles of some alarmingly synthetic-looking beer that she'd found reduced in Lidl.

While they were all thumping around upstairs, I processed the mailing for the Random Book Club, then drove to Newton Stewart to drop the mail sacks off at the sorting office. On the way back the road was blocked on the straight section at Baltersan farm by the dairy herd crossing. I usually try to avoid travelling at this time of day as at around 3 p.m. the cows are moved across the road from the field where they graze to the dairy for milking.

Till Total £85.99
3 Customers

SATURDAY, 24 JANUARY

Online orders: 1
Orders found: 1

Twenty minutes late opening the shop—forgot to set the alarm last night. Fortunately Nicky was here on time to open up, and justifiably berated me for my idleness when I appeared, bleary-eyed and shoeless.

Old friends the brothers Robin and Bernard dropped round at about 11 a.m. and bought some books. Robin always buys books about history and cricket. Bernard is someone I haven't seen for a while. He surprised me by buying several books about the American Civil War, in which it appears he has a keen interest.

One of today's customers—a man in a deerstalker—came in and out of the shop six times in the space of an hour. He didn't buy anything.

Cold day, and it looked like snow was coming, so I told Nicky that she could leave at 4.30.

Till Total £134
14 Customers

MONDAY, 26 JANUARY

Online orders: 7
Orders found: 6

Among the orders this morning was one for Bellenden's two-volume *The History and Chronicles of Scotland*—£225 to a customer in Canada. A good number of the books on Scottish history we list online seem to end up in Canada.

At 9.45 a customer came to the counter and said, 'Graham Greene, Ernest Hemingway, John Steinbeck. First editions. Where?'

When I took today's orders over to the post office, I made a point of saying an effusively friendly 'Hello' to William, who reluctantly reciprocated with an obviously grudging reply. His previously benevolent mood has clearly abandoned him.

Customer: 'I'm looking for a copy of *The History of Rutherglen and East Kilbride*, and a copy of the first *Statistical Account of Scotland*.' We have both in stock, at reasonable prices. He bought neither.

Tonight was Burns Night, so I closed the shop early and went to the co-op to buy haggis, turnip and potatoes, and a bottle of whisky for a Burns supper. Carol-Ann came round with haggis pakoras. She drew the line at drinking whisky, but I had a couple of large glasses of Laphroaig.

Till Total £133.49
8 Customers

TUESDAY, 27 JANUARY

Online orders: 4
Orders found: 2

The wild wind repeatedly blew the door open throughout the day, so I removed the lock plate so that the latch could keep the door closed.

At 10.30 a.m. Callum delivered twelve bags of logs, which should see me through the next three weeks.

An elderly man with a walking stick bought £40 worth of books on a range of subjects. As he was paying, he showed me his stick, which was made from a snooker cue with a snooker ball mounted to the top of it as a handle. He told me that he had come down from Edinburgh to visit his brother, who is convalescing in Newton Stewart hospital. During our lengthy chat he told me that he'd been down two weeks ago to bury his friend Lord Devaird. I was slightly shocked to hear that he'd died, as he was a regular customer, a quiet man with diverse reading tastes. It's often only when someone tells you that one of your regular customers has died that you realise you haven't seen them for some time.

Isabel came in to do the accounts. She couldn't decipher any of the handwriting on my cheque stubs and, to be fair, I struggled to too. Lambing starts next week, so I'll probably see her less frequently now until that's over.

Till Total £60
5 Customers

WEDNESDAY, 28 JANUARY

Online orders: 6
Orders found: 6

All of today's orders were from Amazon; none from Abe.

Clear day with bitter showers. The wind has died down considerably though.

As I was pricing books up, I found a bookplate in an early set of Dickens with the name Fanny Strutt on it. For some reason I imagined the Fanny Strutt being a 1950s American dance craze.

Till Total £21
2 Customers

THURSDAY, 29 JANUARY

Online orders: 4
Orders found: 4

Wet, dull day. The sort that causes me to question why I have chosen to live here.

The Alma-Tadema sketch that I found in the copy of *Catriona* last week sold for £145, about five times what I was expecting. Such is the peculiar way of the second-hand book trade that a scrap of paper found in a 120-year-old book can prove to be worth more than the book itself.

As I was going through the boxes of books from the widow in Ayr (four flights of stairs), I found a pilot's log-book from 1938 and a *QE2* wardroom song book so, following the success of the last RAF notebook, I decided to list them on eBay and googled the name of the pilot in the log-book to see whether he was significant enough to add value to it. His name was John William Mott, and he had been an engineer on the HMS *Exeter* when it had attacked the *Graf Spee* in 1939. The *Exeter* suffered extensive damage and—without any serviceable guns—the captain ordered Mott to steam up and ram the enemy vessel. Luckily for all on board, the *Graf Spee* turned and steamed off towards Montevideo. Mott then managed to guide the vessel to the Falkland Islands and safety. His obituary was in the *Independent*, and makes fascinating reading. He oversaw the construction of the *QE2*, and later went on to manage Culzean Castle, a National Trust property near Ayr, which is where his widow retired following his death.

After work I went for a pint with Callum at the Brig End—a pub down by the River Bladnoch about a mile from Wigtown. We're both invited to Tom and Willeke's for supper tomorrow. Callum is going to drive there, and we'll share a taxi home.

Till Total £49.50
3 Customers

FRIDAY, 30 JANUARY

Online orders: 2
Orders found: 2

Nicky arrived at 8.55 a.m., just as I was switching the lights on. 'Eh, you're up early' was her greeting—fair enough after my lie-in last Saturday. She told me that—despite an extensive search—there was nothing worthy of Foodie Friday in the discount area of Morrisons last night. Considering how low the bar is for Foodie Friday, there must have been nothing but out-of-date dog food in the Morrisons' discount area.

After we'd picked the orders, I dropped off the mail at the post office at eleven o'clock. William studiously ignored me. Perhaps he's embarrassed about his uncharacteristic friendliness of the week before last.

Shortly before five o'clock a customer asked Nicky, 'I'm looking for a book. I don't know what it's called but I read it in school and it was about a koala that keeps stealing jam. Do you have it?' Nicky laughed, pointed at me and said, 'Ask him, I'm away home.' Shortly afterwards, a customer appeared with six boxes of antiquarian books that he told me he'd inherited from his great-aunt. I could see Nicky's interest was piqued, and it was obvious that she wanted to stay and rake through them. I don't think it's possible—once you've worked in the second-hand book trade—to hear from someone that they've got six boxes of antiquarian books and not want to go through them immediately and see what they are, but Nicky has clearly decided that she'd had enough for the day and headed out the door to Bluebottle, her skip of a van.

Callum, Anna and I went to Tom and Willeke's for supper, which turned out to be an extremely entertaining night. Tom and Willeke are more or less self-sufficient when it comes to food, so everything we ate was grown and cooked by Tom. Home at 2.30 a.m.

Till Total £85.50
5 Customers

SATURDAY, 31 JANUARY

Online orders: 2
Orders found: 2

I was an hour late opening the shop. Within five minutes of opening the door, the shop was full. Perhaps this is the secret: inconsistency with opening hours.

Order for book called *Moles and Their Control.*

Callum appeared at 12.30 p.m. and wandered off towards a friend's house, where he thought he might be able to blag a free breakfast.

I dropped off the mail at the post office and picked up a copy of The *Guardian*. I've started to question whether the only reason I buy The *Guardian* is to outrage William's right-wing sensibilities. Every time I buy it, he returns my change, muttering something about woolly liberals, or champagne socialists.

At one o'clock a woman came in with a bag of books, among which was a copy of Ludovic Kennedy's *In Bed with an Elephant* that she'd bought in the shop eight years ago. She made a great fuss about the fact that it had been signed by him. When I checked the dedication on the title page, it read: 'For David and Rosemary with best wishes, Ludovic Kennedy.' David and Rosemary are my parents. He must have given them the book when he was here for the book festival several years ago. They must have given it to John, the previous owner, once they'd read it, and now it has come almost full circle.

Till Total £74
8 Customers

FEBRUARY

About 200 new books are published per week. It's an awful thought. A body would need a deep purse to buy everything he would like to read. The fact is, he doesn't buy. He borrows from a library.

This is the age of circulating libraries. Never before have they done such a thumping trade. I cannot agree with those who say in a deep voice that a book is not worth reading if it isn't worth reading again. I could complete a fat catalogue of the books that are worth reading once only. This is where the public or the private subscription library comes in. Besides, if a man would like to buy a new book, but would prefer to make quite sure of it before he pays good money, he can have a quiet keek through a library copy. I whiles hear folk on the harangue about circulating libraries, and they expect me to agree because I'm a second-hand bookseller. But only a dolt would try to batter down such a useful institution.

Augustus Muir, *The Intimate Thoughts of John Baxter, Bookseller*

From time to time we will come across a small, cheaply produced copy of a book with a sticker—usually on the front—which says 'Boots Library' or, more rarely, 'Mudies Library.' They are usually worthless and go into the recycling, or to the charity shop, but these are the 'circulating' or lending libraries to which Baxter refers. Today is no longer 'the age of circulating libraries,' nor indeed of libraries of any sort. Prior to technological innovations at the end of the nineteenth century that enabled paper, and thus books, to be produced more cheaply, they were an expensive luxury, and only available to the relatively wealthy, and so sprung into existence the circulating library, a service by which—either through subscription or a daily charge—the less wealthy could have access to books. They were commercial enterprises, and enormously popular. Publishers and authors benefited too, as they received a share of the revenue. Their demise came in three waves:

first, the reduced cost of books in the early twentieth century; then the advent of the paperback; and finally, the 1964 Public Libraries and Museums Act, which imposed a duty on local authorities to provide free lending libraries. Boots, the chemist, closed its circulating library in 1966. Scotland's oldest free lending library is Innerpeffray Library, near Crieff, which has been lending books to the public since 1680. I share John Baxter's respect for libraries for similar reasons—if someone reads and enjoys a library book, there's every chance that they'll want to own a copy of that book, so once it has been returned to the library, it's likely that they'll buy a copy. I can't see that libraries could have a significantly negative impact on bookshops. If anything, the reverse. The same argument has been made about e-readers, but I'm not so sure about that.

Baxter would doubtless be astonished to discover that last year in the UK, roughly 3,500 titles were published per week. Arguably this could have a negative impact on the publishing industry—overloading the public with too many titles will inevitably drive down the numbers of an individual title's sales figures—but I suppose it is to be celebrated that so much is being published and, hopefully, read.

MONDAY, 2 FEBRUARY

Online orders: 3
Orders found: 1

Callum came in at 10 a.m. to have a look at the leak in the shop window. During the storms the place was awash from the driving rain.

The wind picked up throughout the day until it became so bad that the Met Office probably ought to have dignified it with a name.

Colette, who's working at The Open Book, dropped in to introduce herself. She's in for a quiet week. I often feel sorry for those who come to run it in December, January and February. If my takings are anything to go by, they'll be lucky to see more than a handful of shivering souls.

Till Total £54.49
3 Customers

TUESDAY, 3 FEBRUARY

Online orders: 8
Orders found: 8

After the storm, a sunny day.

Tom turned up at lunchtime to borrow my shop accounts over the past ten years so that he could produce an analysis of how the credit crunch and the growth of Amazon have affected local retail. It's part of his pitch to raise funds for the Writers' House project.

Sarah from Craigard Gallery (three doors down the street) dropped in two belated Christmas cards, one for Nicky and one for me. Nicky's says, 'Queen of Awesomeness.' Mine says, 'Bah! Humbug!'

The majority of the day was occupied with trying to hammer together the programme for the Spring Festival; a weekend of talks and events organised by the booksellers of Wigtown over the May Bank Holiday.

Closed the shop and went to The Open Book and invited Colette over for supper. She told me that she'd had a great night at the Bladnoch Inn last night, and been the focus of the amorous attention of many of the customers—a large number of whom are farmers who live in rugged isolation.

Bed at 2 a.m.

Till Total £22
4 Customers

WEDNESDAY, 4 FEBRUARY

Online orders: 4
Orders found: 3

Opened the shop, then went upstairs and made a cup of tea at 9.10. Came down the spiral stairs to discover Petra dancing around and singing. She gave me a big hug and told me to look after my chakras before dancing out of the door, singing.

Very few customers, but my favourite customer, Mr Deacon,

appeared just after lunch—his lunch, not mine, the evidence of which had formed a paisley-patterned series of stains down the front of his expensive-looking blue shirt. He asked if we had a biography of David Lloyd George. We didn't. In fact, I sold the last one I had to Roy Hattersley, the retired Labour Party politician much lampooned by *Spitting Image*. He had required it for research into his widely respected biography of David Lloyd George, *The Great Outsider*, published in 2010. I clearly recall the telephone call in which he ordered the book—I knew instantly who it was and made a failed attempt to persuade him to come to Wigtown Book Festival by threatening not to send him the book unless he agreed to be one of our speakers. He never came.

Mr Deacon confided to me last year that he has dementia. Since then I have been worriedly observing him each time he comes to the shop, but so far he seems as usual: somewhat distracted, but a widely interested and voracious reader.

Till Total £47
5 Customers

THURSDAY, 5 FEBRUARY

Online orders: 0
Orders found: 0

After lunch a woman with the bearing of a retired headmistress brought in a box of books. They contained little of any interest, but I picked out two that I thought looked vaguely saleable: a scruffy copy of *Songs of the Hebrides* and an old school atlas. I offered her £10 for them, at which point she snatched them back and stormed off, saying, 'I'll just give them to the charity shop, in that case.'

Tomorrow I'll go to the charity shop and buy them there for £5. There is a type of person who is convinced that everyone is determined to rip them off, and who obviously thinks that, by giving things they've been offered money for free to someone else, they will somehow be punishing the person who offered them the money. This is not how the world works.

I received a telephone call in the afternoon from a woman in the planning department telling me that someone has made a formal complaint about the concrete book spirals at the front of the shop. The spirals are two columns of books, arranged in a helix with an iron rod running through the centre of them, one on each side of the door into the shop. I used to make them from real books, coated in fibreglass resin, but they only lasted a couple of years before needing to be replaced, so I asked Norrie, a former employee, good friend and expert in all things concrete, if he could replace them with concrete 'books.' Possibly the most repeated 'joke' of the many often repeated 'jokes' that customers subject me to is to point at one of the books at the bottom of the column and ask 'Can I have that one?'

The woman from the planning department sounded apologetic and clearly had no personal objections to the spirals but had a process to follow, so she's going to send me a retrospective planning application. She seemed quite positive that it would all go through fine, but that there would be costs attached.

Till Total £139
4 Customers

FRIDAY, 6 FEBRUARY

Online orders: 0
Orders found: 0

Nicky was working in the shop today, a clear, sunny day. She was ten minutes late, as usual, and slung her bag in the middle of the floor of the shop.

As it was Foodie Friday, she produced pakoras and some revolting-looking chocolate pastry thing that could honestly have been anything from an éclair to a body part.

A foreign couple came in just after Nicky. The woman asked, 'So, this is a library?'

Me: No, it's a bookshop.
Woman: So does that mean people can just borrow the
    books?

Me: No, the books are for sale.

Woman: Do you buy the books? Can people just come
with a book and give it to you and take another one
away?

[*will to live seeping away rapidly*]

Woman: Do you sell these old ones over here, or are they
just for display?

We were low on change, so I went to the post office to get some.
Normally Wilma, who works there, is quite happy to oblige on
this front, but today must have been her day off and I was left to
deal with miserable William, who flatly refused my request and
told me, 'We're not a bloody bank.'

After lunch I drove to Ardwell House, near Stranraer (25 miles),
with Anna, my American partner of the last five years, to look at
books. The house belonged to a couple called Francis and Terry
Brewis, both of whom died last year. Terry was the Lord Lieutenant
of Wigtownshire. It's a beautiful large house full of fine furniture
and paintings, and with some interesting antiquarian books on
the shelves, but sadly they weren't the books they wanted to sell.
We picked out about six boxes' worth from the library and gave
Chris, Francis's brother (who has inherited the house), £300. He
asked if we could take away some of the books we didn't want,
so that doubled our load. I will take them to Glasgow and dump
them on Monday when I take Anna to the airport: she's returning
to the States for a while. Sadly, and through no fault of hers, our
relationship hasn't worked out, and despite her love of Wigtown
and the area, and her many friends here, she feels a break from the
place would be a useful thing for her.

The drive back, along the west coast of Luce Bay, with its mix
of shingle beaches and sandy beaches, was stunning with the long
shadows cast by the low winter sun. I could see Anna looking
wistfully across the bay towards the Machars, the landscape she
has inhabited for most of the past seven years.

Nicky stayed the night.

Till Total £83
4 Customers

SATURDAY, 7 FEBRUARY

Online orders: 2
Orders found: 2

Nicky opened the shop, so I had a lie-in until 9.30. When I came downstairs, she had the remains of Foodie Friday's haul on a plate on the counter, and said,o 'Is there any better breakfast than leftover chocolate bomb, pakora and beer?'

I emailed Flo to see if she could cover the shop on Monday morning so that I can drive Anna to Glasgow airport. She assured me that she could, so at least that's sorted. Flo worked in the shop last summer. She's a student at Edinburgh University, and when she's home she's usually happy to help out in the shop if required.

After lunch I went with Anna to Galloway House gardens (an eighteenth-century arboretum about six miles away which leads down to a beach), so that she could enjoy her favourite things in the area before she leaves on Monday. There was a dusting of snow on the ground and the snowdrop flowers were hanging over it, with the wild garlic poking through in patches. Anna is particularly fond of this garden. It was one of the first places we went together when she came here from LA seven years ago. I think the juxta-position of a beautiful garden and a stunning beach appeals to her filmic imagination. She is a film-maker by trade, and whenever we're here, I can see her face change, and I know that in her head she's directing a period drama set in this place.

Email from Anna Dreda reminding me that her Readers' Group is coming up next Sunday. I've offered them the use of the shop and the big room for the week, as February is so quiet it might as well be used. Anna has a bookshop in Much Wenlock in Shropshire, and stayed with me last year with her partner, Hilary, on their way home from a holiday in the Western Isles.

Till Total £349.48
15 Customers

SUNDAY, 8 FEBRUARY

Online orders:
Orders found:

Today was Anna's last day before returning to America, so we went to visit Jessie, who runs the Picture Shop in Wigtown. She has been in hospital for about three weeks, and looked quite frail. We—perhaps optimistically—decided it was her medication rather than failing health that was the cause. Afterwards we returned to the arboretum at Galloway House 'one final time,' where the rhododendron buds are fattening up, ready to flower, then along the deserted beach at Rigg Bay. Home at five o'clock in the thickening winter twilight.

Despite the cultural chasm between rural Scotland and suburban Massachusetts, Anna dropped into life in Wigtown as though she'd been born to it. She has befriended everyone, and her relentless good nature has endeared her to the place and its people. One of her favourite characters is Vincent, who owns the petrol station in town. When she first moved here, she realised that she was going to need a car, so Vincent—famous for his fleet of wrecks—found her a Vauxhall Nova which she adored, and happily drove around in—initially, nervously and painfully slowly (with her face close to the windscreen and her body visibly tense) but latterly at considerable speed and with wild abandon, once she'd grown used to driving on the left. On one occasion she decided to go to the auction in Dumfries on her own (I must have been busy with something) and was almost at the saleroom when she heard a loud metallic noise like an explosion. In panic, she instinctively pulled over to the right, rather than the left, into what could easily have been oncoming traffic. When she got out of the car, she spotted almost the entire exhaust in the middle of the road. She never made it to the auction, but Vincent kindly arranged for her to be picked up by a Dumfries mechanic who repaired the car so that she could drive back to Wigtown.

MONDAY, 9 FEBRUARY

Online orders: 7
Orders found: 6

Up at 7 a.m. to take Anna to Glasgow airport. It was dark, and the wind and rain beat against the van all the way. We bade each other a very tearful farewell. There has been a tension between us for some time, caused entirely by me and a fear of commitment that I don't entirely understand, so we've decided to spend some time apart.

I fear that this may be not just the end of a chapter but the closing of the book for Anna and me. When she first moved here, things seemed perfect: an intelligent, funny, attractive woman who wanted to live in Wigtown and have a life with me. The problem is me, though. I find it hard to see a future except as a cantankerous curmudgeon, living alone. It's not a future that I—or anyone, I suspect—would wish for, but there it is, and to my shame it has caused hurt to Anna and to my family, who embraced her as a daughter and sister.

On the way home I dropped a van load of rotated stock off at the recycling plant. The man who I have to deal with there seems to become more irate every time I visit. Today he was cursing and swearing about having to find me three large plastic tubs into which to deposit the books for recycling. Returned home at 1.30 p.m. to find the shop locked and a message taped to the door from Flo explaining that she had forgotten that she didn't have a key, and consequently had been unable to open the shop, so I opened up and checked the mail. It included the planning application for the concrete spirals, with a demand for £401 to cover the cost of the application. I called Adrian Paterson, a local architect, and asked him if he could deal with the application, since it required scale drawings done to an architectural standard.

At three o'clock an elderly couple came in, the woman clutching a plastic bag to her breast like a feeding infant. Inside, bubble-wrapped, was a copy of Livingstone's *Missionary Travels and Researches in South Africa* (Ward Lock, 1857). She had inherited it from her mother, and they'd been 'watching one of them antiques programmes and someone brought a copy on and it was worth

£10,000.' This is not a scarce book, and when I told them that, and that their copy was only worth about £50, they both looked at me with undisguised contempt, as if I was either a charlatan or a fool. I suspect the copy they saw on television was inscribed by Livingstone. I can't imagine any other reason for it being so highly valued. Books of this period frequently have, as a frontispiece, a portrait of the author, and this is often accompanied underneath by a facsimile of their signature. I've lost count of the number of times customers have tried to sell me 'signed' copies of books that are clearly reproductions of the author's signature.

Bum-Bag Dave called in at 4.55 p.m. He often arrives at inconvenient times. So often, in fact, that I wonder if he makes a point of timing his visits to cause maximum disruption. As always, he was laden with bum-bags and various other forms of luggage. He redeemed himself by buying a book about Fokker aircraft of the First World War. When he opened the door to leave, Captain shot into the room at high speed, leaving Dave looking satisfyingly startled.

Till Total £67.49
6 Customers

TUESDAY, 10 FEBRUARY

Online orders: 3
Orders found: 2

At 10 a.m. I lit the fire in the drawing room above the shop for the old ladies' art class. They meet here every Tuesday during the winter, and paint *en plein air* during the summer.

After lunch I drove to Kirkpatrick Durham, a pretty village about ten miles from Dumfries, to look at some books that a woman had called me about last week. They had belonged to her late husband. The house was a whitewashed cottage at the end of a farm road, and the books were a collection of A. G. Street hardbacks in dust jackets. The woman selling the books seemed reluctant to part with them, as they were clearly her husband's favourite books. He had grown up on a farm in Sussex, she had spent her life in Birmingham, and they'd met on a trip to St Kilda in their fifties. Sadly, he died of cancer two years ago.

A. G. Street was a Wiltshire farmer who wrote about agriculture during the 1930s, and whose works were immensely popular in their time but, like many others, have fallen into relative obscurity. We're still occasionally asked for his books, but the frequency of these requests is decreasing like the intervals of breath of a dying animal. Kirkpatrick Durham too is an interesting place, if for nothing more than the achievement of its most famous son, Kirkpatrick Macmillan. Born there in 1812, Macmillan is credited with inventing the bicycle, an achievement for which he was widely recognised during his lifetime, but for which he took little credit or acclaim, refusing even to patent the invention.

The books weren't in great condition, but I gave her £40 for two boxes and headed home.

My mother dropped in at four o'clock to tell me that Jessie from The Picture Shop died this morning. The gravity of the moment was lightened slightly when my mother decided to tell Elaine, one of the art class (very deaf, and an old friend of my mother), about Jessie's sad demise. I'm not quite sure how, but Elaine misunderstood completely and thought that Jessie was retiring and that Anna was taking over her shop. On hearing what she thought were glad tidings, she announced, 'Oh, that is such wonderful news.'

Just before closing, a man wearing a flamboyant paisley bow tie brought in six boxes of books, mainly hardbacks in excellent condition, with the focus on art and gardening. I told him that I'd go through them and work out a price by tomorrow lunchtime.

Till Total £67.50
4 Customers

WEDNESDAY, 11 FEBRUARY

Online orders: 5
Orders found: 2

At 11 a.m. a tall, thin man with diabolical halitosis appeared at the counter and said, 'Hello Shaun, we've met before. I've got some books to sell.' He then deposited a box of books about cinema on the counter and wandered off, so I went through them and picked out a few. When he returned, I offered him £12 for eight books, at which point he produced a list and started checking each one against it, saying, 'That one's selling for £6 on Amazon, how much are you giving me for that one?' I attempted to explain that, although it might be £6 on Amazon, I would probably be lucky to get £4 for it. I might as well have been explaining particle physics to a chimpanzee. Eventually he left with all the books he'd come in with and a bewildered look on his face. I still have no idea who he was, or where we had previously met.

Among his books, though, was a copy of *This Thing of Darkness*, by Harry Thompson. It's a truly excellent book. A friend gave me a copy about eight years ago. Shortly after I'd finished reading it, and during the Wigtown Book Festival, a visiting author asked me if I had anything in stock about Fitzroy and the *Beagle* (the very subject of *This Thing of Darkness*). I had a look in the relevant sections but we had nothing, so I went upstairs to the Writers' Retreat to let him know. I found him chatting to Fiona Duff, the person who was in charge of the PR and marketing for the festival that year. I waited for a suitable gap in the conversation and told him that we didn't have anything in stock, but that I could strongly recommend *This Thing of Darkness*, at which point Fiona piped up, 'Oh, my husband wrote that.' My relief that I'd said I had enjoyed it was swiftly followed by Fiona embarking on a scathing and detailed description of the end of their relationship.

Very quiet day, even for the time of year, but a huge sense of optimism restored by noticing that—even half an hour after closing the shop—there was still a vestige of daylight in the darkening sky. It's almost worth the miserable, sinking sense of despair of

December to experience the exhilarating elation of emerging from the depths of darkness as February marches on. I remember a few years ago talking with my sister Lulu, who had recently been travelling, about her time in Ecuador, or Peru, or possibly northern Chile. I asked her how she'd enjoyed being there, and contrary to my expectations, she told me that what she had found hardest about being there in summer was the shortness of the days, being so close to the equator. She had longed for the stretching Scottish summer evenings, when the sun sets at 10 p.m. in June, rather than soon after 6 p.m. for most of the year in those countries. Even when I reminded her of the four o'clock December sunsets in Scotland, she assured me that—for her—it was worth it for the pay-off of the endless evenings in the summer.

Till Total £28.49
3 Customers

THURSDAY, 12 FEBRUARY 2015

Online orders:
Orders found:

Opened up as usual, but as I was switching the lights on, I could hear a strange sound from the back of the shop. I followed it until I was close enough to recognise the sound of the flapping of wings and tracked it down to a starling which the accursed cat must have dragged in. It was fine, and it spent the next hour flying around the shop, evading my futile and incompetent attempts to catch it. Eventually, on the top step of a ladder and flailing around with a fishing net, I managed to get hold of it and took it outside and let it go.

The shop computer rebooted overnight, and now Monsoon won't open, so I have no idea if we had any orders. My email to Monsoon requesting assistance was pinged back.

After work I lit the fire in the snug. Looking through my enormous 'To Be Read' pile in the snug, I spotted a copy of *The New Confessions*, by William Boyd, which a friend had given me years ago. I can't imagine it being quite as perfect as *Any Human Heart*, but decided to give it a go.

Till Total £14.30
2 Customers

FRIDAY, 13 FEBRUARY

Online orders: 6
Orders found: 3

Nicky was in the shop today, so I spent a lot of the day tidying up and preparing the house for the people from Shropshire who are coming up for the Readers' Retreat on Sunday. Anna (Wenlock Books) and Emily (who's helping to organise everything) are going to be staying in the house, so Janetta, who cleans the shop and house twice a week, has prepared bedrooms for them. The others are staying in The Ploughman Hotel and the Glaisnock guest house.

At 10 a.m. I had a book deal in a house about two miles from Wigtown. About two thousand books, most of which I didn't want, but they're selling the house and wanted the whole lot cleared, so I boxed them up and took them away, leaving them with a cheque for £750. Some good regimental histories and nice Arthur Rackham illustrated material too. Rackham is one of a handful of illustrators whose work is instantly recognisable and almost universally known. Along with Edmund Dulac, Kay Nielsen, Jessie M. King, Kate Greenaway and a handful of others in the late nineteenth century and early twentieth, they created what is wistfully referred to as the Golden Age of book illustration. Sadly, when you find books illustrated by them, often several—if not all—of the plates have been removed, rendering them practically worthless.

I returned to the shop at two o'clock and unloaded the van. Nicky began going through the boxes, and we played the usual 'Guess how much I paid for them' game. She guessed £200. Perhaps she would be better suited to running the shop than me after all. She stayed the night, and we had a blind beer-tasting session. She still maintains that she doesn't like beers that are named after birds. That didn't stop her from describing a bottle of Corncrake Ale as delicious.

Till Total £57.50
4 Customers

SATURDAY, 14 FEBRUARY

Online orders: 2
Orders found: 2

A clear, still day. Nicky opened the shop.

After work I lit the fire and began re-reading Orwell's *Down and Out in Paris and London*, the Penguin Modern Classics edition. I tend not to re-read books, thinking that my time would be better spent reading something new, but a customer was talking about it just before I closed the shop and I remembered how much I'd enjoyed it, so I picked a copy off the shelf.

There are some titles, and some authors, that as a bookseller you feel you really ought to have on your shelves to differentiate you from the Danielle Steel and Catherine Cookson stock that dominates so many charity shops. And it's not just the obvious classics—Jane Austen, the Brontës, Thomas Hardy, Charles Dickens, Mark Twain and their like. There are books that, as a bookseller, you feel embarrassed to be asked for and not have in stock: Machiavelli's *The Prince*, anything by Hemingway or F. Scott Fitzgerald, Joseph Conrad, J. D. Salinger, Isaak Walton's *The Compleat Angler*, *To Kill a Mockingbird*, *Catch-22*, Milan Kundera's *The Unbearable Lightness of Being*, *Moby Dick*, *Brave New World*, *1984*, *The Go-Between*, anything by Murakami, George Orwell, Virginia Woolf, Daphne du Maurier … The list is endless, but more often than not, when we're asked, we won't have the book the customer is looking for. It's different for shops selling new books: they can pick and choose their stock, provided it's in print. In the second-hand book trade, we're at the mercy of what comes in: we can't 'order' a replacement for *Catcher in the Rye* when the only copy on our shelves has sold. It often feels as though customers consider us to have failed them when we don't have a well-known title in stock, but these are the titles that sell most readily, and replacing them is a matter of sheer luck, depending on when we next chance upon a copy.

It is entirely possible that the reason we never seem to be short of *The Da Vinci Code* and *Fifty Shades of Grey* is that the tendrils of these books don't reach deeply enough into the souls of readers for them to wish to hang on to the books, so they're less reluctant to dispose of them. *The Catcher in the Rye* must surely—over the years since it was first published in 1951—have been published in greater numbers than Dan Brown, but still we don't see them in the same numbers being offered for sale in the second-hand book trade.

Till Total £78
6 Customers

SUNDAY, 15 FEBRUARY

Online orders:
Orders found:

Anna Dreda and Emily from Shropshire arrived at about 4 p.m. The rest of the Readers' Retreat crowd appeared at about six for supper, a vegetarian chilli which Emily had cooked and brought with her. Four of them were staying at The Ploughman, and were really not happy with their accommodation, so I spent about an hour calling around to see if anyone had any spare beds. No luck so far, but I'll try again tomorrow.

One of Anna's Readers' Retreat guests asked me during supper if the house was haunted, possibly shivering through cold rather than fear. I assured her that it was not, and that I was pretty confident that ghosts were nothing more than figments of the imaginations of those who wished them to exist.

MONDAY, 16 FEBRUARY

Online orders: 2
Orders found: 1

Flo was in the shop today. She's the daughter of Jayne, who has the shop next to mine, and has worked for me on and off (largely when it has suited her) over the years. She's a student, and the very embodiment of petulance. The first thing she said—on spotting a dirty rag on the counter—was 'Is that Nicky's scarf?' Her job for the day was to parcel up the random books for this month's mail-out, a job that I used to approach with eager enthusiasm, but which has now become a dull chore.

At 9.30 a.m. I lit the fire in the big room above the shop for the Readers' Retreat and discussed plans for the week with Anna and Emily. Evening meals will be cooked by Emily, as will some lunches, with Maria bringing in the remainder. Maria is an Australian woman who has settled in the area with her husband and children. She runs a small catering business. She bounded in at 9.45, armed with food and equipment and her customary relentless good cheer.

I've managed to resolve the accommodation problem by putting two of the four unhappy Ploughman residents at Beltie Books. The other two are going to sleep here, which means that Anna and Emily will have to vacate their rooms. Emily is going to sleep in the bed in the shop.

Supper here with the twelve from the Retreat, vegetarian shepherd's pie. Up late drinking and chatting. Bed at 1 a.m.

Till Total £378.47
17 Customers

TUESDAY, 17 FEBRUARY

Online orders: 3
Orders found: 2

Flo in the shop again today so I set her the task of setting up mail merge for the Random Book Club spreadsheet.

Me: Flo, have you finished that spreadsheet?
Flo: I've sort of half done it.
Me: Well, you'll sort of half get paid then.
Flo: Fuck off, you should be paying me more.

This is typical of the high esteem in which I'm held by members of staff.

Telephone call after lunch from someone in Edinburgh whose father died recently, leaving 30,000 books, mainly classics. I have arranged to view them on Friday.

Left the shop at 2 p.m. (with Flo in charge again) to look at books in a house near New Abbey, owned by the people who I went to see on my first ever book deal with John Carter, from whom I bought the shop. He kindly accompanied me on my first few buying trips to help ensure I didn't make any catastrophic mistakes. Back then the family selling their books was also selling their home, Kirkconnell House, which had a fine country house library. This time, sadly, the old lady we dealt with had died and her daughter was disposing of the contents of the house she'd moved into after they'd sold the castle. Unfortunately it was mostly rubbish: *Reader's Digest* condensed books, and dozens of books about flower-arranging, that sort of thing. On the way there I stopped to pick up boxes from Galloway Lodge jam factory. Their discarded apple boxes are perfect for books. Ruaridh, who runs Galloway Lodge Preserves, is the younger brother of my childhood friend Christian, and is among the most irreverent of my many rude friends.

Returned home in time to say goodbye to Flo, followed by a meal with the Readers' Retreat guests. Bed at 1.30 a.m.

Till Total £274
23 Customers

WEDNESDAY, 18 FEBRUARY

Online orders: 2
Orders found: 2

The first customer of the day:

> Customer: Do you have a book called *Sports Car Racing 1958 to 1959*?
> Me: Probably not, but you're welcome to have a look in the transport section.
> Customer: Ah, but I bet you've got a special collection of things like that which you don't put on show.

It's astonishing how often customers clearly think that we have the book they're after but—for reasons best known to them alone—we have decided that we don't want to sell it to them. Shortly after I bought the shop, I remember John Carter telling me about an acquaintance of his in the trade who was bemoaning the fact that he couldn't understand why he had £100,000 worth of stock but never seemed to make any money. With his typical pragmatic wisdom John replied, 'You don't want £100,000 worth of stock, you want £100,000 instead.'

A family of five came in at 3 p.m. The children mauled and pawed their way through the books in the antiquarian section in front of their parents before the father spotted the notice requesting that customers handle the books carefully, read it out loud, then finally told them to stop. It's extraordinary that thought didn't enter his head until he'd read the notice. I wonder if he has 'Remember To Breathe' etched onto the inside of the lenses of his glasses.

Supper cooked by Emily: vegetarian curry. I'm starting to crave flesh.

Till Total £273
6 Customers

THURSDAY, 19 FEBRUARY

Online orders: 3
Orders found: 2

Email this morning from an Irish customer who is interested in a
very early Irish railway book we have in stock, dated 1836, asking
what my 'best price' would be. The book is priced at £900. I offered
it to him for £775. He told me that he'd think about it.

On my way up to the kitchen to make a cup of tea, I had the grave
misfortune to be passing an overweight elderly male customer in
grey polyester trousers as he bent over to look at a book on a lower
shelf. That's the first time I've ever seen a visible Y-front line, and
I very much hope it will be the last.

A large man with a beard, ponytail and crutches spent an hour
crashing around the shop, knocking things over, then looking at
me and saying, 'That honestly was nothing to do with me.'

Sara Maitland, author of *A Book of Silence* and many other
excellent books, came to speak to the readers' group this afternoon.
After chatting with her I discovered that my sister used to go out
with her nephew. As she was popping out for a cigarette, she
spotted the Einstein quotation ('Only two things are infinite, the
universe and human stupidity, and I'm not sure about the former')
on the counter and asked, 'Are you sure he said that? It doesn't
sound like the sort of thing he'd have said.'

Supper with readers' group. Bed at 1.30 a.m.

Till Total £184.99
20 Customers

FRIDAY, 20 FEBRUARY

Online orders: 2
Orders found: 2

Nicky worked in the shop this morning. At 10 a.m. Kate the postie
delivered a parcel for her. Kate has a barcode scanner for anything
sent recorded delivery, and it is a constant source of unhappiness for

her. Either it doesn't work or it scans the wrong thing or something else goes wrong with it. Today was no exception. Nicky's parcel contained about ten plastic dolls, which she confessed to having bought from eBay after a few beers. Apparently they're called Bratz, and she disapproves of how over-sexualised they look, so she's intending to redo their make-up and turn them into 'nature girls.'

The Irish railway enthusiast emailed back to say that he wasn't interested in the book at that price as it was 'far too expensive.'

I left Nicky in charge of the shop at noon and drove to Edinburgh to look at the large book collection in a house in the west of the city. The collection had belonged to an academic, and the estate was left to his widow and son, John, both of whom were there when I arrived. It was nearly all classical Greek and Latin material, very hard to sell, and on my estimate, nearer 6,000 than the 30,000 titles John thought they numbered. Among it was some good antiquarian and railway material. I picked out enough for a van load of non-classical shop stock and offered them £600 for that. The widow said that she'd like to get a second opinion before deciding, so I returned empty-handed. Seven hours' driving for nothing.

Thankfully I arrived home in time for supper with the Readers' Retreat group in Beltie Books. Another late night, this time 2 a.m.

Till Total £147
14 Customers

SATURDAY, 21 FEBRUARY

Online orders: 3
Orders found: 2

Nicky opened the shop, so I spent the day repairing things like loose door handles and painting skirting boards.

We sold a book called *Our Friend the Poodle* online. Shortly after I'd found it, a customer came in with a box of books to sell. It was mainly paperback fiction, but there was a first edition of *Three Men in a Boat*. This isn't a rare book—a decent copy sells for around £50—but it was one of my favourite books when I was a teenager, so I gave her £30 for it and put it in my own collection. The Readers' Retreat group left to head back to Shropshire after lunch.

David, a journalist from the *Free Press* (one of the local newspapers), called for an interview about the book spirals and the complaint lodged to the planning department about them. I was careful not to paint a negative picture of the planners and shoot myself in the foot.

After the shop closed, I dismantled the shelves in the gallery (the largest room in the shop) and painted the wall which Callum had insulated before Christmas. I didn't have time to paint it then, so I had just put the shelves back over the drying plaster. I managed to get paint everywhere. I'll put the shelves back up tomorrow.

Till Total £160
19 Customers

MONDAY, 23 FEBRUARY

Online orders: 1
Orders found: 1

Very unusual for there to be only one order on a Monday morning, I'd normally expect six or seven.

Quite often in the winter, if I'm working in the shop, I hear the door open and expect a customer to appear, but at this time of year it is as likely to be a passing local who on seeing Captain, the cat, sitting outside the shop staring at the door handle will open it enough to let him in, then close it behind him. Today it happened three times.

Peter Howie, an engineer from Creetown—across the bay from Wigtown—brought in six boxes of his mother-in-law's books. Went through them. Only about two boxes' worth were of interest, so I offered him £60. One of the more interesting books was a Victorian book of lithographic illustrations of India, but since it had been bound using gutta-percha, the binding had perished and the illustrations had become loose and had been damaged. Most books bound in gutta-percha eventually reach this state; there must be something in its chemical make-up that defies longevity. During the second half of the nineteenth century, gutta-percha (the rubbery sap from the Palaquium tree) was seen as a sort of industrial panacea: it was used to make everything from golf balls to fillings for teeth to electrical insulation (the first transatlantic telegraph cable was insulated in it). It was also used, briefly, in book manufacturing. Traditionally 'gatherings' (huge sheets of paper, with 16 pages printed on them, folded so as to produce 8 leaves in octavo bindings) would be sewn together over cords on the spines to produce books, but it was far quicker (and cheaper) to glue them using gutta-percha. After the discovery of vulcanisation, gutta-percha became all but redundant, but books from this window in history do still occasionally turn up, invariably in the same condition.

My mobile phone charger has become temperamental. Now it only charges when the phone is face down.

Till Total £77.48
8 Customers

TUESDAY, 24 FEBRUARY

Online orders: 1
Orders found: 1

At eleven o'clock a customer came to the counter with a book that was priced at £1. He and his wife then spent four minutes going through all their pockets and purses to scratch the money together. They were 20p short and asked if they could pay the balance on their credit card.

Shortly afterwards there was a telephone call from a customer who had found a book we're selling online for £3, postage £2.80 (Amazon's standard rate): 'Is that really what the postage is going to cost, because I don't particularly want to pay more than the actual cost of postage. Can you do the postage for less if I buy it directly from you? £2.80 seems a bit steep for posting a book.'

The telephone charger is now only working intermittently, even when the phone is face down.

Till Total £203.65
7 Customers

WEDNESDAY, 25 FEBRUARY

Online orders: 7
Orders found: 7

Six out of the seven orders this morning were from Abe, which means that there has been some sort of communication problem between Monsoon and Abe. We sell some books online, mostly through a website called Abe (Advanced Book Exchange). It was set up by some book dealers in Canada, but sadly Amazon bought it in 2008.

While I was eating toast, a customer came to the counter and said, 'Three things: law, philosophy, spirituality.' I complimented him on his numerical skills. He shot me a supercilious look and wandered off.

A customer bought a set of bound *Gallovidian* magazines for £250. *The Gallovidian* was an illustrated quarterly magazine published in the first half of the twentieth century, and is a mine of fascinating information on all manner of subjects written, for the most part, by educated gentlemen of means. Collectors are fewer (and older) than when I bought the shop, but in good condition, copies of *The Gallovidian* are still desirable.

Nicky dropped in to say that she might be late for work on Saturday. Once we had established that, the conversation took a predictably bizarre turn.

> Nicky: I've got two pals who are twins who've been giving
> Bratz dolls makeovers.
> Me: Twins? Are they identical?
> Nicky: Sometimes, aye.

The telephone charger is not working at all now, and there's barely any power left, so I called Vodafone and spent the next hour switching the accursed thing off and back on, changing settings but to no avail. They're sending a replacement tomorrow.

Till Total £293.99
6 Customers

THURSDAY, 26 FEBRUARY

Online orders: 2
Orders found: 2

Glorious sunny day.

The new phone arrived at 9.30 a.m., so inevitably I spent much of the day trying to get all my apps etc. onto it.

Terrible back pain this morning, so I went to the chemist to buy painkillers and received what probably amounts to a hero's welcome in the pharmaceutical industry. I had no idea what it was about until Mae, who works there, mentioned the article about the concrete book spirals in our local newspaper, the *Free Press*. After that a stream of people dropped into the shop to offer sympathy and support. Most booksellers suffer from back pain: the job involves a lot of lifting heavy boxes from the floor, and the inevitable consequence of that is damage to the back.

Till Total £83.39
7 Customers

FRIDAY, 27 FEBRUARY

Online orders: 3
Orders found: 2

Came downstairs at 8.30 a.m. to find a mess of feathers and a dead sparrow on the landing. Captain normally eats what he kills, but he's so fat these days that I wonder why he bothers hunting at all. My friend Carol-Ann gave him to Anna and me about five years ago, and Anna dotes on him with a maternal enthusiasm that borders on the alarming.

Online order for six-volume set called *Canada in the Great War*, nicely bound in red morocco. It sold for £170.

After lunch I went to Vincent's garage to fill up with diesel. Vincent has singularly failed to move with the times over the years, offering lines of credit for fuel which some people took advantage of. He's an incredibly kind man. Recently he was persuaded to install a credit card machine, as people (tourists, mainly) who didn't know that he didn't have one were repeatedly filling up, then having to drive off and get cash to pay for their fuel. The first time I filled up there after the machine had been installed, rather than turn his head away as I typed in my PIN, Vincent kept hold of the machine and asked me what my PIN was, then typed it in himself. He has subsequently learned that it is really for the cardholder to enter the PIN, but he still watches the machine eagerly as customers type their numbers in.

Till Total £24
3 Customers

SATURDAY, 28 FEBRUARY

Online orders: 4
Orders found: 4

Had a lie-in as Nicky opened the shop.

At about 2 p.m. I was chatting to Nicky when a customer came to the counter.

> Customer: This book is £3.50. I want it for £3.
> [*I could see Nicky gritting her teeth*]
> Nicky: No, I'm afraid we can't let it go for that. It's £3.50.
> Customer: Hmm, well, if that's the case, I suppose I'll pay the full price then. Do you have something I can put it in, like a grocery bag?
> Nicky: Yes, you can have a bag, but we have to charge you 5p.

The customer said no, muttered something about being ripped off, then produced a plastic bag from her pocket.

Nicky revealed the Bratz doll which she'd applied a makeover to. It looks exactly like me.

Finished *Down and Out in Paris and London*.

Till Total £292.50
21 Customers

MARCH

I must record that all booksellers are honest. I wouldn't suggest anything different; not for the world. But some are more wide-awake than others. Many a time Mr Pumpherston lets a customer have a bargain, but he's far too clever to tell him so: he always lets the customer discover it for himself, knowing fine he always does. This is the way to get good results.

Augustus Muir, *The Intimate Thoughts of John Baxter, Bookseller*

Augustus Muir is perhaps being unduly generous in his description of all booksellers as 'honest.' There are crooks in this trade, as in every other, but few people enter the book trade with any hope of growing fat on the back of it. Perhaps that is what he meant: it's not a business from which most of us who have chosen it expect enormous financial reward. The benefits come in other shapes. In his book *Bits from an Old Book Shop*, published in 1904, R. M. Williamson observed: 'The few who make fortunes by bookselling are not to be compared to the many who make no more than a modest livelihood. The happiest men in the business are not the wealthiest, but the most contented, the men who love their occupation, who look on it as a high privilege to buy and sell books.'

Oddly, though, it is when I'm buying books that I encounter the greediest people: the person selling his collection who will push to extract every last penny that they're worth from the bookseller they're selling them to, will inevitably be the same customer who will drive the price down to the very margin when he's buying books. And while this is arguably good business sense, it has rather an unsavoury whiff about it. There's no sense of fairness. Conversely, the customer who brings in books to sell and is happy with whatever you offer him will be the one who doesn't attempt to push the price down when he's buying books from you. Like Mr Pumpherston, these are the customers for whom I will happily round the total down from £22 to £20 without their asking, rather than those who demand reductions, pointing out minor defects, such as a small tear to a dust jacket. When I encounter these miserable fiends, my response is always along the lines of 'Yes, there is a tear to the jacket—I factored that in when I was pricing the book. Why should I discount it twice for the same tear?' This usually silences them, but they are the kind of people who won't buy anything unless they feel they've somehow managed to negotiate a bargain. They are the worst kind of people to deal with, and I suspect that this is because, ultimately, it's not about the paltry £1 they're saving, it's about power. It's about them calling the shots, and, whether you're an antique dealer, agricultural supplier or car dealer, it's about the customer feeling that in the dynamic of the exchange they are in charge. They are the people who will demand a 'bulk discount' when they buy two books, who never tip in restaurants, who would boast about going on holiday to a place after a terrorist attack 'because it's cheaper.'

As far as I can see, the trick with buying, if you're a bookseller, is to be fair and consistent. If you acquire a reputation for ripping people off in this trade, word spreads quickly and your supply will dry up. I've walked away from a few deals because a seller has wanted more than I have been prepared to pay, and on most of those occasions they've come back to me having tried several other dealers and been disappointed. Most book dealers are the same when it comes to buying, and I can honestly say that I don't know any who would try to get away with paying a few pounds for a rare and valuable book.

MONDAY, 2 MARCH

Online orders: 7
Orders found: 6

Seven orders, all from Amazon.

At 10 a.m. I had a visit from Jeff, the wild man who lives at the Doon of May—a sort of commune in a forest which he set up years ago. He is both a thoroughly decent man and very anti-establishment in his politics. He looked quite troubled and was pacing about a bit. It turns out that he's been offered a considerable sum of money for the timber on the land he bought for his commune and is now faced with the problem of becoming a capitalist.

There was a half-hour blizzard just after Jeff left. Captain was clearly unexpectedly caught out in it and appeared in the shop covered in snow shortly after it ended.

After lunch a customer came to the counter wielding a book about embroidery and said, 'I don't want to buy this book, but I found it in the philately section, which would seem to me to be entirely the wrong place for it.'

Till Total £68.99
8 Customers

TUESDAY, 3 MARCH

Online orders: 2
Orders found: 1

Only one Amazon order, and no Abe orders again today, so no doubt Monsoon has encountered another technical glitch. With initial enthusiasm (which soon deteriorated into indifference, and has now become extreme reluctance) we began selling books online a few years ago. We use a database called Monsoon, through which we manage our stock, upload to websites and receive orders.

An elderly woman asked, 'Can you get that copy of Mrs Beaton down from that shelf and tell me the price and publication date?' I did as requested, only to be told, 'I have the same edition at home. Now I know what it's worth.' I'm going to introduce a time-waster tax.

Till Total £39.49
5 Customers

WEDNESDAY, 4 MARCH

Online orders: 1
Orders found: 1

Nicky was working in the shop today, so I drove to Glasgow to dump books at the paper recycling plant. Before I left, I asked her to clear the table and do a new window display while I was away.

I arrived at the Smurfit Kappa recycling plant at 2.30 p.m. and dropped off boxes of books from the van into four large square plastic bins (each one can take about twenty boxes). The contents of the bins are emptied onto a conveyor belt, then shredded and baled before being sent to China or Birmingham for recycling, depending on the international price of paper.

Nicky asked me to go to an architectural salvage warehouse since I was in Glasgow to find her some shutters, so once I'd finished recycling the books, I headed off there. Eventually I found the place, after much driving around, during which I accidentally jumped a red light. The salvage warehouse had plenty of shutters, and when I asked what the price was, they told me that they're £75 per pair, so I called Nicky to see if she was happy with that price. She replied 'Eh? What? Have they got the decimal point in the wrong place?' I left empty-handed.

Returned to the shop at six o'clock to find that Nicky had inflicted her customary chaos on the place, with piles of books on the floor, table and even under the table. In a radical departure from her normal behaviour, Nicky had followed instructions and created a new window display, which appeared to be a bewildering assortment of books on golf, cinema and politics.

The combination of five hours' driving and heaving the boxes out of the van hasn't helped my back problems.

The shop has seemed busier than usual this winter, possibly because it has been so mild. Most of our customers are retired and don't like driving in icy conditions, but they don't seem to be put off by rain.

Till Total £61
7 Customers

THURSDAY, 5 MARCH

Online orders: 3
Orders found: 3

Email this morning:

> Hi, I was wondering if you have any books by Paul Barton? I found them on the Internet from Cube Cart. I do not have no credit card so I wrote this fellow last year explaining that I don't have no credit card, asking how I can purchase these books. You know what he did? He sent my letter back didn't even read it, put a bunch of silly nonsense on the outside of the envelope. Not even explaining, no apology, nothing. I think that is very rude! Sounds like he can't be reached. He must be in jail or in some sort of institution. Do you know this man? I have emailed him several times, he has not responded. Maybe he might respond to you. Very odd! Thank you.

I'm not entirely sure how many people would conclude—on receiving an unopened, returned letter—that the intended recipient must be in jail. Several far simpler possible explanations leap to mind, not the least of which is that the person who sent me this email probably ought to be in 'some sort of institution.'

Went into the garden to pick some greenery for a gardening window display and spotted that the chrysanthemum has started to flower. The flowers look gorgeous for about a day, then they begin to turn brown. The soil is too alkaline for it, but it struggles on into flower every year regardless.

The shop computer rebooted overnight, and the anti-virus software has removed something from Monsoon, so now it won't open. I have no idea if we have any orders. Emailed Monsoon, but they're in Portland, Oregon, on the west coast of America, so they're seven hours behind.

Till Total £60.49
8 Customers

FRIDAY, 6 MARCH

Online orders: 2
Orders found: 2

Nicky in. She has hijacked the shop's Facebook page again and left this typically bewildering post:

> Good morning everyone!
>
> With a song in my heart, I skip in to work only to be berated for buying books off a customer for £45, whereas the BGC would have paid £175. Happy customer, happy me, disgruntled tube, sorry, I meant to say 'boss.'

BGC is Nicky's current nickname for me, and stands for Big Ginger Conundrum. 'Tube,' for the uninitiated, is a Scottish insult, the politest interpretation of it being 'idiot.'

One of this morning's orders was for a book called *Moscow Has a Plan*, superb cover design, and I'm sure Mr Putin would be delighted with the title.

Received an email from Monsoon with a Log Me In code so that they can remotely access my computer and fix the problem. Once again, owing to the time difference, this meant that the database was down for most of the day, which meant that Nicky couldn't list our stock online.

Till Total £64.34
7 Customers

SATURDAY, 7 MARCH

Online orders: 0
Orders found: 0

This morning I drove to a house near Maybole (about an hour away) to look at a private library. The books were in a house that I've been to before, owned by a widow. The last time there was some excellent antiquarian material. Today there was nothing much of great value, apart from a 1753 copy of *The Trial of James Stewart*—for what is known in Scotland as The Appin Murder, the story on which Robert Louis Stevenson based *Kidnapped*. Stevenson's father had picked up a copy of the same edition—possibly even the same copy—of *The Trial of James Stewart* in a bookshop in Inverness, and given it to RLS, and from that the seed of what would become *Kidnapped* was planted. Stevenson even obliquely refers to this edition of the book by calling his protagonist (the only important character not based on a real person) David Balfour: *The Trial of James Stewart* was published by Hamilton and Balfour.

In the middle of the afternoon an ex-soldier called Adam Short came to the shop. He's walking anticlockwise around the coast of the UK and has been going for 366 days. He needed a bed for the night, so we put him up in the warehouse, where he seemed delighted, despite the fairly rudimentary conditions. I can't help thinking that timing his trip to be in the north of the UK precisely when the days are shortest and the weather at its worst might not have been the most sensible idea.

Till Total £215.97
17 Customers

MONDAY, 9 MARCH

Online orders: 3
Orders found: 3

I awoke to the sound of howling wind and rain lashing against the bedroom window. When I opened the shop, I noticed that the window was leaking onto the books in the display, so I grabbed some saucepans from the kitchen to catch the drips, then lit the fire and huddled over it for ten minutes in a vain attempt to warm up.

Shortly after I'd opened the shop, a group of about eight youngish people (mid-twenties) came in and wandered about for an hour. Not one of them bought a book.

Tracy (RSPB) came in at 10 a.m. to use the wifi. She spent the morning sitting by the fire looking for jobs.

Till Total £55
7 Customers

TUESDAY, 10 MARCH

Online orders: 2
Orders found: 2

At 9.30 a.m. a vast man in red cords marched into the shop and asked, 'Tell me, is Whithorn open today?' Whithorn is a town of similar size and appearance to Wigtown. It's about 12 miles further down the peninsula. I'm still slightly confused about whether or not a town can be considered open or closed, unless it's under quarantine.

After lunch a couple with two young children came in. The children went straight for a book that came in last year, and which I recently put on a display stand on a table. The book is called *Fausto, impresiones del gaucho Anastasio el Pollo en la representación de esta ópera*, and was published in Buenos Aires in 1951. The fascination for children, though, is that it is an unusually tactile book. It is bound in leather which has been cured, but the hair from the cowhide hasn't been scraped off, making it look like an animal skin, which of course it is. This technique produces what is colloquially known in the trade as a 'hairy binding.'

Today was a warm, sunny day, and shortly before lunchtime a butterfly started to fly around the shop.

Till Total £163.50
8 Customers

WEDNESDAY, 11 MARCH

Online orders: 2
Orders found: 2

Opened the shop to the sound of rain dripping into the window display once again. Buckets etc. in place. Kate the postie delivered the mail, which included a fine and penalty points from Strathclyde Police for jumping a red light in Glasgow last week in my quest for a pair of shutters for Nicky.

That brings me up to ten points. When I first got the new van last year I was unduly thrilled that it had a built-in satnav that provided an estimated time of arrival for journeys. So much so that to alleviate the boredom of long drives to buy books from distant houses, I used to play 'beat-the-satnav' and see how many minutes I could shave off the ETA. This had the unfortunate—but entirely predictable—consequence that I was caught speeding three times. I've had to stop now.

Till Total £134.49
12 Customers

THURSDAY, 12 MARCH

Online orders: 2
Orders found: 2

More torrential rain. The buckets in the window are slowly filling up.

A customer accosted me as I was tidying up the history section, and said, 'I was in here two years ago and you had a book by Roger Penrose. Do you know what happened to it?' There are 100,000 books in the shop, and we probably sell 20,000 books a year. Including rotated stock, books that customers dump on us and the books we've sold over the past fifteen years, I estimate that I must have handled close to a million books. I don't remember Roger Penrose's book.

Telephone call from Anna in the evening. She's clearly missing

Wigtown. We reminisced about the time we went to visit her grandmother in a retirement home in Baltimore and she insisted on taking us out for lunch. Many of the residents there still drove, but with increasingly failing memories and eyesight they often had trouble finding their cars in the home's car park, so when one of them had the bright idea of attaching a plastic toy to the aerial of their car, the others all did the same. It remains one of the strangest sights I've seen: a car park in which every vehicle's aerial was decorated with some sort of child's toy.

Frieda (Bubeh), Anna's maternal grandmother, never lost her Polish accent; even after sixty years in America, she still sounded as though she'd just stepped off the boat with her husband, Max. Both Jewish, they'd survived the war and the Nazi scourge against considerable odds. Bubeh, aged thirteen when the Nazis invaded her small town in rural Poland and rounded up the Jews, had escaped with her sister and spent most of the war on the run, dependent on the kindness of the best of humanity and exposed to the cruelty and vindictiveness of the worst. She ended the war in a work camp before being liberated.

Max, Anna's grandfather, was transported to Auschwitz with his first wife and their two sons. He was separated from them on arrival. He never saw them again. Anna—although she is doubtless unaware of it—bears the legacy of it: sharp shards of sadness occasionally puncture her otherwise eternally optimistic disposition. I see it whenever I look at her, but I wonder if that's just my own sadness for her family's past manifesting itself. Primo Levi, who, along with Anna's grandfather and a few other fortunate souls, survived the concentration camps, witnessed the unbelieving stares of the Soviet liberators who cut the wires of the camp on 27 January 1945. He wrote in *The Drowned and the Saved*: 'Until 1944 there were no children in Auschwitz; they were all killed by gas on arrival. After this date, there began to arrive entire families of Poles arrested at random during the Warsaw insurrection: all of them were tattooed, including new-born babies.' Max's children were aged five and seven, just two of the million estimated to have been killed in Auschwitz.

My maternal grandparents, by contrast, spent the war in rural Ireland, a country so recently freed from the shackles of British dominion that it couldn't even bring itself to recognise the conflict in Europe as a war, preferring instead to refer to it as 'The Emergency.' While hardly living in luxury, they were—at least— in no danger of being executed for who they were.

Till Total £155
10 Customers

FRIDAY, 13 MARCH

Online orders: 2
Orders found: 2

Alarmingly, Nicky was in on the dot of 9 a.m. I had to check my watch three times to make sure it hadn't stopped. Shortly afterwards, Jeff the minister dropped in to trawl through the theology section. He often does this, and inevitably makes disparaging comments about my stock. Nicky's hackles rise when he comes in, but thankfully Jeff is blissfully oblivious to her particular religious predilections.

One good sale today: £220 for two early beautiful leather-bound editions of Lewis Carroll's *Through the Looking-Glass and What Alice Found There* and *Alice's Adventures in Wonderland*. They weren't the more valuable first editions, but they certainly weren't cold on their heels.

As I was going through some boxes of fresh stock, I discovered another RAF observer's log-book from the Second World War. I'll put it on eBay. It won't sell in the shop. These more unusual things tend to disappear into the shelves when they're in the shop, but online they seem to stand out and realise decent prices.

I recently had a copy of *The Little Grey Men*, by BB, published in 1942. On the verso (left-hand page, when you're looking at an open book) of the half-title is a crest that reads BOOK PRODUCTION WAR ECONOMY STANDARD. I think the first time I saw this was on a first edition of *The 39 Steps*, published in 1915, although I may be wrong about that. Certainly, the production values of *The 39 Steps* were not high. The War Economy Standard came into force because of the need to prioritise resources for the war effort, so publishers were forced to cut their paper consumption by 60 per cent, and print size, blank pages, words per page etc. were dictated by the Ministry of Supply. Most books published between 1942 and 1949 will bear the compliance stamp on one of the preliminary pages.

The War Economy Standard is also responsible for a legend in the world of publishing. Pan Books came into existence in part because of the regulations: the rigours and demands of the war meant that cheap paperbacks were more compliant than heavy hardbacks. Pan commissioned Mervyn Peake to design a logo for them, which he duly did—the iconic silhouette of Pan playing the pipes. They offered him two options: a one-off payment of £10 or a percentage of every book sold under the Pan imprint. Graham Greene advised him to take the £10 because he believed that 'the paperback book was just a temporary solution to the paper shortage.' He took Greene's advice, which, it turns out, was a costly mistake.

Denys Watkins-Pitchford wrote and illustrated many natural history books under the pseudonym BB (the size of the shot in a shotgun cartridge used for shooting geese). His books—or, at least, some of them—are highly sought after by collectors, and even for people not interested in the subject matter his writing is engaging and, at times, exquisite. One of my earliest reading memories is of being entranced by a story he wrote for children called *The Pool of the Black Witch*. I couldn't put it down, and the picture he painted with words is still clear today, thirty-five years later. The landscape, the tension and excitement were so rich and real that perhaps, more than anything, that book taught me the joy that reading can bring.

Nicky stayed the night.

Till Total £366.50
9 Customers

SATURDAY, 14 MARCH

Online orders: 2
Orders found: 2

Nicky and I had breakfast together, then she opened the shop, so I went back to bed for an hour.

After lunch there was a telephone call from Maria (who takes care of the catering in the Writers' Retreat during the festival) in as much of a panic as she ever gets (a mild fluster) to ask if she could use the shop as a venue for her pop-up restaurant, the Galloway Supper Club. Apparently the place she had lined up had double-booked so she can't use it. I happily agreed to let her use the shop. The event is next Friday night.

After lunch a customer—an elderly woman—was tutting loudly and complaining in the orange Penguin section of the shop, so I asked her if there was a problem. She embarked on a lengthy complaint about the fact that some of the titles on the spines read from bottom to top, and some from top to bottom, so she kept having to tilt her head in different directions, and told me that I should arrange them all so that the titles could be read from top to bottom. This would mean putting quite a few of them upside down, and since she's the only person ever to have made this complaint, I told her that I wasn't prepared to indulge her request.

As far as I'm aware, there is no convention in the world of publishing as to whether spine titles read in a particular direction. On the whole, they tend to read from top to bottom, with the publisher's name or logo at the base of the spine, but plenty of them read the other way. The only convention seems to be that the publisher's logo appears at the bottom.

Before she left, Nicky gave me a small booklet called *What Does the Bible Really Teach?* Apparently it's standard issue for Jehovah's Witnesses when they're doorstepping people. Her parting words were 'Right, you. I want you to read two paragraphs of that every week. And I'll be testing you next time I see you.'

After she'd gone, I took advantage of the ever-lengthening days and went for a walk down along the old railway line. It's a pretty walk, even from the shop down to the bottom of the hill, past the row of Georgian houses on the sloping Bank Street, then the ruined Norman church with its view south down across the frequently flooded fields, and after that along the railway line, with the salt marsh to the left, heavily populated with thousands of geese at this time of year, waiting for their breeding grounds in Greenland and Iceland to thaw before they migrate north again.

Till Total £165.50
12 Customers

SUNDAY, 15 MARCH

Online orders: 0
Orders found: 0

Phoned Nicky in the morning about searching for a lost ruin near her house. I met her at Whitefield Loch, and we scrambled around looking for the remains of what was once a beautiful Scottish Baronial castle. The house has been totally destroyed apart from part of a wall. She then took me to a beautiful Arts and Crafts house nearby which someone is clearly restoring. When I asked her how she knew about it, she replied, 'One of the perks of being a Witness.'

Afterwards we drove to Knock Fell, the highest point on the peninsula, to look for a chapel which Nicky was convinced would be in good condition. I assured her that it would be no more than a pile of stones. I managed to get the van stuck and had to walk to the nearby farm to seek help. By the time I returned with the farmer's wife in her 4×4 Nicky had found a sheep's skull, which she was proudly displaying on the bumper of the van. After a bit of an effort we managed to get out and head home.

MONDAY, 16 MARCH

Online orders: 3
Orders found: 1

Only found one of the orders. One of those unlocated was a 1970s Highland Region winter bus timetable.

The first customers of the week were a German couple who bought £37 worth of cookery books, mainly by Jamie Oliver.

An American customer came to the counter at 4 p.m. and asked 'Do you have any old maps?'

> Me: Yes, how old?
> Customer: Quite old. What's your oldest book?
> Me: At the moment it's this one here. It was published in 1582.
> Customer: Wow. That's, like, 300 years old.

He was only out by 133 years.

This is the time of year when the River Cree, which flows through nearby Newton Stewart, sees its annual migration of sparling. These are small fish that come up the river with the tide (they're notoriously bad swimmers—a bit of a bummer if you're a fish) for a few hours, just once a year, to spawn. The Cree is the only river on the west coast of Scotland that still has a sparling population, and their appearance is one of the positive signs that we're slowly creeping out of the long winter.

Till Total £179.05
14 Customers

TUESDAY, 17 MARCH

Online orders: 2
Orders found: 2

It was a quiet morning, the peace broken at 11 a.m. by a middle-aged woman in a duffel coat who kept shouting at her husband:

Woman: Barry! … Barry! … Barry!
Barry: Yes dear?
Woman: Barry, have I read *Nineteen Eighty-Four*?

Unsurprisingly, Barry wasn't sure whether or not she had read it, so she decided not to blow £2.50 on a mint Penguin copy, just in case she had.

I listed the RAF observer's log-book on eBay and noticed that the Colwyn Bay bookshop in Wales has clearly failed to sell their stock as a job lot on eBay again at the second attempt, and they've now split it into two smaller lots. Selling shop stock as a single lot is increasingly difficult, as every other dealer will assume that the best of the books have been removed.

Till Total £94.20
9 Customers

WEDNESDAY, 18 MARCH

Online orders: 1
Orders found: 1

By 12.30 p.m. the only person through the door was Kate (the postwoman) with today's mail, which included a parcel for Anna, so the inevitable battle with barcode technology ensued until she eventually managed to scan it.

Spent much of the day packing the random books, mainly selected from the books bought from New Abbey a few weeks ago, which included a box of orange Penguins. Among them was the wonderfully titled *The Breaking of Bumbo*, by Andrew Sinclair.

At about 2 p.m. I needed to get my chequebook to pay a customer for some books that he'd brought in. I'd left it in the van. It was a sunny spring day, and the moment I opened the door of the van I was hit by a foul stench caused by the sheep's skull that Nicky had left in the cab from our adventure on Sunday.

Till Total £44.50
3 Customers

THURSDAY, 19 MARCH

Online orders: 2
Orders found: 1

I spent the morning stamping, labelling and bagging all the books for the Random Book Club, which currently has 176 subscribers.

No Nicky tomorrow, because she's away at a Jehovah's Witness convention this weekend, so I've booked Flo instead. I have two private book collections to look at tomorrow—one in Dumfries, one in Thornhill.

In the evening I set up the big room for Maria's Galloway Supper Club tomorrow night. Twenty-three expected, and so far I've only been able to make space for twenty. I'll do some furniture moving in the morning.

Till Total £131.95
8 Customers

FRIDAY, 20 MARCH

Online orders: 3
Orders found: 3

Flo in at 9 a.m., uncharacteristically punctual for her. Nicky's away at her Jehovah's Witness convention.

I spent the day driving around, looking at the book collections. The first was near Dumfries (50 miles away): a woman who had about a hundred books. I took about forty away and gave her £50, then on to Thornhill (40 miles away), to a beautiful old house. As I drove up the driveway, I could see an elderly man pushing a wheelbarrow, wearing a pair of what appeared to be tight black leather trousers. He and his wife are downsizing, and were utterly charming, keeping me supplied with a steady stream of tea and biscuits. The library contained a good collection of gardening books, including two eighteenth-century herbals, but an awful lot of unsellable books, and many in poor condition. I left with about 200 books. He wanted me to clear the lot, but I ran out of boxes, so I told him that I'll collect the remainder (roughly another 500) the next time I'm passing. The leather trousers still seem remarkably incongruous.

Home at 5.30 to find that Katie, a former employee and now a medical student at Glasgow University, was waiting in the shop. I'd forgotten that she'd said she was coming round for tea at 4.30. Flo had locked her in.

Shortly after Katie had left, Maria and her cohorts turned up to set up for the Galloway Supper Club. I lit the fire and gave the big room a blast from the industrial space heater before the guests started to arrive at 7.30. It was a very entertaining evening, and Maria's food was—as always—exquisite. Crawled into bed at about 1 a.m., once we'd finished clearing up.

Till Total £115.49
8 Customers

SATURDAY, 21 MARCH

Online orders: 1
Orders found: 1

Flo in, and it was a beautiful day, so I spent most of it gardening. The garden behind the shop is a long, fairly narrow maze of lawns, beds and trees. Since I bought the shop in 2001, I have replanted and redesigned most of it, and despite the long, gloomy winters, at this time of year it brings me enormous pleasure as it awakens into spring.

In the evening I checked the emails and found this one from Nicky:

> Oh what a disappointment to make a return visit to IKEA after 18 years, the place was FULL of whinging, squalling toddlers & sold out of the stuff I was so excited about .... HOWEVER, who was at the next checkout ...? None other than the mountaineer Jamie somebody who was stranded on the Eiger (or some other mountain) for days, & lost his climbing partner & his hands & feet. He was buying a plant.

Katie came around again after work, and we watched the final match of the Six Nations rugby tournament. After she left I spotted my copy of *The New Confessions*, which I'd only managed to get fifteen pages into before putting it down behind a pile of other books. Read it for an hour and discovered that—as with *Any Human Heart*—Boyd captures the oppressive nature of boarding-school like nobody else I've read. His description of the narrator running away from school—'It was a fresh cool evening with high, heavy cloud. There was a smell of honey in the air from the sycamores and a woodlark whispered high above us. A dull, bluey light lay over everything'—took me straight back to the age of ten, and the smells and sounds of the summer night when a friend and I briefly escaped my boarding-school in the middle of the night. Unlike Todd, Boyd's protagonist, we were—of course—discovered and returned to captivity.

Till Total £106.30

15 Customers

MONDAY, 23 MARCH

Online orders: 3

Orders found: 2

Order for a book called *Save Your Own Seed*.
Telephone call at 9.30 a.m.:

> Good morning to you, sir. I've got some books I'm interested in selling. I'll read you all the titles and you can tell me what you're going to offer me for them. *Harmsworth's Universal Encyclopedia*, volume I, *Harmsworth's Universal Encyclopedia*, volume II, *Harmsworth's Universal Encyclopedia*, volume III, *Harmsworth's Universal Encyclopedia*, volume IV…

Every time I attempted to interrupt him to tell him that none of them was worth anything, he'd just get louder and carry on reeling out his list of worthless books.

Two elderly customers came in at 11 a.m. and left after five minutes, saying 'Eeeh, you could spend all day in here, couldn't you.' Well, apparently not.

Spent the afternoon listing books on the database to sell online.

At four o'clock a customer appeared at the counter with two books, one priced at £20 and the other at £8.50 and asked 'Will £20 buy the two?'

Till Total £189
13 Customers

TUESDAY, 24 MARCH

Online orders: 3
Orders found: 3

One of the orders was for a book I'd listed yesterday. It's surprising how often this happens.

Till Total £153.39
16 Customers

WEDNESDAY, 25 MARCH

Online orders: 2
Orders found: 1

This morning a customer found a scarce book called *Cairo to Persia and Back*, dated 1933, with beautiful illustrations. We had it priced at £30. He brought it to the counter, slapped it down and said, 'If you're interested, I'll give you a tenner for this book, which I think is vastly overpriced.'

I was far from interested.

Shortly after he'd left, an old man in Lycra cycling trousers, puffer jacket and wide brimmed leather hat came into the shop and headed straight for the antiquarian section, where he spent a lot of time taking books off the shelves, opening them, tutting, then putting them straight back.

By lunch the takings were £2.50.

Telephone call from a woman inquiring about a book called *La vida breve*. She'd seen that we have two copies listed online and asked if I could put them aside. She'll be in on Saturday to 'have a look at them.' I hadn't really looked at our copies when I bought them, but it's a very attractive, cloth-bound privately printed book of poems, all set in this area, with well-executed woodcuts, and printed on handmade paper. Our copies are priced at £100 each.

At closing time I checked the RAF observer's book on eBay—it has four bids, 218 views, thirty watchers and is at £26. One day to go.

Loaded the van with forty boxes of dead/rotated stock to take to the recycling plant in Glasgow tomorrow on the way to a book deal in Hawick.

Till Total £40.50
5 Customers

THURSDAY, 26 MARCH

Online orders: 2
Orders found: 1

Nicky arrived on time, unusually, and immediately told me that I looked like a tramp. As I was reaching up to draw the curtains in the shop, my T-shirt must have exposed a bit of flesh. She told me that she'd 'never seen anything so disgusting' in her life.

In the afternoon, I set off for Hawick for the night so that I can look at two collections of books in private libraries tomorrow morning.

Checked Facebook in the hotel to discover that Nicky had hijacked the shop account again and written the following:

> Dear friends, having been away for 2 weeks, I was happily talking away to the BGC while he ignored me & smoothed down the puffy door-drapes; I was so happy that it took me a minute to realise that the putty/stilton/foxed endpaper effect which was confusing me was his MIDRIFF—in a CROPTOP! YUCK! How distressing is that?

Supper in Hawick, where I attempted to read *The Bankrupt Bookseller Speaks Again* as I worked my way through an enormous bowl of mussels. I say 'attempted to read' because I was competing with the background sound of a very loud Canadian woman regaling a group of people who looked stunned, bored and vaguely afraid in equal measure as she dominated every conversation at their table.

Till Total £199.40
19 Customers

FRIDAY, 27 MARCH

Online orders: 2
Orders found: 1

In the morning I left the hotel at 9.30 a.m. and headed to the first house—a beautiful big country house whose owner was a very well-spoken man called Christopher Ward, a retired journalist and one-time editor of the *Daily Express*. He'd been to Wigtown in his capacity as an author during the festival a couple of years ago. He wrote a biography of his grandfather, who had been a violinist in the band that played on as the *Titanic* sank. The book's called *And the Band Played On*. There were a considerable number of books, mainly modern and in good condition. I advised him to remove everything he wants to keep, then call me in a few months, I'll come and assess what's left. Over a cup of tea we discussed (at length) the state of the publishing industry and the problems facing writers, whose average income is now £11,000, below the Joseph Rowntree Foundation's 'minimum standard of living.' This is something that I hear repeatedly from writers during the book festival, several of whom—twenty years after they embarked on careers in writing—are earning the same as they were back then, and not just in 'real terms,' but in terms of their actual income.

I left Christopher's at 12.30 p.m. and arrived at the next house on my list (an hour early) at 1 p.m. The house belongs to a friend's aunt who was widowed last year. Again, a gorgeous house—this time an old manse—and in beautiful grounds. I took away a few boxes and parted with £300. Nice set of *The Gentleman's Magazine* from the early nineteenth century.

Left Hawick at 2.30 p.m. and got back to the shop at 5.30 to discover Nicky still pottering away. When she (eventually) unlocked the door and let me in, it transpired that she had made the unholiest of messes—even by her appalling standards—and was busily trying to tidy up before I got back. There were books everywhere, pens all over the place, rags on the floor ('I use them for cleaning up the dirty books') and boxes strategically distributed so as to cause as much of a nuisance as possible.

Once Nicky had finished tidying up, I checked the emails and found one from a customer regarding a book, *A Haunted Inheritance: A Story of Modern Mysticism*, which we have priced on Abe at £75: 'Hello, would you consider selling this book at 45 GBP plus shipping, etc? Please let me know your thoughts on this. Thank you in advance.' I replied and told him no, I would not consider selling at that price. That would be a 40 per cent discount, meaning that we'd lose money.

Went to the pub for a pint with Callum after Nicky had gone home and reminisced about the time we canoed down the River Bladnoch, the river that cuts through the land at the base of the hill on which Wigtown sits. It's a gorgeous river, lined with native broadleaf trees, and the higher reaches of it contain some fast-flowing rapids before spilling into the wide flatness of the salt marsh. Callum is always the instigator of these adventures, and he'd managed to borrow a canoe for me from a friend. On a warm summer's day we navigated our way down without incident until we got to a particularly fast section and I managed to put a hole in my canoe. Or, more accurately, Callum's friend's canoe. From then on it was a question of seeing how far I could get before I sank and had to upturn the canoe and empty it. Fortunately the distillery and the pub were less than a mile away, so it wasn't too tortuous a final leg.

Till Total £127.78
18 Customers

SATURDAY, 28 MARCH

Online orders: 2
Orders found: 1

Typically, of the two orders, the one I couldn't find was the more expensive, a £50 book about Mohammed.

In one corner of the shop we have a few shelves of small antiques: jewellery, decanters, ornaments, that sort of thing. There's a little sign that says Antiques above it. A man came to the counter with two unpriced penknives from there and asked, 'How much for them two? I got them from your junk shelves over there.' Oh, customer-beating stick, where art thou?

Checked eBay to see what the RAF log-book made. To my surprise it was £156.09.

The customer who had asked me to put aside our two copies of *La vida breve* came in with her husband. I gave her both copies to look at. They spent an hour poring over them, then left, saying 'We'll have a think about it,' which, as every bookseller knows, is code for 'they're too expensive.'

This afternoon I discovered that Nicky has reinstated her 'Homefront' shelf, despite clear instructions not to do so. A year ago she discovered a box of romantic fiction set during the First World War and decided to invent a genre of her own—'Homefront novels'—none of which sold, so I told her that I didn't want to see them again. They kept reappearing over the year, and I kept removing them. I've replaced it with a shelf of green Penguins. Penguin has always been an innovative publisher, and the simple, elegant covers—a single colour with a white band through the middle—as well as their reputation for publishing good books make them still sought after. Each colour on the distinctive covers denotes a different subject, so orange is (usually) fiction, green is crime (the best-selling of the Penguins in my shop), purple is biography, black is classics, pink is travel, and so on.

After lunch I received an email from an Italian woman:

Dear Sirs,

I would write this mail hoping to not disturb. My name is

Emanuela Maranci and I am an Italian student at the University of Turin. I studied cinema and arts and I am looking for a job (even occasional, at the moment). In these years of study and sacrifice I had the privilege to observe closely books world, experience that allowed me to understand the true value of every page and every word written. Especially the job in Film and Resistance National Archive required more skills: having to make a Catalog dedicated to Italian Cinema of 1964, I was involved in the research and selection of articles (also digital), research material in magazines, organization of layout with use of Photoshop (also useful to improve the quality of some articles damages by the passage of time). I am twenty-five years old, and I feel I must do something in my life, because, unfortunately, study is not enough. Expand my knowledge, work in contact with books, in a country like Britain, would be a real dream. You need a help?

Thank you for your time and consideration. CV attached.

Respectfully yours,
Emanuela Maranci

I'll reply tomorrow and see if she's prepared to work in the shop in exchange for bed and board.

An enormous man with a tiny dog (smaller than Captain) spent half an hour in the erotica section before relocating to the theology section.

Till Total £268.94
18 Customers

MONDAY, 30 MARCH

Online orders: 3
Orders found: 3

The clocks went forward last night, but I forgot to change the time on the alarm clock so I was half an hour late opening.

The shop was busy all morning, so it must be school holidays.

Among the usual mountain of Monday morning emails was one from the man who wanted the £75 book for £45 asking me to counter-offer. I told him that £60 was the least I could let the book go for and still make a profit.

Before lunch I spotted that Nicky had taped a bit of paper over the 'Follow us on Twitter' sticker which is on one of the glass panels in the door. Further investigation revealed that she'd tried to pick it off and made a complete mess of it, so had stuck something over it in the hope that I wouldn't notice.

I replied to Emanuela, the Italian woman who had emailed looking for work, and told her that I have already agreed to take someone on for the summer, but she's welcome to come and work if she doesn't mind not being paid. I've never done this before and feel deeply uncomfortable about it, but I can't afford two sets of wages.

Till Total £114.98
15 Customers

TUESDAY, 31 MARCH

Online orders: 2
Orders found: 2

Wild, windy day, showers and glorious sunshine in equal balance. I was reminded of Anna's favourite comment on the weather at this time of year: 'April showers bring Mayflowers, and what do Mayflowers bring? Pilgrims.' I suppose it must be a New England thing, and similar to our 'March comes in like a lion and goes out like a lamb.'

Both orders today were from Amazon.

The customer who wanted the £75 book for £40 replied agreeing to pay the £60 as long as it included shipping to America. I replied that he could not have the shipping for free as I'd already explained about my margin, and that if he looked online he'd find that the only other copy available was £250.

A customer came in at 9.15 and hovered about the place, looking as though she was about to ask a question, and making it impossible for me to go and make the cup of tea that I was desperately in need of.

The place was full of more screaming children rampaging through the shop throughout the day.

Just before closing, a customer brought in four bags of wild-fowling books. He left his number and I said I'd work out a price and get back to him.

Till Total £138.54
23 Customers

APRIL

When she described the second-hand bookshop where he had
worked for the best years of his life I was able to tell her that I knew
her husband quite well, for I had been in the habit at one time of
browsing among the bookshops in that maze of narrow streets near
the Old University buildings in Edinburgh. At one time there were
a considerable number of these shops: a number which has now, alas,
been much reduced.

Augustus Muir, *The Intimate Thoughts of John Baxter, Bookseller*

If Augustus Muir, who wrote these words in his spoof diary of
Baxter in 1942, could have foreseen quite how much more significantly the number of bookshops would be reduced in the decade
following 2005, he would doubtless have been horrified; their
number has almost halved in the UK since that date, and this is
the tenth year in a row that has seen a decline.

Those who have weathered the storm of the advance of online
technology have largely done so because they've adapted, or
diversified, or because their original business model is impervious
to the vagaries of changes in shopping habits, like the established
top-end antiquarian bookshops—Maggs, Harrington, Jonkers
and their like—whose customers tend to not feel the ravages of
economic cycles in quite the same way as those of us considerably
lower down the economic food chain. And, by way of green shoots,
there are still independent bookshops opening up: perhaps the best-
known of these in the past few years has been Mr B's Emporium
of Reading Delights, which opened in Bath in 2006, and whose
owner, Nic Bottomley, is happy to concede that the considerable
tourist footfall of the city lends itself to the continuing success of the
business. That, though, is not to detract from the innovative ideas
that have sprung from his opening the shop, such as customised
reading lists and a 'reading spa.' These are the threads which it

seems most surviving bookshops have woven in common—making the bookshop an 'experience' and offering something fresh and different, which online shopping can never provide, whether it's a café or a model railway running through the shop (Barter Books), or Sarah Henshaw's amazing Book Barge, or having regular live events, such as stand-up comedy, poetry or music. Customers expect more, and unless bookshops continue to offer more, our numbers will continue to dwindle. My own business has survived in part because of the Random Book Club, whose members receive a book a month from my stock but have no control over what they will receive, and while this generates a good deal of extra work for me, it saved the business a few years ago.

WEDNESDAY, 1 APRIL

Online orders: 2
Orders found: 2

Both of today's orders are Abe. None from Amazon.

Kate the postie delivered the mail at 10 a.m. It included a letter from Dumfries Infirmary confirming the appointment for an MRI scan on my back at 12.45 p.m. on 14 April.

Emanuela, the Italian woman who emailed me about working in the shop, replied to say that she'd be delighted to work for free in exchange for bed and board. I spent the day thinking about it. I have grown quite accustomed to my privacy and space, so I spoke to Callum about the possibility of converting the back of the Garden Room (a remote part of the shop which generates very few sales) into a self-contained bothy.* We worked out that the cost of doing it would be recouped in saved wages within two months. It would originally have been living-quarters for a member of staff when the house was home to George McHaffie and his family, who built it in about 1830.

Sandy McCreath, a local farmer, dropped in to discuss an idea

---

* Traditionally a bothy is a small cottage used to house farmworkers, but in recent years it has become more associated with renovated crofts in the mountains, used as refuges for climbers and hill walkers.

he's had for getting four farmers to keep a video diary for a year and make a series about the reality of farming, rather than the sanitised version as portrayed on *Countryfile*.

The first customers of the day, a family of four, arrived at 11.30 and stayed for about ten minutes before leaving empty-handed.

I went through the wildfowling books that came in yesterday, which I'd neglected to value. Their condition wasn't great, but there were some reasonable books among them. Ten years ago I'd have bitten his hand off for this lot, but now prices for shooting books seem to be in free fall, as is demand. I think a price of £200 is fair in today's market. It would have been double that a decade ago.

A customer with a ponytail that stuck out near the crown of his head leaving a sort of mullet-style around his neck bought a bookshop bag. I thought twice about selling him one, as I suspect seeing him with it might put more people off than it attracts.

Till Total £287.47
25 Customers

THURSDAY, 2 APRIL

Online orders: 4
Orders found: 4

Four orders, all Amazon.

Beautiful sunny day.

Kate the postie delivered a letter from Anthony Parker of Dumfries asking if I can look at his books as he's moving into a care home. I have another book deal in Dumfries tomorrow, so will try to tie it in with that.

At 11 a.m. an old woman brandishing a Scottish National Party badge haggled over an old hardback copy of *Pinocchio* in pristine condition. It was £4.50. 'You can't honestly expect me to pay that, not in these straitened times.' It clearly hadn't occurred to her that bookshops are more exposed than most to the strictures of 'straitened times.'

Three people brought boxes of books in, nearly all rubbish. It's that time of year when people start to clear out, move house and spring clean, so we're invariably inundated with books in March and April.

I worked my way through the boxes of books that Nicky had bought in East Kilbride (she happened to be up there at exactly the time someone called to tell me they had books to sell, so she did the deal on my behalf). They were mostly in very grubby condition, but that could as likely be from spending two weeks in Nicky's van as anything else. I still have twenty boxes in my van from the Hawick deals to unload, and the shop is piling up with boxes of books.

After I'd closed the shop, I replied to Emanuela, asking her when she thought she might be able to start.

Till Total £98.50
8 Customers

FRIDAY, 3 APRIL

Online orders: 2
Orders found: 1

Good Friday, Bank Holiday. Thankfully Nicky is happy to work on Bank Holidays and came in to 'help.' In fact, so oblivious is she to holidays of any kind—even religious ones—that I can call on her pretty much any time, and if she's free, she'll come in.

This morning I telephoned the man who'd brought in the wildfowling books and offered him £200 for them. He wasn't happy, and had clearly been expecting a lot more. In fact, he said that someone had offered him £250 two years ago for just one of the books in the collection. I suspect this may have been a ploy to push me to increase my offer—I'd checked them all against online prices to reach our figure, and among them there was no book which was anywhere near £250. So either he was lying to try to get more from me, or—if he was genuinely offered £250 for the book two years ago—he was greedy and thought he could get more.

Either way he's lost out. He's going to collect them on Tuesday.

Wildfowling is a reasonably popular sport around these parts; the creek-riven flats of the salt marsh at the bottom of the hill that Wigtown perches on are a huge habitat for geese in winter, and often—after squatting in the muddy trenches as dawn breaks—wildfowlers come into the shop dragging clods of clay on their boots. They always ask for wildfowling books but never buy any of our stock of them, claiming that they're overpriced, yet when they wish to sell their own books, they expect me to pay considerably more than they're worth. It's rare that people selling their books don't accept what I'm prepared to offer, except with wildfowlers, who seem to have a hugely inflated sense of their value.

After lunch I went to view the library of Anthony Parker, who had written to me to ask if I'd come and buy his books as he's moving into a care home. As I drove up the rough farm track to his remote cottage I realised that I'd been there before several years previously and had bought books from him back then. His wife had been alive then, and he had been quite mobile. Today he was alone. His sight was deteriorating daily, and he could only shuffle about using a frame which he had clearly made himself out of an old wooden trolley with two walking sticks gaffer-taped to it. It was an impressively utilitarian contraption with shelves and wheels. He's moving to Surrey to a care home nearer his children. He turns ninety tomorrow. I bought a box of books from him and about fifty Ordnance Survey maps.

I made it back home at about 5.30 p.m. and went to the pub with Callum and Tracy, who I hadn't seen in quite a while. She's been busily job-hunting, but there's so little industry in the area that most people I know work for themselves.

Checked the emails when I returned from the pub later and found one from Emanuela asking if she can start on 2 July, to which I readily agreed. Now I have to deal with the problem of converting the Garden Room. There are probably two thousand books in there, and I have nowhere to store them. I'll have to get the place ready before she arrives.

Cloda and Leo arrived from Ireland at 11 p.m. with their baby, Elsa. Bed at about 2 a.m. Cloda is an Irish friend who I met when

I lived in Bristol. She's a pharmacist and now lives in Dublin with Leo, her Argentine partner. We often share stories about customers, although hers tend to be of a slightly more criminal disposition than mine, frequently stealing narcotics or attempting armed robbery.

Till Total £228
22 Customers

SATURDAY, 4 APRIL

Online orders: 0
Orders found: 0

Nicky was in again today, and the sun was shining. Cloda and Elsa were up and in the kitchen when I came down.

Today was the first Wigtown market of the year. There seemed to be better stalls than in previous years. The market runs from April to October, and is a motley affair with stalls selling everything from country music CDs and tartan travel rugs to locally grown vegetables.

Just after lunch there was a telephone call from someone in Castle Douglas with a northern English accent who wants to bring some banana boxes of books over on Tuesday. 'I've only just moved here, how do I get to Wigtown?' Getting to places in Galloway is pretty straightforward: it's a thinly populated place with few roads, so I just told him to aim west.

Went to the Steam Packet in the Isle of Whithorn for lunch, with Cloda, Leo, Callum and his friend Murray, and Murray's girlfriend Vivien. The Isle of Whithorn is a beautiful fishing village about 15 miles away, and the Steam Packet is an excellent pub on the harbourside. Visitors always ask why it's called 'the Isle' when it isn't, in fact, an island. Local lore has it that it was once an island, separated from the mainland by a shallow sandbank, and shallow-drafted smuggling boats being pursued by customs vessels in the eighteenth and nineteenth centuries would—if the tide was right—head for the sound between the Isle and the mainland.

They could cross it, but the deeper-drafted customs boats would run aground, so the authorities built a causeway connecting the Isle to the mainland to prevent such smuggling escapades. Much as I like the colourfulness of this explanation, I would question its veracity.

The shop was refreshingly busy all day. People start to emerge from hibernation at this time of year, and the movable feast of Easter always brings visitors to the town.

Till Total £672.93
52 Customers

MONDAY, 6 APRIL

Online orders: 3
Orders found: 2

Easter Bank Holiday.

Cold, grey morning, with a thick sea mist over the town, but an abundance of customers—mainly families with young children and not spending any money. A very different day from Saturday.

I couldn't find one of the orders: *Two Sons of Galloway* by McKerlie. I've had a few copies of this, but they must be scarce online as this one sold for £120. One of the other orders was for a two-volume set, *The Works of Lucy Hutchinson*, which sold for £152, which slightly makes up for the lack of the McKerlie, and is a vast improvement on our usual average online sale of £7.

Two Sons of Galloway is a title that raises the issue of identity for me. Locals around here don't describe themselves as 'coming from' a place; they say that they 'belong to' a place, as if it owns them, rather than the other way around. Janetta (who keeps the shop and the house clean and tidy) has lived in Wigtown for most of her life, but she would say that she 'belongs' to Mochrum, a tiny village about 8 miles away. Growing up here with an Irish mother and an English father, I've always felt that—despite being born in Galloway—I could never really say that I 'belong' here. Not because I don't feel that I do, more because there's a sense among others that to be entitled to say that, you have to have several generations of Gallovidians behind you before you're permitted to feel that sense of identification with the place.

Many years ago, when I was helping my father with the 'clipping' (sheep shearing), one of the clippers—a man called Lesley Drysdale—asked my father how long he'd lived in Galloway. He replied that he and my mother had been here for twenty years. The clipper told him that in another five years he'd have served enough time to be considered 'settled.' It's a strangely displacing sensation, the feeling that—in the place that feels more like home than anywhere else—others see you as not belonging there. The rolling drumlins, the meandering rivers and the rugged coastline of the Machars are so integral to my sense of self that I suspect that if I was living anywhere else, I would feel that part of me was absent.

By two o'clock the mist had burned off, and the sun came through, at which point the customers deserted the shop for the hills and beaches. I didn't see anyone after three o'clock.

I cycled to my parents' house (six miles) after work, as my sister Vikki was down visiting them with her husband, Alex, and their three daughters. Made it back home at around 11 p.m.

Till Total £155.49
19 Customers

TUESDAY, 7 APRIL

Online orders: 0
Orders found: 0

No orders again today. This is extremely unusual under any circumstances, but twice in three days, and over the holiday period, leads me to suspect that Monsoon is having problems again.

Awoke with a rheumy and productive cold. I wonder which one of the ill-behaved snotty brats in the shop over the Easter period was kind enough to share that particular virus with me.

At 9.45 a.m. a short fat man appeared clutching a piece of

paper. He came nervously to the counter and asked, 'Have I got the right place?' He turned out to be the banana box man who had telephoned on Saturday. He brought the boxes in, whispered conspiratorially 'Where's the nearest public toilet?', then scampered off to find it.

I spent twenty minutes going through the six boxes. All the books were in pristine condition and an extremely unusual mix of subjects: predominantly transport, pest control (twelve books) and the Pierrepoint family of executioners. We agreed a price of £120.

In the afternoon, after I'd priced up and shelved the banana box books, I started going through boxes I'd bought from the house in Hawick two weeks ago and came across a handsome 25-volume set of the Swanston edition of Stevenson, limited edition. Unfortunately there isn't space for it in the shop, so I've listed it on eBay.

Email from someone wishing to dispose of her late father's books:

> I know some of the hunting books have a fair amount of resale value and I need to generate as much off the books as I can—just as you want to pay as little as possible! There will always be a compromise position.

I feel vaguely insulted that this complete stranger's perception of me is of an almost criminal mendicant.

Vikki and Alex came to the shop with the girls, the youngest of whom, Lily, proceeded to chase Captain around the place, and insisted on climbing into the window display at the front of the shop. It wasn't long before there was a squabble over a tube of Pringles, and the other two joined in and generally made themselves as irritating as they could possibly manage. I have no idea how Vikki puts up with it. She maintains that any combination of two of them is fine, but add a third in and the mix becomes volatile.

Two people asked to pay for £1.50 purchases with credit cards. Up until recently—and in line with many other businesses—we refused to accept credit cards for purchases under £10. This was in part because it is a bit of a pain, and also because we incur a small charge from the bank, but since Transport for London introduced contactless payment on the Tube in 2014 an increasing number of people seem to find it acceptable to pay for even the smallest of transactions this way. I suppose we will have to adapt to the inevitability of the cashless society.

By closing there was still no sign of the man who said he'd collect his wildfowling books today, so I went for a pint with Callum and Tracy, who has finally managed to get a job interview. She's going to Turnberry to apply for a receptionist's job. Despite his best efforts, most of the people of south-west Scotland refuse to refer to the hotel and golf course as the egomaniacally renamed 'Trump Turnberry.' I suspect his proposed refit of the hotel will turn the place into a monument to diabolical taste. My old housemate Martin and I used to exchange Christmas presents when he lived here. One year—by total chance—we both gave one another a copy of a book by Peter York called *Dictators' Homes*. I have no doubt that Donald Trump uses it for designing interiors like normal people would use Terence Conran's *House Book*.

Till Total £162.89
17 Customers

WEDNESDAY, 8 APRIL

Online orders: 6
Orders found: 5

One of the orders was for three books, one of which was brought in by the banana box man yesterday—*Outrage*, by Ian Nairn, an unusual book. Nairn was an architectural critic who coined the word 'subtopia.' One person ordering three books online means that the total number of books that went out today was eight: total value £99. Unusually high for our online sales, but it compensates for the two zero days we've had in the past week.

At 10 a.m. a young Italian woman came in to discuss life in a bookshop for an article she's writing for a blog. While we were chatting about the hardships facing bookshops today, a customer was browsing and came to the counter with three books. The total was £23. He said, 'You'll do them for £20, won't you.' The Italian woman's jaw dropped in disbelief. Which reminds me, haven't heard from Emanuela for a while. Perhaps she has changed her mind about coming to Scotland.

A young woman spent a long time in the erotica section, and bought five books from it. This is a refreshing change from the bearded men in polyester trousers who normally haunt this particular section.

Till Total £293.27
30 Customers

THURSDAY, 9 APRIL

Online orders: 3
Orders found: 3

This morning I was pricing up and putting out recently acquired stock when I spotted the missing McKerlie *Two Sons of Galloway*. Fortunately I hadn't cancelled the order from Monday as I suspected the book was around somewhere. A customer must have picked it up, read it, then returned it to a different shelf. Sadly, this is far from uncommon.

Email from Emanuela:

Shaun,

I don't know how to thanks you for your help. Tomorrow I'm going to book the flight (July 2)

I'm very happy.

Emanuela

Also in today's inbox was this from someone who is after some Penguin books:

Hello,

I'm getting married next month and we're having a bit of a Penguin book theme.

We're going to have some Penguin books at the reception
venue as decoration. We have managed to get hold of
some orange books online, but need to get a few more, as
well as some other colours—greens, blues, yellows, lilacs
etc. We really want the iconic solid background with white/
cream horizontal stripe across the middle.

Is this something you might be able to help with? We're not
in Scotland so would need to arrange delivery.

Ideally, we'd probably look at getting another 5 orange books,
then 20–25 of other various colours.

The internal condition of the books is unimportant and if
they're a bit battered on the outside, providing they're in
one piece and not too faded, would be fine. We're prepared
to pay 20–25 pence per book.

It's interesting to note that in this sort of situation, because they
just see the books as place mats, or decoration, or whatever they're
going to use them for, people see the books as being relatively
worthless. Why would I sell books that I can get £2.50 each for
one-tenth of that?

Just after lunch a well spoken teenage girl rushed excitedly to
the counter and said, 'This bookshop is amazing, I've just bumped
into my best friend's cousin here. She lives in Dundee and we live
in Newcastle.' There really does seem to be a serendipity about
bookshops, not just with finding books you never knew existed, or
that you've been searching for for years, but with people too. Often
customers—not locals—will bump into people they know from a
totally different walk of life in the shop. I've overheard dozens of
conversations along these lines.

At 4.45 p.m. a thin man with a wispy beard appeared and
wandered about the shop, making the occasional grunting noise,
and seemed to be engaged in a wrestling contest with his cardigan.
It wasn't clear whether he was trying to put it on or remove it. He
left twenty minutes later, empty-handed, with one arm in a sleeve
and the other not.

By closing there was still no sign of the man who'd brought in the wildfowling books, so I telephoned him to remind him that they're cluttering up the shop. He's going to pick them up on Saturday now. The shop is groaning under the weight of boxes of books that have come in recently, and his books are not only in the way but in danger of being priced up and shelved, or thrown out.

Till Total £432.20
16 Customers

FRIDAY, 10 APRIL

Online orders: 4
Orders found: 4

Nicky appeared at 9.10 a.m. She immediately started raking through the boxes of stock I've earmarked for recycling, and taking books out and putting them back on the shelves. Then, when I was upstairs making her a cup of tea, she spent £60 of my money on three ex-library books that a customer brought in to sell.

In the inbox today was this email from an Amazon customer:

Im looking for a book but I can't remember the title.

Its around about 1951.

Part of the story line is about a cart of apples being upset, that's all I know, its for a friend who I want to surprise.

Can you help please?

Kind regards

As I was pricing up books, I came across Shirley Jackson's *The Haunting of Hill House*, a book that several people have recommended. Flicking through it, I came across this passage and was reminded of Joyce's assertion that The Bookshop is haunted:

There is a manor in Scotland, infested with poltergeists, where as many as seventeen spontaneous fires have broken out in one day: poltergeists like to turn people out of bed violently by tipping the bed end over end, and I remember the case of a minister who was forced to leave his home because he was tormented, day after day, by a poltergeist who hurled at his head hymn books stolen from a rival church.

Closed the shop ten minutes early and went to the pub with Callum and a few others.

Till Total £177.99
17 Customers

SATURDAY, 11 APRIL

Online orders: 2
Orders found: 1

No Nicky today. I forget what her reason was, but it was predictably bizarre. I think it may have involved either her pet rabbit or her cat. Or possibly both. The missing order today was for a £40 book about the clearance of Raasay which Nicky listed recently. I searched the surrounding shelves but could find no sign of it.

At 10.30 Callum turned up for a cup of tea. He was in town to pick up his car, which he had driven to the pub last night. After a few pints he decided that it was prudent to cycle home.

Shortly after Callum had arrived, Fenella and her children turned up for a chat, shortly followed by Tris. Fenella and Tris are friends I've known since childhood. Although I knew them both from an early age, they didn't know each other particularly well, which is unusual in a place so thinly populated. We decamped to the kitchen as the shop was filling up with customers, so I left Callum in charge of tea duties and returned to the shop as they all chatted and caught up with one another in the kitchen.

The man who'd brought the wildfowling books in came to collect them just after noon. I helped him load them into his car. He reappeared five minutes later angrily claiming that *Snowden Slights*, the most valuable of the books, wasn't there. I asked him if he'd mind looking again while I looked through the shop's stock in case it had been accidentally priced up and shelved. Five minutes later he reappeared clutching the book apologetically.

A customer brought in a leather bag full of books and asked if he could have credit in the shop in exchange for them, so I fished out a few and offered him £20 credit for them. The rest were Alexander McCall Smith—stock that is increasingly appearing in almost every box or bag that customers bring in and which is selling poorly—like most best-sellers—in the second-hand book business.

At 4 p.m. a man arrived with a carload of books. They were mainly unsellable, but I found two interesting titles among them: *Marijuana Potency* and *Marijuana Botany*. I already know which of my customers is going to buy them.

Till Total £316.87
36 Customers

MONDAY, 13 APRIL

Online orders: 4
Orders found: 4

Today's best order was for a Frank Brangwyn illustrated *Rubaiyat*, at £75.

By 11.20 a.m. there hadn't been a single person through the door—not even Kate, the postie.

I read the letter from Dumfries Infirmary about the MRI scan again. There's a questionnaire about general health which included a question about piercings. At the bottom there was an instruction that read, 'If you answered "yes" to any of these questions please telephone the MRI unit before your appointment,' so I called them and explained that I have a piercing. The specialist advised me to find a magnet and see whether or not it responds to a magnetic force. If it does, then it will be ripped from my body when the MRI passes over it. Slight cause for concern, so I searched the house but couldn't find a magnet.

An old man approached me as I was pricing up stock and asked, 'I wonder if you can help me, I'm looking for self-help books.' I'm almost certain that he failed to see the irony, so I asked him what sort of self-help books he was looking for, to which he replied, 'I don't know.'

At four o'clock the telephone rang. It was a woman who'd tried to buy a book that we have listed on Amazon, but her computer had crashed during the process, so she thought she'd do it over the phone instead. I took down her name, address, credit card details and telephone number. After the call, as I was manually inputting her card information to the machine, I couldn't understand why it consistently failed to complete the transaction until I finally realised that I'd typed her telephone number in instead of her card number.

Just before closing, an elderly couple brought in an old family Bible. These are rarely worth anything, even in good condition. Almost every household had one in the Victorian age, and there is no demand for them whatsoever, as far as I can see. The only Bible I've had that has proved to have some value, and been relatively easy to sell, has been the 'Breeches Bible,' an edition of the Geneva Bible published in 1579 (preceding the King James Bible), and so known because Genesis Chapter III Verse 7 reads: 'Then the eies of them both were opened, and they knew that they were naked, and they sewed figge tree leaves together, and made themselves breeches.'

Till Total £130.29
15 Customers

TUESDAY, 14 APRIL

Online orders: 3
Orders found: 3

Flo was working in the shop today, as I needed cover for the MRI scan on my back. I left Wigtown at 10 a.m. and drove to Dumfries. After much searching I managed to find a magnet in Homebase. Uncertain whether or not the piercing would prove to be magnetic, I bought a pair of pliers too, just in case I needed to remove it, then drove to the Infirmary and found the MRI unit. There was nobody there, so I went into the loo with the pliers and magnet. The piercing appeared to be unresponsive to the magnet, so I left it in, then waited a very nervous half-hour before I was summoned, given a hospital robe and asked all the questions on the question-naire another two times, each by a different person. Eventually I went into the room where the scanner was and was slid slowly into the coffin-like machine, unable to move for the next twenty minutes while the thing made hideous noises, like some sort of machine from *Doctor Who*, all the while terrified that my piercing might prove to be magnetic after all.

I left Dumfries at about 2 p.m. and was back in the shop by 3 p.m. to find Flo sitting reading a book, surrounded by boxes of books that customers had brought in to sell. One day I must take the time to teach her about the business, so that it doesn't all fall to me and Nicky.

> Flo: The takings always go up when I'm working in the shop.
> Me: It's not because you're here, it's because I'm NOT here.

Till Total £297.08
22 Customers

WEDNESDAY, 15 APRIL

Online orders: 1
Orders found: 1

Telephone call at 8.20 a.m. from Radio Scotland. They wanted to do a piece about people using bookshops as a browsing facility, then buying books online. They called again at 10 a.m. and I contributed to a live chat with Sara Sheridan, a writer who by coincidence was my landlady when I was at university in Dublin. I was shaking nervously throughout the whole thing—I have a paralysing fear of public speaking and I hate doing live radio. No doubt I came over as a complete moron—certainly from the tone of the texts and emails that the show was receiving live and reading out there were plenty of people who felt that browsing in shops, then buying online was a perfectly acceptable thing to do.

A family of four came into the shop after lunch. The mother

looked at me and said, 'So you've finished being on the radio for the day, have you? We were listening to it in the car on the way over here.' They browsed and bought a few books. As she was paying for them, she told me that we'd met when I was a child. We'd been on a family holiday to visit some friends in Jersey when I was ten, and she'd been their *au pair*. I refrained from reminding her that our host had a rule that women had to be topless in the swimming pool, and hers had been the first breasts that I'd ever seen.

I had totally forgotten that I'd listed the Swanston set of Stevenson on eBay. I hadn't bothered putting a reserve on it. It sold for £20, a dismal figure for a complete set of this limited-edition Stevenson. I've unquestionably lost money on it, but I suppose if that's what the market is prepared to pay for it, then that's all it's worth, and it was taking up a lot of space in the shop.

In the afternoon I noticed a young girl staring up at the skeleton that is suspended from the ceiling in the gallery in the shop. Her mother told me that she refused to walk underneath it. The girl asked me if it had a name, something that nobody has asked before and which I'd never considered, so I asked her what she thought its name should be. She instantly replied 'Skelly,' which, coincidentally is how Stuart Kelly (literary critic, writer and Wigtown Book Festival institution) is referred to by his cohorts.

A very tall American couple came in late, just as I was contemplating closing early. She bought a book. As they left (at 4.55), she asked, 'Is there anywhere around here we can grab a late lunch?' It's hard enough to get lunch at lunchtime in Wigtown, let alone at nearly five o'clock.

Callum called to say that he's going climbing in the Highlands tomorrow, so I emailed Nicky to see if she can cover so that I can get away for a couple of days.

Closed up and went for a pint with Tracy, who had a job interview at Turnberry today.

Till Total £146
15 Customers

THURSDAY, 16 APRIL

Online orders: 3
Orders found: 2

Nicky came in to cover so that I could get away for a couple of days. Callum arrived at 9 a.m., so I packed my climbing gear and we headed off, arriving at Lochinver at 5 p.m., at the same time as Murray and Vivien, two of Callum's friends, who are joining us. Callum and I usually share a room on these trips.

Till Total £200.99
18 Customers

FRIDAY, 17 APRIL

Online orders: 4
Orders found: 3

The four of us set off from our B&B at 8.30 and headed for Suilven. On the walk we discussed the possibility of Callum doing the work to convert the Garden Room into a bothy in which Emanuela can stay during the summer. He seemed quite keen on the idea. We will have to start a.s.a.p. if it's going to be ready in time.

Till Total £205
16 Customers

SATURDAY, 18 APRIL 2015

Online orders: 3
Orders found: 3

Spent an exhilarating but exhausting day walking in the mountains of Assynt, in glorious sunshine in shorts and T-shirts.

Till Total £337.92
29 Customers

MONDAY, 20 APRIL

Online orders: 3

Orders found: 1

Callum and I drove back down from Lochinver yesterday. Arrived back home at 6 p.m.

Today was another beautiful, sunny spring day.

Monsoon appears to have stopped working again; the anti-virus software keeps mistaking it for some sort of infection and removing essential parts of it so that it won't open.

Nicky left a note of her activities during my absence:

Bought some books

Turned some away

Swept outside

Emptied shelves in Railway Room

Brought Heraldry in from Garden Room

Entertained Captain

Attended to lovely customers suffering from diarrhoea

Smiled at everyone

Processed boxes

So, did very little as always

Dealt with many numpties

Took down ALL the Biggles books for a lovely old man

Listened to Mr Needy again

Lots & lots of swooning customers absolutely ADORING the shop.

There were a few other comments, but litigation would be hot on my heels if I included them.

Monsoon eventually replied to my emails with a Log Me In pin and took over my computer and fixed the problem.

An older man in trousers that were clearly designed to be worn by someone considerably younger than he was spent a while staring at the antiquarian section saying, 'If only these books could talk, and tell us of the things they've seen.'

Till Total £74.50

9 Customers

TUESDAY, 21 APRIL

Online orders: 0
Orders found: 0

No orders, but yet another glorious sunny day. Jeff called in at 10 a.m. He was on his way to the funeral of one of his parishioners, but as a friend rather than in his capacity as a cleric. 'Aye, she was one of the better ones,' he remarked sombrely as he left. He normally drops in when he's waiting to pick up a prescription from the chemist, and is usually in a light-hearted mood, but today was different.

At eleven o'clock a customer came to the counter, demanded my attention and said, 'There's a bigger bookshop than this one in Alnwick,' then walked out. Customers often mention Barter Books in Alnwick in comparison to my shop. I've never been, but really ought to visit. As well as its superb reputation as a bookshop, it deserves recognition (or eternity in the fires of Hades) for the discovery of the now ubiquitous 'Keep Calm and Carry On' Second World War poster, which the owner found in a box of books he'd bought at auction.

Sandy the tattooed pagan came in with seven new sticks, so I notched up £42 credit in his ledger. While I was chatting to him, a customer came to the counter with three books and told me that he'd always 'had a relationship' with books, and asked me what my relationship with books was. I was unable to answer—I couldn't really think what to say, or what it was, other than as the objects that I buy and sell. There's much more to it than that though.

Mr Deacon called in to order a book about Henry IV. It's been some time since I've seen him, and he seemed his usual self, despite the recent, uncharacteristically candid revelation that he has Alzheimer's. After we'd discussed the details of the book he wished to order, another regular customer, known to the staff here as 'Mole-Man,' came in and spent his customary £35 on a diverse range of books. I attempted to engage him in conversation, but he wasn't having any of it. Mole-Man is like Mr Deacon's shorter, impecunious, myopic cousin: patchily shaven, and dressed in polyester rather than the silk of a QC, but no less rapacious in his thirst for knowledge than Mr Deacon—in fact, if anything, more so. He burrows and ferrets his way silently through the shop, almost invisibly, before popping up at the counter, dishevelled and blinking through milk-bottle glasses. The pile of books he brings to the counter is always eclectic in subject matter, and rarely consists of fewer than ten books. But, unlike Mr Deacon, he never speaks or makes eye contact. He hasn't uttered a single word in our transactions in the five years or so that he has been a customer, and he always pays with cash, which he wrestles eagerly from his battered, tatty leather wallet. He is, unlike Mr Deacon, small in height, and—apart from occasional moments during his tunnelling exercises through the shop—I've only ever been able to see the top half of his face when he comes to the counter to pay. I don't know his name, and I doubt very much whether he knows—or cares—to know mine. He is, I imagine, an inveterate reader who has indulged his passion for reading at the expense of learning rudimentary social skills. I like him enormously. I have no idea why he comes to Wigtown; perhaps he has family here. I don't suppose I'll ever know.

There was a new review of the shop on Facebook this morning from a customer called Jenna Fergus. I don't even remember her.

> I am totally disgusted at how rude and arrogant the owner is. He refused to help me access books that were out of reach due to his lazyness and complete disregard for customer satisfaction.

Till Total £128.50
9 Customers

WEDNESDAY, 22 APRIL

Online orders: 0
Orders found: 0

Nicky was in today. The first thing she said when she arrived was 'I brought you a present last week, but you were away. Organic pork sausages.' I asked her what she did with them, given that she's vegetarian. 'I ate them. They were lovely.'

No orders again today, so I've emailed Monsoon to see what the problem is.

A man pulled up in front of the shop in an ancient, noisy Land Rover, then brought in a box of books about clocks. Nicky went through them and checked values online. She told me to offer him £70, which I did on his return to the shop following a walk. All he said was 'I don't think so,' as he picked them up and left without another word.

It was a lovely sunny day, so I called Tracy to see if she wanted to go for a walk. We got back to the shop by lunchtime to find Nicky and Petra standing outside the shop with their mouths open in gormless wonderment, staring at the sky. They appeared to be looking at what they clearly thought was a rare bird. Petra pointed at it and asked Tracy (RSPB member) what it was. She told them it was a seagull.

While we were out walking, Nicky had the following exchange with two customers:

> Husband: Do you own this shop?
> Nicky: No.
> Wife: Do you own this shop?
> Nicky: No.
> Husband: bla bla bla bla biggest store bla bla can I take
> your photo? [*sticks camera phone in my face*]
> Nicky: No. Are you buying a book? [*spoken from behind
> hand*]
> Wife: Oh, you'd let me take a photo if I bought a book.

Both walked out, bookless.

In the afternoon I had a short meeting with Davy Brown, local artist, about the Spring Fling event he wants to hold here in the shop. Spring Fling is an annual event in which artists and makers open their studios to the public. It has grown in numbers every year, and (like Wigtown Book Festival) is one of the cultural highlights of the Galloway calendar. Thousands of people descend on the area in the hope of snapping up a bargain from one of the participating artists (without gallery fees they can afford to drop prices), and out of curiosity to see the space in which the artists create their work. There are several suggested routes, and one of them passes through Wigtown. It usually brings good trade to all the businesses in the town, particularly the restaurants and cafés.

I left the shop at 2.30 p.m. to go to the paper recycling plant in Glasgow. Unfortunately I arrived at 4.40, to find that its closing time was 4.30, so I stayed with a friend in Glasgow.

Till Total £66
6 Customers

THURSDAY, 23 APRIL

Online orders: 1
Orders found: 1

Dropped off the boxes of books at the recycling and headed home. Back in shop by noon. A spectacularly quiet day, but almost every customer bought a book.

Till Total £64
12 Customers

FRIDAY, 24 APRIL

Online orders: 3
Orders found: 1

The only order I could find today was for a copy of a book called *The Camper's Hand Book*, dated 1908, which contained a superb advert for Burberry, featuring a man wearing clothes that wouldn't have looked out of place in the Boer War.

The other two orders were for books we had sold years ago on Amazon, but which Monsoon has somehow magically decided we still have. This causes massive headaches—we will now have to cancel the orders and risk negative feedback on Amazon (which we will almost certainly receive) because of a technical glitch with third-party software.

Callum came in to ask if I wanted to go to a talk about St Kilda in the County Buildings in Wigtown, but as Nicky has already worked her two days this week I was stuck in the shop. When I moved back to Wigtown in 2001, the place had a very different appearance from today. The Georgian gardens in the middle of the square had been hideously defiled by 1970s municipal planning, with raised beds built from reconstituted granite blocks, full of alpines and roses, and the County Buildings—arguably the architectural jewel in the town's crown—were closed and fenced off. Now, though, the gardens have been restored to their former grandeur, and are far more used by visitors and locals alike than the granite monstrosity that they replaced; and the County Buildings, the former municipal seat of power—the grand Hôtel de Ville—has been renovated beautifully, and is in constant use by all sorts of community enterprises.

At 10 a.m. a customer brought three books to the counter:

> Me: That comes to £24 please.
> Customer: £24? What? Those two are £2 each.
> Me: Yes, but that one is £20.
> Customer: But it looks just like the other two.

Tracy called to say that she's been offered the job at Turnberry. She starts on Wednesday and tells me there are rumours that Donald Trump plans to visit some time soon. Hopefully there's more truth in those than the rumours that he's going to run for the US presidency.

In the afternoon, a man brought in three books on Lee Harvey Oswald and asked, 'Are you buying at the moment?' I gave him £5 for them, to which he rather depressingly told me, 'I've reached the point in my life where I'm not going to re-read my books.'

Till Total £48
7 Customers

SATURDAY, 25 APRIL

Online orders: 1
Orders found: 1

For most of the morning a customer who clearly had no intention of buying a £400 antiquarian book about Scottish heraldry sat by the fire reading it, then left it on the table.

A customer brought a pile of books to the counter, then removed one and said, 'I'll put that one back, I've just remembered that I already downloaded it onto my Kindle.' This has inspired me to produce some mugs with 'Death to the Kindle' printed on them, so I emailed Luise (occasional customer and excellent designer in Edinburgh) to see if she'd mind coming up with a design.

I have devised a new strategy for dealing with hagglers. When they ask for a discount, I'm going to ask them what they do for a living. Based on some spurious guesswork, I'll judge whether they earn more than I do, or less. In the extremely unlikely event that they earn less, they can have a 10 per cent discount. In the almost inevitable event that they earn more, they can pay me 10 per cent extra. That's progressive economics.

After the shop shut, Katarina (a young photographer who has moved to Wigtown from Bristol) appeared and asked if she could use the shop for a photo shoot, so I gave her the key and let her get on with it. She left at 7 p.m.

Till Total £334.89
23 Customers

SUNDAY, 26 APRIL

Shop closed. This morning I began boxing the contents of the Garden Room so that Callum can make a start on converting it back to a bothy, hopefully some time in the next few days.

Luise sent two designs for 'Death to the Kindle' mugs, so I've emailed them to Bev, who has the mug printing machine, and asked if she can produce twenty for me.

MONDAY, 27 APRIL

Online orders: 7
Orders found: 3

In the orders this morning was one for Lucy Inglis's *Georgian London*, published in 2013, original price £20. Our copy sold for £11. It's highly unusual for something so relatively recent not to have dropped to a penny on Amazon.

Typically, one of the unlocated books was the most expensive order of the day.

Mr Deacon came in at 3 p.m. looking for his book about Henry IV, which has yet to arrive.

Lisa, the local doctor's wife, dropped in a box of books, so I gave her £10 for them. As we were chatting, a customer asked, 'What was the Shakespeare play with the Moor in it?' Before I could admit that I couldn't remember, Lisa had answered '*Othello*,' sparing me considerable embarrassment.

This afternoon there was a very satisfying encounter involving a customer who began requesting a discount on a pile of books about the Rolls-Royce company. His friend prodded him in the back and said, 'You've got some nerve, asking for a discount from this poor bloke while you drive about in your fancy Rolls-Royces.' He didn't get a discount.

Went for a pint after work to send Tracy off—she starts her new job at Turnberry on Wednesday. She is now an employee of Donald Trump.

Till Total £214
18 Customers

TUESDAY, 28 APRIL

Online orders: 3
Orders found: 3

Callum arrived at 9 a.m. to begin the conversion work on the Garden Room.

Two elderly customers came into the shop at 9.30 a.m. and

wandered about for a while, then—as they were heading towards the door—started saying 'No, no, no' to one another. I can only assume that they were unimpressed with the shop. Or me.

Mr Deacon's book arrived in today's post, so I left a message on his answering machine.

Bev dropped off twenty 'Death to the Kindle' mugs. They look fantastic. Luise did an excellent job with the design. Now I just need to sell the damned things. I've realised that the only way to circumvent the ferocious competition on Amazon, which squeezes your margins to the limit, is to control the supply of the product you're selling, which means creating the product yourself; the mugs are perfect for this.

At noon a customer telephoned looking for an Edinburgh Telephone Directory from 1966. We don't have one for that year, but strangely, old directories—particularly trade directories—sell quite well online. I have one for 1974–75, but not 1966. Just after I'd put the telephone down from the directory caller, a man came to the counter with the £400 Scottish heraldry book and bought it—no haggling. Perhaps I had been slightly uncharitable about the customer who had spent the morning reading it by the fire last week. Perhaps he'd told this person—the man who bought it—about it.

There was a monstrous camper van parked in front of the shop all day, not only blocking the view but also hiding the shop from potential customers. The owner of it came into the shop and said, 'You've got a disarticulated set of Baines's *Lancaster* on the shelves. It's priced at £60. Would you take £40 for it?' I had to look up 'disarticulated' shortly after I'd told him that his offer was not agreeable.

Till Total £650
19 Customers

WEDNESDAY, 29 APRIL

Online orders: 2
Orders found: 1

Today's missing book was *The Mystical Flora of St Francis de Sales*, priced at £75. An early listing. These are always the hardest to find, as the longer the book has been on the shelf, the higher the chance that it has been sold (and not de-listed) or moved to a different shelf by a customer.

A Glaswegian woman, wearing a pair of trousers so incredibly tight (and flesh-coloured) that I initially thought she was naked from the waist down, asked for a map of the area so that she could 'avoid the roads.' By which, it turns out, she means the single-track roads. She's the wife of the motor home owner.

A customer wandered about the shop for an hour this afternoon repeating to his wife 'There doesn't seem to be anything in German' before leaving without asking whether—in fact—we had anything in German. It's tempting to interject and point out that we do have a section of German-language books, but to be honest, in these situations, if the customer doesn't even have the sense to ask, then there's probably only the slenderest of chances that they'd buy something.

Went to the pub after work to meet Samara, who's running The Open Book for two weeks.

Till Total £78
5 Customers

THURSDAY, 30 APRIL

Online orders: 2
Orders found: 1

Katarina (the photographer who used the shop for a shoot) sent me some of the photographs. I had no idea that her willowy model was going to be nude for the entire shoot.

Till Total £67
6 Customers

MAY

It is queer how my fancy is tickled by the oddities of human nature.
Perhaps this happens because I am so ordinary myself. It would give
me the shivers if I thought I was kenspeckle, or that folk considered
me eccentric in any way. I hope I give them no cause to talk about
any oddity of mine behind my back. In the shop I once heard a
University student, a very rude young man, mutter to his companion
'Go and ask that funny-looking tyke.' At first I thought he was
meaning me, for he was looking in my direction, but presently I
noticed that McKerrow was directly behind me. It must have been
McKerrow that was referred to. The old fellow can't help his looks.

Augustus Muir, *The Intimate Thoughts of John Baxter, Bookseller*

Of course the student was referring to Baxter as a 'funny-looking
tyke,' but his observation that his fancy is tickled by the oddities
of human nature is probably a result of working in a bookshop for
several decades. I shudder to think what most of my customers
think of me, but I suspect 'funny-looking tyke' would be at the
more flattering end of the descriptive spectrum.

Most retail involves dealing with all manner of people but, as
Orwell pointed out in his essay 'Bookshop Memories', 'Many
of the people who came to us were of the kind who would be a
nuisance anywhere but have special opportunities in a bookshop.'
It seems to be a common thread of books that are set in or which
are about bookshops that the writers seem to group customers into
almost Linnaean taxonomic groups: R. M. Williamson did it in
Bits from an Old Bookshop in 1904; Will Y. Darling did it in *The
Private Papers of a Bankrupt Bookseller* in 1931; Orwell did it in
"Bookshop Memories"; and Augustus Muir did it with Baxter in
1942. And, in a more generous manner, Jen Campbell did it with
Weird Things Customers Say in Bookshops in 2012. Perhaps everyone
does it, but it seems somehow easier to categorise customers in

a bookshop; people seem to fit more neatly into boxes, possibly because you can form a sense of what a person is like from the books they buy, although Darling contradicts this in *The Bankrupt Bookseller*, saying, 'Some of my customers are frankly a mystery to me, and the darkness of their mystery is not lightened by the books they buy.'

It is probably less about the books they buy and more about the human interaction that Darling is describing, and—very broadly speaking—people can be divided into two groups: those who have worked in a bar, or café, or restaurant, or shop, and those who have not. And while it would be both unfair and untrue to say that everyone in the latter category treats those in the former as a second-class citizen, it is probably accurate to say that virtually nobody from the first category will do so.

FRIDAY, 1 MAY

Online orders: 3
Orders found: 1

Nicky was in the shop today, so I packed up and left for Edinburgh for Alastair Reid's memorial service, which took place at 6 p.m. in part of the university. I drove to Lockerbie, left the van and took the train to Edinburgh rather than driving. Alastair was a hugely talented writer, originally from Galloway (a place to which he returned every spring in his twilight years). He became a good friend during that time, and he will be terribly missed in these and many other parts. Finn, Eliot and a host of other people were at the memorial service. After the event I went to my youngest sister, Lou's, at about 10.30 p.m. and drank whisky with her husband, Scott, for a while, then bed by midnight.

The AWB (Association of Wigtown Booksellers) Spring Festival started today. This is a small festival with a tiny budget, organised by the booksellers. We usually have a dozen or so talks and events held in various venues—mainly bookshops—around the town, and it's always on the weekend of the May Bank Holiday.

Till Total £126.60
9 Customers

SATURDAY, 2 MAY

Online orders: 2
Orders found: 1

Awoken at 7 a.m. by Daniel and Martha, Lou and Scott's children, playing outside my door. Left at 9 a.m. and headed for Waverley Station, via a café for breakfast. I arrived at the station to discover that all trains to Lockerbie had been cancelled and buses had been put on instead. Rather than the pleasant one-hour train journey I had expected, we were sardined onto a pretty uncomfortable bus, where immediately a scrawny man deposited himself on the seat next to mine and proceeded to spend the entire journey sniffing, sometimes several times a second, both in and out. The journey took two and a half hours before the bus finally snailed its way into Lockerbie.

Returned to the shop at about 3.30 p.m. to a scowling Nicky: 'You told me you'd be back by lunchtime.' I apologised and sent her home early. Just before she left, a regular customer brought in a box of books. They were mostly things I wouldn't stock, but I bought a few things. Nicky spotted a battered Book Club edition of *Poldark* in the box which I had rejected. There ensued an argument in which she insisted that it would sell. When I told her that we'd had multiple copies of Winston Graham in the Penguin section for years but never sold a single copy of *Poldark*, she ignored me and gave the man a pound, telling me, 'This will sell by the end of next week.'

The shop was busy all afternoon, and I spent the last hour tidying up the predictable chaos to which I had returned.

I think the cat has worms, so I dug out the worming tablets, at the sight of which he shot off like a bolt of lightning.

Till Total £375.98
35 Customers

SUNDAY, 3 MAY

Online orders: 3
Orders found: 3

I opened the shop at 11 a.m. to find a customer waiting outside: a man with a beard, who on entering the shop asked, 'Have you got anything special in mountaineering?' I replied that it was quite a subjective question—'special' could mean different things to different people—to which he responded 'Well, I suppose I mean expensive,' so I told him to just double the price of the books on the shelves. He eventually explained that he's a dealer who specialises in polar exploration books.

The wonderfully named Ayrshire local historian Dane Love arrived to give a talk about his latest book, *The Galloway Highlands*. Thankfully it was a wet day and the event was well attended, with about thirty people turning up. Unfortunately, being on my own running the shop, I was unable to attend Dane's talk, and shortly after it started, a customer came to the counter with a book: 'This book has three price stickers on it, which one is yours?' One of the stickers had WATERSTONES on it, another OXFAM.

The days are noticeably lengthening, and—though still chilly—the air temperature is rising, to the point at which I no longer need to light the stove in the evening.

Till Total £330.98
26 Customers

MONDAY, 4 MAY

Online orders: 3
Orders found: 3

All three orders today were from Abe, so I processed them and took the mail sacks to the post office, arriving there to discover that it was closed because of the Bank Holiday.

As I was pricing up books, I came across one by a woman called Kay Brellend. I sincerely hope the 'R' key works on her typewriter.

To my fury, and doubtless to Nicky's delight, the first customer of the day bought the copy of *Poldark* that she had bought on Saturday. I am choking back bitter tears as I type this.

Letter in the post this morning from the back specialist in Dumfries. The results of the MRI scan show the problem is wear and tear, and that the only way to deal with it is pain management (Ibuprofen) and exercises, so she's referred me to the physiotherapist in Newton Stewart.

The rep from Nicholson Maps, from whom I buy Ordnance Survey maps for the shop, arrived at noon. Our stock was low, so I ordered forty maps. The Ordnance Survey maps of the region sell fairly well in the shop, largely to visitors who come here for walking holidays.

A woman came to the counter with a pile of books after lunch and said, 'I'd like a trade discount on those' as she slapped her business card on the counter with neither a 'please' nor a 'thank you.' I was very amused later when I read the blurb on her card:

Greyladies Booksellers and Publishers—well mannered books by Ladies Long Gone.

After the shop had closed, I spotted the cat with his head in the food bowl, so I slowly went to the Welsh dresser and removed a worming pill from its wrapper, sneaked over to him and grabbed him by the scruff. Every time I tried to push the tablet into his mouth he'd snarl and scratch so viciously that eventually I had to let him go before I collapsed from loss of blood.

Till Total £347.38
18 Customers

TUESDAY, 5 MAY

Online orders: 1
Orders found: 1

Today was a cold, wet day, more like a January day than one in May. Davy Brown phoned to see if the big room was available. The ladies' art class normally meets outdoors in the summer, usually in one of their gardens, but since it was so miserable Davy decided to hold it inside today.

A middle-aged woman in Ugg boots came in at 10.30 a.m. and asked, 'Do you have anything about the history of land ownership in the area? I'm doing some family history research,' so I showed her to the Scottish room, where there is a five-volume set of McKerlie's *Lands and Their Owners in Galloway* (1877), £100. One hour later she came to the counter and said, 'Thank you very much, I'll borrow that from the library.'

As I was tidying up a shelf in the theology section, I came across a slim pamphlet published by an organisation called AOL. Shortly after I'd bought the shop, a woman came in with a box of pamphlets privately printed about a hundred years ago under the imprint AOL, which—judging from its iconography and the language of the texts they contained—appeared to be some sort of secret society. I vaguely remember it was devoted to Osiris. I had no idea what they were, so I gave her £50 for them and listed them online. They sold incredibly quickly, and all went across the Atlantic to a woman in Canada, but not before I'd received a very menacing email warning me that these were not mine to sell and should be destroyed rather than fall into the wrong hands. I recall the words 'you have no idea what you're dealing with. This is a very powerful organisation. Desist from selling these or you will face serious consequences.' To the best of my knowledge, I haven't faced any consequence. Or perhaps fourteen years of bookselling has been my punishment.

Till Total £134.50
17 Customers

WEDNESDAY, 6 MAY

Online orders: 1
Orders found: 1

In the inbox today, an inquiry about a copy of *The Merrick and the*

Neighbouring Hills which we have listed online for £30, asking if I was prepared to sell the book for £15. Will it never end?

After I closed the shop, I drove to Dumfries to collect Anna from the railway station. I think she feels more at home in Scotland than America now, and despite the end of our relationship, an incredibly strong friendship has emerged from its ashes.

A few years ago—on 26 March 2010, after we'd been living together for a couple of years—on re-entering the country after a trip back to visit her parents in Boston, Anna was held and questioned by an officious Border Agency employee at Glasgow airport. I was kept waiting in the arrivals lounge for three hours, with no idea what was going on. I knew her flight had landed, but there was no sign of her. Eventually someone came out and found me, at Anna's request, and explained that she was being detained, and might be sent back on the next flight. When she finally emerged, she was visibly upset. She had been questioned for hours, the official had even gone through her personal diary and highlighted the entries in which she'd written about the occasions on which she'd helped me in the shop for an hour here and there. Under the terms of her visa (a holiday visa) she was not permitted to do any kind of work.

She pleaded with the official to allow her a couple of days to return to Wigtown to collect her things before deporting her, and eventually they conceded. We had to be back at the airport by noon on the Monday of the following week.

Those were awful days, fraught and emotional, but they were a trifle compared with what was to come. On the Monday morning I drove her back to Glasgow airport, and we made our presence known to the immigration department. It was a farce; they didn't seem to have any idea what they were supposed to do, and hadn't even booked her onto a flight. At one point the officer told her that they'd found her a seat on an Iceland Air flight to Boston, via Reykjavik, but that she would have to pay for it herself. I remember the sense of pride I felt when she told them that if they wanted her out of the country, they could 'fucking well' pay for her flight. Initially, they agreed to pay for her to travel as far as Reykjavik, but from there she would have to make her own way back to Boston. Even when she explained that this would leave her homeless in Iceland without enough money to get back to America, they were unmoved. Only when the two of us threatened to go back to the van and drive back to Wigtown did they finally agree to pay for the full fare. The way the Border Agency dealt with it was an embarrassment from start to finish: a litany of incompetence, insensitivity and mismanagement. The look of profound sadness, tinged with indomitable optimism, on her face as they led her away will remain with me forever.

The following months were awful, particularly for Anna, desperate to return to Scotland and everything she loved, but prevented from doing so by petty bureaucracy. From this end I did what I could—I met with MPs and MSPs, tried to speak to people from the Border Agency—but to no avail. The Border Agency is an impenetrable organisation, and even MPs have no influence over their decisions. One of the reasons I voted for Scottish independence in the referendum was because of the way Anna was treated by them. Rural Scotland needs people like her—intelligent, hardworking, passionate about the place—yet she was forcibly removed because of rules designed for the south-east of England.

After several failed attempts to get her back into Scotland, including paying exorbitant amounts of money to a lawyer who falsely claimed they could organise an 'expedited visa,' and several months, including weeks spent sleeping in her car, there was only one option remaining: the one neither of us wanted to pursue—the fiancée visa. We filled in the forms and she returned, happy, to Scotland with six months to try to find an alternative or be forced to marry. Not, arguably, the worst fate in the world, but one that terrified me beyond imagination.

Several months later, and overriding my every instinct, we were married in the typically bland municipal surroundings of the registry office in Castle Douglas, with Carol-Ann as our witness. That event—more than any other—is the root of the problems we later faced in our relationship.

Till Total £210
13 Customers

THURSDAY, 7 MAY

Online orders: 5
Orders found: 5

Miraculously, I found all five orders this morning. All were from Amazon. Total £40.

Anna seems really delighted to be back in Galloway. She spent the day going around the place visiting people. We've decided that it would be best if she split her time here between staying above the shop in one of the spare rooms and staying with friends. All of my friends have become her friends, and she is infinitely more popular with them than I am. Thankfully, she didn't get round to selling her car before she left, so it was here awaiting her, all rusty and moss-covered, just as she had left it. Once, about three years ago, when we were planning to go for a walk on a wintery Sunday afternoon, as I was locking the shop behind us, Anna flew into a panic and announced that her car had been stolen. I tried to calm her down and reassure her that there had to be another explanation: cars don't get stolen in Wigtown, particularly old bangers. I suggested that perhaps Vincent (who has the spare key) might have picked it up to check on something, so we walked the short distance to his garage and explained the situation. His response was to tell us that it hadn't been stolen, and that he'd just seen it parked outside the co-op, so we wandered up there and sure enough, there it was—less parked, more abandoned, in the middle of the road. We finally worked out what had happened. Anna had been visiting Finn a few days previously and, on her way home, had stopped outside the co-op for bread and milk. She had double-parked because there was no space (normal practice in Wigtown's wide main street) and on leaving the co-op had completely forgotten that she'd driven there. Her car had been sitting, abandoned, in the middle of the road for four days. Nobody had complained; people had just driven around it, as though it was a roundabout.

To my knowledge the only car to have been 'stolen' in Wigtown belonged to my parents, and that was over twenty years ago. It had been in the garage for an MOT, and the mechanic had left the key in the ignition overnight (perfectly normal here in those days).

A fifteen-year-old schoolboy had been passing, and—attempting to impress a girl—had jumped in it with her and driven around the quiet country roads for ten minutes before neatly parking it where he had found it. The only reason his crime had been discovered was because a sheet of paper with his homework on it had fallen out of his pocket and the mechanic spotted it the following morning when he was adjusting the seat.

A customer came to the counter and put £1 on it and said, 'Have this back, we came here last year and we were undercharged by £1, and since you're always complaining about being skint on Facebook we thought we should give it back.' I thanked him and asked who was it who undercharged him, to which he replied 'That dark-haired woman you're always arguing with.'

At 4 p.m. a customer brought a beautiful full-calf Victorian binding to the counter. Someone (no prizes for guessing who) had priced it at £9.50. It ought to have been £45 at the very least, but the customer seemed so excited about it that I let her have it for the marked price.

Till Total £106
13 Customers

FRIDAY, 8 MAY

Online orders: 1
Orders found: 1

Nicky in today. Foodie Friday has reared its ugly head once again; this time she brought in a box of chocolate donuts, which I'm quite certain she'd sat on at some point. Or perhaps her cat had slept on them. In any case, all the chocolate had melted into a runny sludge.

There was a pile of feathers under the kitchen table this morning, which means that one of the unfortunate swallows that undertook the epic journey here from Africa has become Captain's latest victim. Under the kitchen table is his preferred spot for devouring them.

This afternoon there was a telephone call from a woman in Cumbria who informed me that she would like to sell two boxes of children's paperbacks from the 1960s. I told her that it would be unlikely that the cost of the petrol to get here would be compensated for by what she'd get for the books, and advised her to find somewhere closer to home to sell them. There's a bookshop in Carlisle that will probably take them, so I gave her their contact details. At least she had the good sense to call and check before embarking on the journey. Far too often people turn up at the shop without having called first, and are often extremely unhappy to be told that their books are worthless after they've made the effort to bring them.

After lunch I drove to Newton Stewart and bought some Spot On cat wormer. Might be easier to apply it to his skin than try to force a pill down his throat.

Went to the pub with Callum and Tracy. Fairly late night.

Till Total £64
7 Customers

SATURDAY, 9 MAY

Online orders: 0
Orders found: 0

No orders this morning.

I dragged myself out of bed at 8.45 to find a bright and cheery Nicky downstairs, keeping the Facebook followers updated on my hangover and bad temper.

At the moment Nicky disappeared for her lunch break, a very elderly man, walking using two sticks to help him get about, bought a copy of a book called *Advanced Sex: Explicit Positions for Explosive Lovemaking*.

Managed to pin down the cat and get the worming liquid onto the back of his neck. He stalked off, looking back at me with cold, accusing eyes.

Till Total £242.99
30 Customers

MONDAY, 11 MAY

Online orders: 2
Orders found: 2

Today we had an order for a £4 book that was listed in the Railway Room on shelf D3. I eventually found it after twenty minutes on shelf B2. We never had this problem with books in the warehouse; it's only in the shop, where customers can take books off shelves and re-house them somewhere different.

Every year I try to do something in the shop to make visitors, even returning visitors, take notice. Usually it's something that people will find sufficiently interesting to photograph and share on social media. A few years ago, when Norrie and I were replacing the rotten wooden floor in the railway room, we found a large stone-walled cavity underneath it. I'm convinced that it was a brandy-hole, for hiding smuggled alcohol. Norrie came up with the idea for building a model railway in the space and putting a piece of toughened glass over it so that customers could see it. We built the model railway, and then I discovered the cost of toughened glass; to cover it would have cost £600, so it remains there, unseen. One day I will buy the glass so that customers can see it.

This morning I spent half an hour explaining to an old woman that we don't have the copy of the Orwell title that includes the essay about a hanging in Burma (I imagine that it's in *Burmese Days*), yet still she ploughed on telling me that she needs it to give to her granddaughter, who is writing a thesis on capital punishment. Eventually she left, muttering darkly about the stock in the shop.

Till Total £306.79
25 Customers

TUESDAY, 12 MAY

Online orders: 1
Orders found: 1

At 11 a.m., a customer asked if he could bring his dog into the shop.

As always, I said yes, then immediately regretted it when it became evident that the creature was a huge, ancient, reeking hairy beast, leaving enormous muddy footprints all over the freshly cleaned shop (Janetta comes in on Mondays and Thursdays to clean).

As I was mopping up the Hound of the Baskervilles' footprints, a woman came to the counter and asked, 'Are you Shaun?' When I confirmed that I was, she told me that Anna Dreda from Wenlock Books sent her best wishes, and that she was here on holiday because Anna had recommended Wigtown.

At 2 p.m. I nipped out to drop the mail off at the post office and returned to find that a customer had come in to collect a book she'd ordered. She had probably been there for a minute or two, and was standing in a doorway, impatiently shouting 'Hello!' I replied with a similar greeting, to which she responded, 'Where are you? I can't see you.' I was standing behind her. She'd been in the shop a few weeks ago and had ordered a book. She'd given me a scrap of paper on which she'd scribbled down the author, title and ISBN. The book had arrived last week, so I dug it out from behind the counter and gave it to her.

Till Total £379.50
13 Customers

WEDNESDAY, 13 MAY

Online orders: 1
Orders found: 1

This morning's order was for *Mochrum: The Land and Its People*, by John McFadzean. John is a retired local farmer, and his son Ian is married to my cousin. He wrote this comprehensive and impressive local history book a few years ago, and asked me to publish it for him. With literally no experience of publishing, I turned to John Carter, from whom I bought the shop, for advice. John was—as always—incredibly helpful and gave up a considerable amount of his time to steer me through the process, and eventually the book came out in a limited edition of 500 numbered copies in 2009. It was well received locally, and although I still have a few copies left, it broke even in a surprisingly short time.

The woman who came in to collect her book yesterday was back again this afternoon. She was furious, because the book isn't the one she thought she'd ordered. When I produced the hand-written piece of paper showing the title, author and ISBN that she'd given me she calmed down slightly, and admitted that I had made 'an understandable mistake.'

Till Total £170.48
14 Customers

THURSDAY, 14 MAY

Online orders: 4
Orders found: 4

The orders took over an hour to locate this morning; only one was on the correct shelf.

A young customer wearing a baseball cap asked, 'Where's your travel section?' as I was putting a recently priced book onto a shelf in that very section. I replied, 'It's right in front of you. In fact you're looking at it now.'

> Customer: Where? Here?
> [*He pointed to the shelves to the right of the shelf he was looking at, which is the history section.*]
> Me: No. Right in front of you.
> Customer: What, here?
> [*Pointing to the shelves to the left of the shelf he was looking at, which is the India section*]

Eventually I had to put my hand on the shelf label that read TRAVEL and was about six inches in front of his nose.

Lisa, the doctor's wife, came in with two sets of graphic novels, *Blake and Mortimer* (17 volumes) and a French series called *Adèle Blanc-Sec* (8 volumes) along with some other books. I gave her £70 for the lot, and listed the two sets of graphic novels on eBay in the afternoon with reserves of £50 and £40 respectively. Although I'm the first to admit that I'm out of my depth when it comes to graphic novel values, I would hope that they sell by this time next week.

Eliot arrived at 8 p.m. while Anna and I were out visiting Carol-Ann in Dalbeattie. We returned home at 10.30 to find him munching his way through a pizza in the kitchen (which Janetta had tidied earlier). Every cupboard door was open, and there was cutlery on almost every surface. Before I'd even had a chance to say hello to him, I'd tripped over his shoes.

He greeted Anna like a long-lost friend, which I suppose she is.

Till Total £69
12 Customers

FRIDAY, 15 MAY

Online orders: 3
Orders found: 2

Eliot was in the bath from 8.30 to 9.20, so I had no chance to brush my teeth before opening the shop. He's here this time because there's a book festival fundraising auction tonight. It has become an annual affair, and supporters of the festival donate lots, such as a day's fishing on one of the local rivers, or a weekend in a flat in Edinburgh—whatever they can afford.

Nicky arrived at 9 a.m., wearing a top that bore a striking resemblance to a small hot air balloon. I told her it was less than flattering. Needless to say, she'd made it herself.

As I was sweeping the pavement in front of the shop, two women walked past. One said to the other, 'There's no point going in there, it's just books.'

At closing time I went to Newton Stewart to pick up wine and food for a pre-auction drinks party, to which nobody came. Perfect. Wine supply sorted for a month.

The auction took place tonight in the main hall of the County Buildings, with Finn in charge. I donated two lots: a drone flyover video and membership of the Random Book Club. The first made £140, the second £45.

After the auction several of us went to the pub, including Nicky. When we got back to the house, she assured me that she would open the shop so that I could have a lie-in.

Till Total £295
15 Customers

SATURDAY, 16 MAY

Online orders: 4
Orders found: 3

Awoke at 8.55 to no sound of any activity from below, so I came downstairs and opened the shop. Nicky eventually appeared at 10, looking bedraggled and hungover.

Customer in a beret and monocle: Have you got anything by Eric 'Winkle' Brown?

> Me: I can't say I've ever heard of him.
> Customer: What? You've never heard of Eric 'Winkle' Brown?

And so it went on.

Captain—not usually protective of my welfare—appears to have formed a line of defence between me and the customers, and spent much of the afternoon lying on the counter, attacking anyone who dared approach with the intention of buying a book.

Till Total £100.48
8 Customers

MONDAY, 18 MAY

Online orders: 8
Orders found: 4

Thankfully the orders we found this morning were the more valuable of the eight. The total from the successfully picked orders was £180.

Callum came in to continue the demolition of the Garden Room and its steady conversion to a bothy for Emanuela, so the back of the shop was filled with the sound of hammering and drilling all day.

Anna had a visit from Carol-Ann to discuss an idea for a new business to market the region. Carol-Ann is currently working as a business adviser, and she and Anna have been close friends since Anna first moved here. Between them they are forever hatching unlikely business ideas.

At 4 p.m. a customer walked into the shop, looked around, spotted me and said, 'Oh, you're there. You used to be over there,' pointing at the other side of the room. The counter has been exactly where it is ever since I bought the shop, and probably a decade before that. It has never been where he pointed, but memory is a curious thing and I really didn't want to get into a discussion on the matter, so I nodded politely and went back to reading my book.

There are no bids on either set of graphic novels on eBay, but there are quite a few watchers, which usually means that bidding will start at some point.

Till Total £113.50
14 Customers

TUESDAY, 19 MAY

Online orders: 2
Orders found: 1

Davy Brown delivered his paintings in preparation for Spring Fling this coming weekend. He's going to hang them in the big room that we use for the Writers' Retreat during the September festival and which, for the few months of the year in which it is warm enough, functions as my drawing room.

A woman with short, bleached blond hair came in and bought

a book of copperplate prints of William Hogarth illustrations. I recognised her from a previous visit, and we started chatting. When I told her that I remembered her being here about a year ago, she told me that it was exactly three years ago to the day.

A few years ago, even when I first bought the shop, prints sold very well, and many a good book has been 'broken' over the years to extract them. Copperplate is particularly desirable, partly because it is an older technology, which invariably means the prints will have greater antiquity, but partly because it has a warmer aesthetic than the later, harsher, steel-plate technology. Prints, mounted or unmounted, rarely sell nowadays, and the woman who bought the Hogarth book could probably have sold the prints inside it for £10 each fifteen years ago. Not now, though. If they sell at all, it is for £3 or £4 each.

After she'd left, as I was pricing books for the mountaineering section, a customer asked, 'Have you got a section on older books?' I replied, 'Do you mean books about old books? Bibliographies and that sort of thing? Or are you asking if we keep the older books in one place?' Customer: 'I don't know.'

A man brought in a complete set of the first *Statistical Account of Scotland* (21 volumes, 1791–9). They were mostly in poor condition, but good internally. We currently already have a set on the shelves in the Scottish room which haven't sold since I bought them two years ago. For some reason I gave him £200 for them.

Most of the afternoon was taken up with packing the Random Books.

Till Total £187
15 Customers

WEDNESDAY, 20 MAY

Online orders: 2
Orders found: 1

In an attempt to cut postage costs I've been in touch with someone called Gary at Royal Mail. Today—after a review of the 'postage situation'—he telephoned to suggest that 'we replace your OBA with a DMO, that way your STL will migrate to a CRL.' Following a lengthy silence from my end, Gary clearly sensed my rising bile at being subjected to so many three-letter acronyms in a single sentence, and reassured me, 'Don't worry, there will be a lot of training.' Training. A word guaranteed to send a shiver down the spine of most self-employed people. I never, ever want to be subjected to training again. Not that I'm averse to learning new things. It's just that invariably 'training' when you're in paid employment means listening to someone stating the obvious for three days while you think of all the other, far more productive, things you could be doing instead. It's one of the reasons I don't think I could ever go back to working for someone else. That, and the fact that nobody in their right mind would ever employ me.

As I was sorting through boxes and pricing up books, I found a letter tucked into the dust jacket of a copy of Auden's *About the House*:

> Flat no 150.
>
> To: the tenants of no. 158.
>
> I should be most grateful if you could avoid the noises, like a door being closed and the turning off of electric switches which seems frequently, as due to an accident which I sustained recently, breaking my arm and hand, this has caused my nerves to become very bad and I have to receive treatment daily at the hospital. My doctor has told me I should keep as quiet as possible and have as much sleep as I can, so I am writing you this now to ask you if you will be so kind as to prevent the sounds I refer to, particularly after 10 p.m.
>
> Probably you do not know that they penetrate my flat.
>
> Thanking you in advance for your kind co-operation.

I wonder if the copy of Auden belonged to the recipient, or whether the sender decided against the idea of sending it and put it there safely out of the way.

An American woman came in looking for our 'section of books on the McConnell clan.' Clan and family histories are what most Americans visiting Scottish bookshops seem to be in search of. A group of Americans came in later during the day, this time looking for anything about *Outlander*.

The woman who bought the Hogarth prints yesterday came back into the shop to sign up for the Random Book Club.

Till Total £221.99

12 Customers

THURSDAY, 21 MAY

Online orders: 1

Orders found: 1

One month to go until the longest day of the year.

Callum came in at 9 a.m. to work on excavating the floor of the Garden Room for the conversion. Norrie (former employee) dropped by at ten o'clock to borrow the van, and Isabel appeared at 10.30 to do the accounts. Davy Brown arrived at eleven to set up his paintings in the big room. So, plenty of action about the place, but most of it costing me money rather than generating it.

The sets of graphic novels sold on eBay, but not before someone emailed me with an offer of £30 for a set on which I'd put a reserve of £40. Sensing that he was chancing it, I replied that if the set failed to sell I would break it and sell the volumes individually on eBay. He ended up as the only bidder and paid the full £40. The other set met the reserve of £50.

In today's inbox:

Since leaving London for Australia in 1950 I have sporadically sought to identify the series of books I had to leave behind of illustrated histories of e.g. Prehistoric Britain, The British Empire, The Americas. I thought they might be Museum publications, perhaps quarto, soft cover, btw 100–200 pages illustrated with engravings from multiple sources scattered across the pages each with a short caption/note. Can you help? A publisher, some correct titles?

Frankly, they could be any number of series of books.

Till Total £162.50
14 Customers

FRIDAY, 22 MAY

Online orders: 1
Orders found: 1

Nicky was in again. Mercifully no Foodie Friday treats today. I loaded the van and drove to the paper recycling plant in Glasgow. The place was heaving with lorries and vans coming and going, and I had to wait an hour before it was my turn on the weigh-bridge, and about the same again weighing out.

I drove home via a house in Crosshill (about 30 miles from Wigtown) that I'd bought books from before, years ago. The current occupant is the daughter of the people from whom I'd bought the books; they had moved into a retirement home. I remember from my first visit buying two very unusual books about Ming porcelain, both of which fetched prices that far exceeded my expectations. The books today were mostly average shop stock, but some W. W. Jacobs with illustrated bindings, and several P. G. Wodehouse firsts (no jackets), so I gave her £170 for three boxes, but not before she'd gone through the books after I'd made her the offer and removed about twenty of them, so we had to renegotiate the price. It's incredibly irritating when this happens.

It's Wigtown Food Fair tomorrow, so I've loaded the marquee I bought several years ago into the van. It has been in a shed for most of that time, and as I was shifting it I noticed an alarming number of mouse droppings fall from it. No doubt it will be revolting, and probably a health hazard. Bev and Fiona are going to put it up in the morning. Wigtown Food Festival is the event that bridges the gap between the end of spring and the start of summer, and invariably falls on one of the most pleasant days of the year.

Till Total £40.50
8 Customers

SATURDAY, 23 MAY

Online orders: 2
Orders found: 1

Nicky wasn't in today: her brother is visiting, and she wants to show him around. That should be a treat for him, being driven around in a van with the sack of manure that habitually inhabits the back of her van.

Today was a glorious sunny day: perfect for the Wigtown Food Festival, which took place in the square this year for the first time. Bev and Fiona came over to collect the key for the van at 9 a.m. and put the marquee up. Robbie, Fiona's husband, appeared too, as he always does when an extra pair of hands is required, as did Bev's husband, Keith. The booksellers of Wigtown are markedly split into those who do things and those who don't, although I'm not sure into which category I fall.

Davy Brown arrived at 9.30 a.m. with more material for his Spring Fling show. I had completely forgotten that I'd agreed to let a writing group use that space too, so I was taken slightly aback when a raven-haired American woman called Marjorie introduced herself as its host at 10.30. At eleven o'clock the writers turned up, so I left them to fight it out among themselves.

Just after eleven a tall blonde woman came to the counter. She'd found a book that must have been here since long before I bought the business. It was a tatty Observers book, priced at 50p: 'Two questions, firstly can I have a discount because it is in pretty grotty condition, and secondly, can I pay for it by card.' When I told her that it must be the only book in the shop priced at 50p and that there was no possible way I could discount it, she looked horrified and left it on the counter. Most of our Observers books are £4 without jackets, and £6 if they have jackets, and they sell well at those prices.

At lunchtime a fat man with a ponytail managed to get wedged between a pile of boxes and the sci-fi section. I had to move several boxes to extricate him.

Till Total £279.91
33 Customers

SUNDAY, 24 MAY

Online orders: 1
Orders found: 1

I opened the shop at 9 a.m. Tricia and Callum (Davy's daughter and son) turned up at 10 a.m. to staff the Spring Fling exhibition.

The first email of the day began with the ominous words 'Hi i have a collection of 96 readers digest leather bound condensed books, and a lot of single ones would you be interested. I can provide more info if needed thanks.' *Reader's Digest* books, particularly the condensed fiction series, are possibly the least desirable things you will ever come across in the second-hand book trade. They are worthless, and in fourteen years in the trade I think I've only ever been asked for them once.

Just before lunch a man came to the counter with a small pile of antiquarian local history books which Nicky had seriously underpriced, including a two-volume set of Sir Herbert Maxwell's *A History of the House of Douglas*, which she'd put at £40. The last set I bought I paid £80 for and sold for £120. He asked, 'If I buy all of these, how much will it come to?' I had no idea that adding £40, £25 and £45 could be such an intellectual challenge for a grown man.

A man with a Crocodile Dundee hat and a white goatee which he'd dyed blue picked up a copy of *Tripe Advisor*, read a bit, chuckled and told his friends, 'That appeals to my sense of humour,' before putting it back and buying a book about child abuse.

Callum, Gerald (my cousin, who is visiting from Ireland), Anna and I went to the pub after closing. There must be some sort of sidecar rally going on as the entire street was lined with motorbikes and sidecars.

Till Total £224.92
33 Customers

MONDAY, 25 MAY

Online orders: 0
Orders found: 0

No orders, so I suspect Monsoon is playing up again.

Today was a Bank Holiday, and the final day of Spring Fling. The shop was heaving with children messing the place up. Danny (my neighbour and a plumber) came to look at some work that I'm planning on doing in the bothy out the back. I apologised to him for bothering him on a Bank Holiday—he just laughed and told me that Bank Holidays were no different from any other day. For the self-employed—and for most people in retail—they are nothing like most people's perceptions of a Bank Holiday. For the majority of the country they are a long weekend: a break, a holiday. But for my business they are the time when there are people around, and people who want to spend money, so, rather than take time off, I end up working longer hours than I usually would on an ordinary weekend. This normally coincides with having a houseful of visitors who want to stay up late and drink and chat.

An ex-girlfriend's mother, Anna Campbell, came in with four boxes of books to sell at lunchtime, so I sorted through and picked out £25 worth. Often when they're selling books, people will tell me that they want their books to 'go to a good home,' as though they were a much loved pet or family heirloom. I have no idea whether the books I sell end up in a 'good home' or not, and were I to be so particular as to insist, indeed even ask my customers if they had a 'good home' to take the books to, I suspect I'd lose a great deal of business.

Sandy the tattooed pagan brought in four more sticks and spent £12.

A Northern Irishman spent four hours in the shop, managing to position himself in front of every shelf I needed access to. In the entire time he was there I didn't even see him take a book from a shelf. Eventually he asked where the theology section was, so I told him that it was boxed up and piled in front of the music section. Since the time I boxed it up and piled it in front of the music section (so that there's no access to the music section any more either), pretty much every second customer who has come into the shop has asked for either music or theology. He didn't buy anything.

A woman came to the counter at 5.30 and said, 'You only have one R. S. Thomas title.' I thanked her for letting me know and carried on pricing up books.

Just before closing, a large family turned up—probably fifteen of them. They were wonderful, and all bought books. One of the daughters had insisted they come to the shop, eschewing all other Galloway tourist attractions in favour of here.

Till Total £357.37
44 Customers

TUESDAY, 26 MAY

Online orders: 2
Orders found: 2

Callum was in at 9 a.m. to work on the bothy.

Today I sold a book called *The 100 Most Pointless Things in the World* for £2.50. It was a hardback a year old in a mint dust jacket, original price £14.99. Nicky had priced it at £2.50. I would have had it at £6.50. Her argument that we should price to compete with Amazon doesn't stand up when so much is available for a penny there. I'm going to try to persuade her that we shouldn't be considering penny listings, but instead think of what the book would cost if it was brand new today, and divide that by three.

An Amazon customer emailed to say that he was disappointed because the book that he ordered from us does not have a dust jacket, unlike the one in the photograph on the Amazon listing. I explained that Amazon uses generic stock photographs, and that there were twelve other copies of the same book on that listing. They couldn't all possibly be that very same copy.

A man who looked exactly like Captain Mainwaring from *Dad's Army* came to the counter and said, 'I'm 89 and I live in Minnigaff.

I'm moving house and I've got a lot of books to get rid of. Is there a market for second-hand books?'

Till Total £193.98
16 Customers

WEDNESDAY, 27 MAY

Online orders: 1
Orders found: 1

Callum came in at 10 a.m. to work on the Garden Room conversion. As he was walking through the shop he sarcastically commented that the place was busy. There wasn't a soul in the shop but the two of us.

At 11 a.m. a customer brought in a box of books, 'All first editions.' They were all first editions, but mainly things like Dick Francis, which are largely worthless because they were produced in such huge numbers, but I picked out a few Miss Read and Terry Pratchett novels, and an interesting old book on the Sandwich Islands. There are only two online, and the cheapest is £200. I've listed ours for £125.

It started to rain heavily this afternoon and the shop—previously quiet—suddenly filled with customers. Callum came through to ask me a question about the position of a door at this point. There must have been forty people in the shop. When he eventually made it to the counter, inching through the crowded shop, I reminded him of his words of this morning: 'Busy in here, isn't it?'

A very tall French woman bought £4.50 worth of books and insisted on paying by card, and covering the entire PIN handset with her hand so that nobody could see her number, even though there was nobody other than me in the room at the time. After she'd gone, Mole-Man appeared, scuttling past the counter into the history section where he began his literary excavations, before moving silently into the railway room. By the time he came to the counter his pile of books had reached a dozen, and—clutching the base against his belly—they almost reached his nose. It was the usual eclectic mix and included an odd volume (volume 5) of Virginia Woolf's *Diary*, a book on the history of mining in County Durham, three Penguin novels by Evelyn Waugh and an illustrated book of the misericords in Bristol Cathedral, among others. As he was plunging his hands into various pockets in an effort to extract the correct amount of cash, I noticed that a large drip had formed on the end of his nose, and I watched with fascination as it lengthened and began to swing pendulously to mirror his movements. Fortunately, shortly before gravity was to have a final say in its destiny, he deftly ran his sleeve over the tip of his nose, and transferred it to the less than absorbent polyester of his jacket before passing me the £37 required to cover the cost of his books.

Till Total £429.83
45 Customers

THURSDAY, 28 MAY

Online orders: 1
Orders found: 1

There was a reply from Monsoon in today's emails telling me that I'm getting orders for books we've already sold due to a technical problem with Amazon, and that I need to delist and relist my entire stock. All done at the click of a mouse, apparently.

When I opened the shop this morning, the small, bearded Irishman was sitting on the bench waiting for me. I know little about him other than that he comes in his large, battered blue van two or three times a year and sells me books, usually fairly interesting stock and in decent condition. I'm pretty sure he sleeps in his van, although it has not a single trapping of luxury, not even a mattress. He's a quiet man, and I would say that if you described him as 'feral' he would be quite flattered. I bought six boxes of mixed stock and gave him £180.

Heavy rain last night, so I checked river levels and the Cree is 3ft 6in., which means that the Minnoch would have been perfect this afternoon, so I emailed my father to see if he wanted to go fishing.

He replied saying that his back is too bad. I've never known him to miss an opportunity to go salmon fishing.

Just before lunch a man came in and asked if I wanted to buy some books—'I've got three bags, then the same again.' So, six bags. It turned out to be a collection of very saleable modern paperback fiction in mint condition, including a copy of Martin Amis's *Time's Arrow*, which I recall an old flatmate from my time in Bristol recommending. I've never read any Martin Amis, so I put it on my ever expanding 'To Be Read' pile.

As I was sorting books on the table, an elderly customer decided to sit on it, despite there being seven chairs placed throughout the shop.

Till Total £323.90
32 Customers

FRIDAY, 29 MAY

Online orders: 2
Orders found: 2

One of the orders today was for the Sandwich Islands book. A quick turnaround is always both a relief and a reassurance that you've bought and sold something at roughly the right price. Customers often come to the shop with a book they want to sell and tell you that they've seen a copy on Abe for several hundred pounds. A quick check usually reveals that there are dozens more, ranging in price from £10 to hundreds. Even the copy at £10 is probably overpriced because it's still there.

Nicky was in today, so inevitably the day began with an argument about the books the Irishman had brought in, for which I had paid £180. They were pretty average, and I threw about a quarter of them out. The first thing she did was to start going through the books that I had rejected, despite the fact that we have a massive backlog of about thirty boxes of decent fresh stock to sort through.

In the front of the shop is a beautiful Georgian bureau which

I bought from the Dumfries saleroom about two years ago. The lid is open, but several times today I noticed that Nicky had closed it, claiming that 'wee children keep bashing their heads on the corner.' It has been open for weeks, and no such incident has occurred during that time when I've been in the shop.

Monsoon was still showing our stock as 'Delisting' on Amazon. After twenty-four hours I emailed them to ask if this was normal, as the 'Relist' button needs to appear for the 10,000 books we have listed on line to be active again.

After work I went to the pub with Callum.

Till Total £187.50
18 Customers

SATURDAY, 30 MAY

Online orders: 1
Orders found: 1

Nicky was up early and opened the shop this morning.

The order today was for one of the books that I had rejected and Nicky had salvaged from the boxes she'd bought from the Irishman. It sold for £30, and she made no attempt to disguise her glee that I had made a mistake.

While Nicky was on her lunch break, a couple (about my age) came in with two boxes of books that had belonged to the woman's father. They were in a terrible state, and mostly between 100 and 200 years old. It transpired that her father had been teaching himself how to become a bookbinder and had been going to auctions for a few years, looking for books in poor condition to repair. These were the books he hadn't got round to before he died last year, and they weren't sure what to do with them. Because of their condition, there were only a couple that I could have got any money for, and the cost of repairing them would be prohibitive, so I gave them £20 for them and hopefully I'll be able to get Christian, the local bookbinder, to repair a couple of them for me in exchange for the rest.

Over the years, seeing books in this sort of condition has taught me a lot about how books are made. With the boards and spine off an early-nineteenth-century book, you can see exactly how the sewing part of the process is done, over the cords which then— once the leather of the binding is hammered over them—become the 'raised bands' on the spine. Typically, five is what you'd expect on a leather-bound book of this period. Even the 'gatherings' become obvious when you look at a disbound book.

Traditionally, the size of a book was determined by two factors— the size of the original sheet that the text was printed on, and the number of times it was folded to produce a 'gathering,' or number of pages:

> 1 fold would produce a gathering of 2 leaves, and this is known as folio
>
> 2 folds would produce 4 leaves, making it quarto (abbreviated to 4to)
>
> 3 folds would produce 8 leaves, hence octavo (8vo, the most common size of book, even today)
>
> 4 folds would produce 16 leaves, known as sextodecimo (16mo)

There are other variations on this: 12mo, 32mo and 64mo.

Once printed (for an 8vo gathering, the compositor would have to have prepared 16 pages of type, 8 for the top and 8 for the bottom of the sheet), and, folded into a gathering, the numbered gatherings would be placed in the correct order and sewn together over the cords on the spine. Once complete, the binder has the option of trimming the book, which not only gives a uniformity to the edges but also detaches each individual leaf from the others in the gathering. Occasionally books appear where the pages are still joined together (untrimmed), but this is usually just on the fore-edge. The top and bottom edges are nearly always trimmed.

After Nicky had gone I poured myself a G&T, then went into the garden and started reading *Time's Arrow*. Now that spring is here and the days are lengthening, and the ground is beginning to warm under the sun, quiet evenings in the garden are once again an appealing way to pass the time after a day in the shop.

Till Total £189.99
16 Customers

JUNE

It is mostly old theology we get from the Cloth, and they are dumb-founded when we offer them thirty-five shillings or so for the lot. They usually write back in a fine huff, and tell us that they paid more than that, forty years back, for Cruden's *Concordance* and Smith's *Travels in the Holy Land*. Cruden still sells for a few shillings, but they can't understand that old theology is—well, just old theology.

I nearly told a minister the other day that the best use I could think of for these old tomes was to dig them into the garden for manure.

Augustus Muir, *The Intimate Thoughts of John Baxter, Bookseller*

Not much has changed in this regard since Muir wrote these words. Theology remains a difficult subject to sell: even Cruden doesn't shift from the shelves these days. Most of the theological collections I've acquired have not been from the ministers themselves but from their widows, who are often just keen to be rid of them to make space for other things. But ministers' widows aren't the only people who try to sell us theology; on an almost daily basis we are approached by people wielding enormous Victorian family Bibles, often elaborately bound and with metal clasps. They must have cost a pretty penny in their day. Bunyan is the same. There is an abundance of old copies of *The Pilgrim's Progress* out there but, again, largely worthless. There is no market for them today, and I can't see it ever recovering. Very early theology, though, does have a value, but that's largely because of its antiquity: a single page from the Gutenberg Bible (1455) sold for $74,000 at an auction in 2007. This, though, is exceptional, and its value is in the fact that it was the first book ever printed using movable alloy type.

When it comes to customers, we are often asked for theology, or 'religious books' or—more common still—'Christian books' but the customers rarely buy anything. More frequently nowadays, we are asked for books on spirituality and eastern religion. Of those who ask for theology, the overwhelming majority have Northern Irish accents, doubtless in part because of our geographical proximity to the province where interest in matters theological is kept alive thanks to the fact that for many people there religion, politics and identity are grimly intertwined. More often than not these customers are after post-Reformation literature attacking Rome.

Aside from theological libraries, the other single-subject collections that we're often offered are law libraries. Over the years I've bought several of these, although I'm not sure I'd touch another one unless it contained something very interesting. Generally, they are made up of Scots Law Times reports and Public Statutes. Normally, they are in calf bindings and if I'm lucky I can sell them to someone who has a library to fill with attractive-looking books or, as once, to a company that builds sets for films. Their value is purely as bindings.

MONDAY, 1 JUNE

Online orders: 1
Orders found: 1

Email in this morning from someone who has clearly never been to the shop:

> Dear The Bookshop,
>
> Firstly, I'd just like to say what an exquisite shop you have. I absolutely love The Bookshop's focus on unique, quality goods and innovative design—it's precisely these qualities, in fact, that have inspired me to reach out here.

Unsurprisingly he was a self-published author trying to persuade me to stock copies of his novel about mermaids, or fairies, or some such nonsense. He can 'reach out' elsewhere.

Jeff the minister called in at 11 a.m. During the warmer weather he travels on an electric bicycle rather than the bus—his winter mode of transport. He told me that his sermon on Sunday was about the perils of infidelity, inspired by a rumour that he'd heard about one of his parishioners.

Spent an hour on the telephone to the Royal Mail helpdesk after unsuccessfully setting up their DMO system to replace the clunky dinosaur that is OBA. Finally had everything in place and up and running only to discover that the much promoted DMO is even worse than OBA. The Royal Mail's legacy of being publicly owned is that it appears to have a profound affection for abbreviations. I have no idea what any of them stand for. These systems are unquestionably designed by people who never have to use them.

Till Total £330
29 Customers

TUESDAY, 2 JUNE

Online orders: 2
Orders found: 2

Two orders, one Abe and one Amazon. *Municipal Buildings of Edinburgh*, a beautiful Victorian architectural hardback with bevelled edges, gilt titles and 13 plates, 1895 sold for £60. The Amazon order was for a small, unremarkable paperback titled *Antar, the FV12000 Series British Army Service*—a book about a military vehicle that sold for £58. The days in which the former could be reasonably safely assumed to be worth around £50 while the latter would perhaps reach £8 are long behind us. Now it could easily be the other way around, and it's almost impossible to pick out the valuable modern paperbacks from the crowd without checking almost everything online.

An old woman came to the counter and said, 'Can you help me? I'm looking for a book but I can't remember the title. It's called *The Red Balloon*.' A predictably confused conversation followed.

Mr Deacon came in just before closing and bought a biography of Nelson. He's never a chatty man, but today he didn't even say hello.

Till Total £322.97
23 Customers

WEDNESDAY, 3 JUNE

Online orders: 7
Orders found: 6

Seven orders this morning. There must be a surge after delisting and relisting the Monsoon database on Amazon.

Isabel was in to do the accounts. She found a black cat in the office. We spent ten minutes chasing the little bastard around the shop.

Two American pensioners came in at three o'clock wearing nauseatingly tight Lycra cycling gear. They did what all cyclists do, which is to go straight to the Ordnance Survey maps, have a good look at them and plan a route, then leave empty-handed. More American cyclists came in later, one of whom spent a good deal of time telling me that you can use old books to make interesting craft objects. If Nicky had been here they would have waffled on together for hours.

Picked up my copy of *The New Confessions* from the 'To Be Read' pile again and read some more of it after work. I normally read a book right through once I've started it, but I appear to be interspersing this with other books. Perhaps I'm subconsciously trying to make it last longer. It's remarkably similar to *Any Human Heart* in some respects, although John James Todd (the narrator) lacks some of Logan Mountstuart's charm. It is a narrative of a full and fascinating life. He has now joined the army and is experiencing some of the full horrors of the First World War. Will return it to the 'To Be Read' pile and resume later. The way the book is structured oddly lends it to being read in this way; it's almost like several books in one. At almost 600 pages it could easily be several books.

Till Total £154
12 Customers

THURSDAY, 4 JUNE

Online orders: 4
Orders found: 3

Callum was in today to work on the bothy. It's getting closer to completion, but I don't think it will be ready in time for Emanuela.

An Australian man came to the counter mid-morning and told me that he'd got a bargain in a shop in Sydney: a five-volume set of Scott's Waverley novels in poor condition, published in 1841. He asked me what I would sell them for, so I told him £20 at the very most. He looked crestfallen. He'd paid £23 and was convinced that he'd bagged something worth a fortune. Waverley novels—however old—are rarely worth much unless they're in a fine binding. They are ubiquitous and have undergone so many reprints that—like Burns—very few editions of them have any value. The rule of thumb for Burns is that if they were published before his death (1796), then they probably have some value. After that they decline dramatically. Burns has one principal bibliographer, J. W. Egerer, and the list of editions of Burns's works he details in his book is astonishing. Several years ago a customer came to the counter with a very tatty two-volume set of Burns from about 1820. He asked me what I thought it would cost to rebind it, so I told him that it would probably be cheaper just to throw it away and buy a replacement set of the same edition. His unexpected response was to shout 'How dare you! This belonged to my great-grandfather!' Quite how he expected me to be privy to that information, I have no idea.

Fibre-optic engineer turned up at 10 a.m. and installed the new wiring for super-fast broadband.

Carol-Ann arrived at about two o'clock to run the shop while I'm away for her fiancé Craig's stag weekend. We're sailing in the Clyde. I drove up and stayed with friends near Ayr. I'll meet them early tomorrow morning on the boat in the marina.

Till Total £229.54
21 Customers

FRIDAY, 5 JUNE

Online orders:
Orders found:

Arrived at the marina at 8 a.m. to find everyone looking pretty hungover. They'd been drinking on the boat last night. We set sail at noon from Largs and headed for Tarbert, on the Cowal peninsula. Arrived at about 5 p.m. with a following wind in fairly pleasant conditions. Moored up and went to a bar, where Craig, considerably the worse for wear from the previous night, managed to drink less than a quarter of a pint.

Till Total £230
17 Customers

SATURDAY, 6 JUNE

Online orders:
Orders found:

Telephone call at 10 a.m. from Carol-Ann to say that the landline in the shop is dead and the credit card machine isn't working. This can only be related to the fibre-optic technician messing about with things, so I told her to call my broadband supplier and the phone company to sort it out.

Tremendously windy wet day, so we stayed in Tarbert until about 3 p.m., then set sail for Portavadie on the opposite side of the bay. Managed to rip the mainsail as we were putting it up. Limped into Portavadie and went for a meal and a few drinks in the fancy new marina they've built there.

Till Total £310.98
36 Customers

SUNDAY, 7 JUNE

Online orders:
Orders found:

Up reasonably early and sailed back to Largs. Cleared the boat and headed back to Wigtown. Home by 6 p.m.

MONDAY, 8 JUNE

Online orders: 2
Orders found: 2

Today was Flo's first day of working in the shop for the summer. The telephone and credit card machines were still out of action at lunchtime, so I checked all the new sockets and discovered that there was a cable that should have been plugged in but wasn't, so I connected it and everything worked again.

I logged on to the shop's Amazon seller account to check messages to find that, because of some new legislation, we now have to give them something called a Unique Business Code, a scan of my passport and a scan of a bank statement linked to the account into which they pay us their paltry pittance every fortnight. Failure to do so will result in the account being suspended and no sales online, so I emailed the Inland Revenue and requested a UBC. I suspect that the purpose of it is to tighten up the behaviour of Amazon, but it will inevitably have the consequence of penalising small businesses, onto whom Amazon dumps any extra costs.

Till Total £265.50
24 Customers

TUESDAY, 9 JUNE

Online orders: 4
Orders found: 2

Flo was in today, the day was warm and sunny: the diametric

opposite to her disposition. By lunchtime she hadn't uttered a single word in answer to my questions or requests, merely a series of shrugs and grunts in response.

Callum came in. He's working as many hours as he can in an effort to complete the bothy conversion before Emanuela arrives.

A woman called into the shop and made a massive fuss about the condition of a £4 book. She'd found it online and had decided to come to the shop to see it before she invested such a vast sum. When she brought it to the counter and started complaining about the torn jacket, and the previous owner's signature, I showed her the listing, in which every defect she'd complained about was outlined. She refused to pay more than £2 for it, so I relisted it at £8 (the next cheapest copy online is £12).

The book in question was called *The Princess in the Castle*, published in 1885 by the Religious Tract Society. Their books always look interesting and possibly valuable at first glance, but as soon as you see the name of the publisher, you can guarantee that they'll be worth very little. The Religious Tract Society was established in 1799 with the intention of evangelising women, children and the poor. Their later publications—from about 1850 onwards—are fairly saccharine and preachy. *The Princess in the Castle*, for example, contains a story called 'The Boy Who Obeyed His Mother.' I've got about a dozen RTS books on the shelves, but I can't recall ever selling one.

Spent the evening reading *Time's Arrow*.

Till Total £166.38
9 Customers

WEDNESDAY, 10 JUNE

Online orders: 5
Orders found: 3

Another hot day, sun shining. Flo made it in on time. Callum came in shortly afterwards.

I came downstairs with a cup of tea for Flo at 11 a.m. to find her staring in open-mouthed horror at a man wearing an unusual red beret. Her withering sartorial critique is usually directed towards me, so it was a refreshing change to see her glare directed at someone else.

Callum and I spent most of the day working in the bothy. At one point we were putting up some plasterboard when a customer appeared in the doorway—to get to which involved scrambling over rubble and building materials. He asked Callum 'Is this the Garden Room?' to which he replied that no, he had walked straight past the Garden Room. Customer replied 'Oh, is it through the door which has "Garden Room" written on it?'

Till Total £223.99
17 Customers

THURSDAY, 11 JUNE

Online orders: 2
Orders found: 0

Flo was in the shop today, surly and uncommunicative as always.

Till Total £40.50
7 Customers

FRIDAY, 12 JUNE

Online orders: 0
Orders found: 0

Hot sunny day. Nicky was in, but thankfully without a Foodie Friday treat. Callum came in just after 9 a.m. He'd climbed Cairnsmore yesterday, a nearby hill of 2,000 feet and a beautiful walk with stunning views in all directions. Ashley and George appeared at 10.30. Ashley assured me that they would be finished by Tuesday, or Wednesday next week at the latest. Ashley and George are boiler fitters and work for Ashley's father's company,

Solarae, based in Dumfries. They're fitting a biomass boiler at the back of the shop.

I spent much of the day helping Callum with the bothy. As the labourer, I was banished up in the crawlspace that passes for a loft, with electrical cables. I managed to rip my T-shirt on a loose nail while I was reversing out of it. It is a hot and hideous space, lined with fibreglass and full of dust. Today, with the summer sun beating down on it, it was almost unbearably still and stifling up there.

No orders from Amazon, so I suspect the account was suspended for non-compliance with the new regulations. The post arrived with the UBC form from the Inland Revenue, so after lunch I spent an hour filling in forms on Amazon. By the end of the day the account status had now changed to 'Pending.'

After work I took the van to Vincent's garage for a service, then went for a pint with Nicky and Callum. Nicky stayed the night, declining my offer of a comfortable bed in favour of her tramp's nest in the old warehouse.

Till Total £176.48
16 Customers

SATURDAY, 13 JUNE

Online orders: 4
Orders found: 4

Nicky was up and re-organising the music section when I came down at 9 a.m. She's unilaterally decided that we should use the space in the sci-fi section for the extra music books which are piled up on the floor. The sci-fi section—unlike most other sections— always appears to have a big gap. It is also one of the hardest sections to keep tidy. Whether this is because it is out of sight of the counter, and people don't feel they're being observed, or because sci-fi fans are naturally messy I'm not sure.

All of today's orders were from Amazon, so the 'Pending' status must have been updated. One of the orders was for a book about

Hammer studios, whose leading actor, Christopher Lee, died the day before yesterday.

Today's post included a letter from the British Library acknowledging receipt of their copy of *Tripe Advisor* which they requested. Because we ascribed an ISBN to the book when we produced it last year, we are obliged to (like every publisher) to supply a copy free of charge to all of the UK and Ireland's copyright libraries. There are six of these:

· The British Library, London
· National Library of Scotland, Edinburgh
· Bodleian Library, Oxford
· Cambridge University Library
· Trinity College, Dublin
· National Library of Wales, Aberystwyth

After lunch I went to collect the van from Vincent's, only to find that it was still up on the lift awaiting new brakes, due to arrive on Monday.

Till Total £235.96
23 Customers

MONDAY, 15 JUNE

Online orders: 5
Orders found: 3

Flo in, sarcastic and hostile, as usual.

Callum is working on the bothy, and Ashley and George were also in, putting in the new boiler, plus—at one point—Janetta cleaning the shop. This is going to be an expensive week.

I posted a request on Facebook for further contributors to submit book titles for the concrete book spirals and received five straight away. The idea of using this as a means of funding the planning application was Anna's and has proved remarkably successful. The concept is that anyone who wants to 'buy' a book title can pay £20 and either make up a title or suggest a real one.

Ian, at the engravers, then cuts them onto a piece of plastic, and I glue them to the concrete books.

Vincent came round with the van—complete with new brakes— at 3.30.

Finished *Time's Arrow*. I loved it—dark and absorbing, and a very unusual narrative device of a life lived backwards. Going to try something by Kingsley Amis next.

Till Total £208.98
23 Customers

TUESDAY, 16 JUNE

Online orders: 3
Orders found: 2

At 9 a.m. Flo, Callum, George and Ashley appeared simultaneously.

I spent the day working with Callum again, mainly back up in the hellish crawlspace that passes for a loft, this time with the water pipes for the new boiler. I spent half an hour up there in the dust and heat trying to push the alkathene pipe through a tiny hole that George had made for it. I emerged, as always, sweating, thirsty and scratching from the dust, so I stole Callum's cup of tea by way of petty vengeance.

In the early afternoon, as I was helping Callum put some plasterboard on the ceiling, Flo appeared in the bothy:

> Flo: There's a man here to see you.
> Me: Who is he?
> Flo: Dunno.
> Me: What's it about?
> Flo: Dunno.

So I dragged myself into the shop, leaving Callum balanced precariously on a stool trying to drill some drywall screws into the plasterboard above his head, to be met by a grinning old man with a Farmfoods bag full of old *People's Friends*.

Till Total £124.49
12 Customers

WEDNESDAY, 17 JUNE

Online orders: 5
Orders found: 3

Flo in at 9 a.m., and Callum was already working on the bothy before I opened the shop. George and Ashley appeared at about 10.30, but not before the electrician, who had been there since 9.30, expecting their arrival. He had to sit in his van until they arrived. No doubt I'm paying for all of this slack time.

The electrician managed to blow the electrics several times and plunge the entire shop into complete darkness. He also caused a minor flood when he inadvertently switched the pump on, and black water blew out of the open pipes which George and Ashley had been working on, soaking poor George.

A customer brought in a box of bound *National Geographic* magazines from the 1960s while I was out working in the bothy with Callum, so I told Flo to phone and tell him that we don't take magazines. We've tried selling them, but other than 1970s *Playboy*, *Penthouse* and *Mayfair*, they don't do well at all in the shop. Older magazines—for example, very early *Scots Magazine* (the first one was issued in 1739) and early *Tatler* (first published in 1709), and even *National Geographic* (first issued in 1888)—sell reasonably well, but apart from '70s soft porn, twentieth-century magazines are a bit of a non-starter. By far the most valuable of the *Scots Magazines* is the August 1776 issue, which was, I think, the first publication in the world to print the American Declaration of Independence in full.

There was no hot water in the house tonight—no doubt due to the plumbing changes for the new boiler.

In the afternoon I drove Anna to Lockerbie to catch the train to Edinburgh for a film course she's been invited to attend. The road was closed at Carsluith (about 15 miles from Wigtown) following an accident in which two lorries collided. There was debris everywhere, and the traffic was diverted through the tiny village and along a very narrow road, not remotely suitable for the ferry freight traffic, but we squeezed through and just made it to the train on time. The road was open again by the time I came home.

Till Total £144
10 Customers

THURSDAY, 18 JUNE

Online orders: 0
Orders found: 0

I came into the shop at 5 p.m. so that Flo could go home and found
her staring in fixed horror, this time at a customer in shorts, white
socks, pulled right up, and sandals. She was visibly relieved to be
going home. She's fascinated by what she sees as wardrobe trans-
gressions. The man in the red beret last week was almost too much
for her, but today's combination was clearly far worse.

After she'd gone, I started pricing up some books that had
come in several months ago, and which included nine volumes
of the *Highways and Byways* series. These were published by
Macmillan in the early twentieth century, and were distinctively
(and uniformly) bound in blue cloth with gilt titles to the front
boards and spines. They were regional guides written by people
with comprehensive knowledge of each area, and though they are
packed with information, they are quite informally written in the
style of a guided tour of each area, and filled with illustrations.
Other publishers tried to emulate the success of the series, most
notably Hodder and Stoughton with Arthur Mee's *The King's
England* series, and Robert Hale with *The County Books* series, but
none of them, for me, comes close to matching the aesthetic, the
production values or the content of *Highways and Byways*.

The volume local to Wigtown, *Highways and Byways in
Galloway and Carrick*, was written by Revd Charles Hill Dick and
published in 1916, with illustrations by Hugh Thomson, a well-
known artist of the period. Of Wigtown, Dick writes, 'one looks
up to it with a certain respect, not only because the situation is
dignified, but also on account of the dust of the martyrs lying in its
churchyard,' before examining elements of the town's history and
architecture. He also compares Galloway with Rockall in the way
it is overlooked—the forgotten corner of Scotland—a sentiment
echoed in a 1950s guide to the region that I recently discovered,
which reads: 'Even for Scottish tourists there is a smack of
adventure in invading Galloway on foot or by car, for no other
part of Scotland is so far off the beaten track, and, geographically

speaking, it is nearer to Ireland and more closely knit to it than to Central Scotland.'

As with most second-hand books, though, they've dropped in value over the past fifteen years, and whereas in 2001 I could expect £25 to £30 for a decent copy, nowadays £10 to £15 is all customers are prepared to pay for one.

Till Total £151.75
14 Customers

FRIDAY, 19 JUNE

Online orders: 3
Orders found: 2

Nicky arrived in Bluebell, her van, at 9.12 a.m.

George and Ashley came in to commission the new boiler. Now I just have to build a waterproof shelter over it.

We have about twenty boxes of fresh, exciting stock in boxes, which needs to be sorted and shelved. In another corner we have five boxes of books that are destined for the dump. As always Nicky went straight for the boxes we're throwing out and started rummaging around in them. For her this is the literary equivalent of the Morrisons skip.

Closed at 5 p.m. and went to the pub with Callum and Bob. In the pub I spotted the woman who is running The Open Book—an American woman who was scribbling in a notebook on the table in the corner. Introduced myself and invited her to join us. She has a bookshop in the States, and after the others had left, she and I chatted about the trials of bookselling in the twenty-first century.

Till Total £260.99
22 Customers

SATURDAY, 20 JUNE

Online orders: 2
Orders found: 2

Nicky arrived late and carrying a small plastic bag, which she thrust in my face and announced, 'Eh, look at that. I picked them from my garden this morning.' Expecting some fruit, or at least flowers, I leaned forward to be greeted by a bag of slimy snails and the words 'I'm putting them in your garden.' After some negotiation, she agreed to release them in a field.

Callum was already working in the bothy when I got there. He's reached a bit of an impasse and is waiting for Danny, the plumber, who was supposed to be here today.

At 2.30 p.m. Nicky reminded me that we had a Gaelic choir booked in to rehearse in the big room, so I hurriedly prepared it for them. They arrived at three.

Since it was a sunny day, I decided to eat my lunch in the garden but was slightly put off when I discovered a dead crow in the middle of the lawn, so I dug a small hole and gave it a decent burial. The cat will probably exhume its corpse and drag it into the house.

Till Total £250.96
21 Customers

MONDAY, 22 JUNE

Online orders: 5
Orders found: 2

Flo was in today, so I left at 10 a.m. to catch the ferry to Belfast to look at some books for a probate valuation. I arrived at the house (near the Botanic Gardens) at about 3 p.m. and met the executor of the estate, the dead man's brother, a much younger man than I had expected, with an impressive ginger moustache. There were books all over the house, and a lot of antiquarian Scottish material. By five I was only about a quarter of the way through them, so I told him that I'd need to stay the night and finish them in the morning.

He recommended a nearby hotel, which thankfully had a vacancy. I called Flo and she's agreed to open the shop tomorrow.

Till Total £120
12 Customers

TUESDAY, 23 JUNE

Online orders: 3
Orders found: 0

Flo opened the shop, so I continued to work my way through the rest of the books in the house in Belfast. The total for probate valuation came to £10,000, which is by far the highest probate valuation I've ever given. The collection contained two copies of Camden's *Britannia* and a number of other books that were in the high hundreds. As always with probate valuations, it was a lower figure than I would expect the books to realise at a sale. The deceased man's brother and I discussed what to do with them; I told him that I'm not in a position to offer anything like that amount and that they should go into a Scottish saleroom.

Caught the 3.30 ferry and was back home by 7 p.m.

Went for a walk in the garden (avoiding the spot where the dead crow had been) and picked a large bowl of strawberries from the polytunnel.

Till Total £247.25
20 Customers

WEDNESDAY, 24 JUNE

Online orders: 2
Orders found: 0

Flo was in again today. I'm not sure why we're managing to find so few of our orders. I will contact Monsoon again and see what the problem is.

The shop has been a complete mess for several weeks now, with piles of books everywhere—partly because the contents of the back of the Garden Room (now the bothy) are now scattered throughout it, partly because people keep bringing boxes of books in to sell.

Telephone call from a woman at Radio Scotland at 11 a.m. to see whether I had any thoughts on Amazon's latest controversial policy: only paying authors of books that sell on Kindle a royalty based on the number of pages that the purchaser reads. I suspect she wanted me to say that I thought this was wonderful and would drive people back to books, but this is not the case and the consumer rarely cares about such trifles as whether the author receives a royalty or not. I posted the news on Facebook and the following discussion ensued:

> **John Francis Ward:** Hmm … and if I order a meal and only eat part of it, could I only pay for that bit? It rather takes us back to Victorian times, with serialisation—maybe I could start selling my books to Amazon a page at a time? It is an extension of an uncertainty that already exists, in that a book is never sold till someone buys it from the shop—up to that point, it might yet be returned. The one good thing about it is that it might put more writers off dealing with Amazon.
>
> **Page & Blackmore Booksellers Ltd:** I think Amazon's idea is that you will pay for the whole meal you ordered but that the cook will be paid only for however much of it you actually eat.

Callum was in, working on the bothy. The plasterer came in and did about two-thirds of the plastering and said that he'd be back next Thursday to finish it off.

A customer wearing Crocs and red shorts and with a squat, aggressive dog spent an hour going through the boxes on the floor, leaving everything in piles all over the place while the dog growled at passers-by. They left without buying anything.

I was shovelling sand from the large tote bag (which has been on the pavement between my shop and Fiona's next door since we started work on the bothy about a month ago) when her husband, Robbie, appeared and told me that he was disappointed to see it going, and that it had made a welcome addition to the landscape of the high street. It has been there for so long that weeds have grown in it and are now setting seed.

Before closing the shop, I went to the bank in Newton Stewart and stopped at the baker's on the way back to the van to buy a sausage roll. The woman behind the counter told me, 'I love the music video you did in the shop.' Anna, Nicky and I had done a parody of 'Rapper's Delight' last year and put it on Facebook. I forget whose idea it was—either Nicky or Anna—but I remember walking into the kitchen one night after work to find the pair of them excitedly planning the choreography and the lyrics. Apparently our version is very popular in China.

After I shut the shop I drove to Rigg Bay, about 7 miles away, and went for a swim. It was completely deserted, and although the sea has yet to warm up noticeably, it was a refreshing end to the day, after shovelling sand for most of the afternoon. My friend Michele refers to Rigg Bay as 'the Kate Moss of beaches' because it is impossible to take a bad photograph of it.

Till Total £407.98
37 Customers

THURSDAY, 25 JUNE

Online orders: 7
Orders found: 7

At lunchtime a lorry arrived with a delivery of ninety-six sacks of pellets for the new boiler. At exactly the same time the carpet fitter turned up to fit the new doormat at the entrance to the shop. Callum and I were wrestling with removing the front door so that the fitters could get to work when the map rep appeared too and stood patiently by as we struggled. The final player on the crowded stage was a customer, who repeatedly said 'Excuse me' until I reluctantly let go of the door and politely asked what she wanted—'What's your wifi password?'

At 3 p.m. a couple came in; hard to tell the gender of either of them from either their appearance or their voice. One of them asked, 'Where is your palmistry books?'

Once everything had settled down, and the carpet fitters were working away, I bought a box of books from a woman. Included a first edition of *The War of the Worlds* (1898, Heinemann).

Till Total £165.98
16 Customers

FRIDAY, 26 JUNE

Online orders: 2
Orders found: 2

Nicky arrived at 9.15 a.m., late as usual. She hijacked the Facebook page and commented, 'First disappointment of the day ... 2 beer boxes and 8 wine boxes filled with ... yup, books.'

Appointment with the physiotherapist in Newton Stewart at 2 p.m. She gave me two pages of exercises to do, three times a day.

Closed the shop at 5 p.m. and went to the pub with Callum. Returned at seven to find a tiny dog turd on the doorstep. I know exactly whose dog is responsible.

Till Total £298.36
28 Customers

SATURDAY, 27 JUNE

Online orders: 2
Orders found: 2

Nicky's decided to update Facebook about our progress with the bothy:

Garden Room Bothy update at 5.10 p.m. yesterday ...
'So, shall we put the door on tonight?'
'Ummmm.'

'You could collect it in the van and we could hang it tonight.'
'Ummmm.'
'Or we could just do it tomorrow.'
'Yes, although I do have the van.'
'Yeah, and we could put it on tonight.'
'Maybe we should.'
'Or we could do it tomorrow'…
No door has been hung.

All a bit rich, considering that she'd been 'tidying up' the English topography section and it looked very much like a freshly ransacked house.

After lunch I drove to Dumfries to catch the train for Eliot's son's christening, or naming ceremony, as it is being euphemistically called. On the way there the road was closed and diverted through Carsluith due to an accident. There was a Land Rover in the middle of a field, but it didn't look too bad. An hour later, as I was on the train, I received a message from Anna telling me that Robbie Murphie—whose wife, Fiona, has the shop next door to mine—had been killed on his motor bike in the accident. Robbie was a thoroughly decent man, and an excellent GP. Everyone who knew him had the utmost respect for him, and although it always sounds trite when someone young has died, he was so well known and liked in the community that his absence will be keenly felt. He was a rare combination of relentless good humour, quick wit and kindness.

Till Total £286.27
19 Customers

MONDAY, 29 JUNE

Online orders: 4
Orders found: 1

Checked Facebook first thing this morning to discover further hijacking of the page by Nicky on Saturday:

yee heuch! Traditional musicians in the square (loudspeakers on!—in yer face Radio 3), the smell of sweaty horses as they canter past the door giving a cheeky wee buck to thrill the crowds, as the Riding of the Marches is introduced after an absence of 60 years! Beer! Can it get any better? Yes! Shaun's in London!

Flo in. As always, she made the bare minimum of effort to find today's orders, in part owing to the fact that today is her eighteenth birthday, which in her world absolves her of the requirement to do anything productive in the workplace.

The garden is in full bloom, and the scent of blossom fills the evening air. A particular favourite is a shrub I planted next to a gateway, *Viburnum x Burkwoodii*. According to the retired gardener of Galloway House (the seat of the earls of Galloway), the last incumbent to live there insisted on having them planted next to the French windows of the dining room, so that he could savour the scent while he ate.

At almost eleven o'clock it was still light enough to sit outside on a bench with a beer and read as the bats flitted by.

Till Total £260.47
27 Customers

TUESDAY, 30 JUNE

Online orders: 2
Orders found: 2

Flo in, mildly hungover after her eighteenth birthday last night.

A customer with a braided beard asked, 'How much is this copy of the *Edinburgh and Leith Post Office Directory 1938*? I'm quite interested in it.'

Me: It's £35.
Customer: What! That's outrageous. Who would want to buy that?

Well, you for a start.

As I was getting changed into my work clothes (painting, gardening sort of work, rather than pricing books up), I spotted several moths flying around the bedroom, so I checked my kilt and tweed suit. Both have suffered heavy losses in the war of moth attrition, so I will unleash the Doom moth killer when I'm next away for a few days and fumigate the room.

Must get round to doing my back exercises. They look so boring that I keep making excuses for not doing them.

Till Total £193
13 Customers

JULY

It is not often we second-hand booksellers go into one of these spick-
and-span places where books are garbed in their paper jackets like
women in coloured waterproofs on a crowded railway platform. As
like as not, the seller of new books nowadays has to go nap on a Fancy
Department where you can buy anything from pen-nibs to photo
frames. It's a sad fall, and a sign of the times. Will the day come,
I wonder, when second-hand booksellers must run a department
where you can buy cough-drops, aspirin and pickles? God forbid. We
have our pride. Mr Pumpherston never uses the word second-hand;
he says it reminds him of an old clothes shop. The lettering above his
door tells folk that he is an Antiquarian Bookseller. I wonder what
some of the shabby books on the sixpenny stall outside think when
they take a keek upwards. Maybe they puff out their tattered chests
and reflect after all there is some dignity in death.

Augustus Muir, *The Intimate Thoughts of John Baxter, Bookseller*

Muir is correct that we second-hand booksellers don't darken the
doors of 'spick-and-span places,' but that's largely because most of
our businesses are owner-run and can no longer afford staff, so we're
stuck in our own little worlds most of the time, surrounded by dusty
books. I can't really think of a more pleasant environment, but it has
drawbacks, and whenever I have the opportunity, if I'm travelling,
I'll nose out other second-hand bookshops to see what they're doing,
and whether they have any ideas I can steal or diversify.

He's also right about sellers of new books having had to adapt
and sell other things. It seems like a remarkably prescient observation, and could have been written just a few years ago in its
relevance to the changes ravaging both the new and the second-
hand book industries thanks to the icy grip of Amazon, but to
talk of Amazon is to start ploughing a field that is already well
furrowed. I sincerely hope, though, that I won't end up having

to sell cough drops, aspirin and pickles in order to provide the financial security to allow me to continue selling books.

Muir was uncannily prescient though, in his prediction that 'cough-drops, aspirin and pickles' would be sold beside books on the shelf. He could have added almost any product to his short list and described the modern supermarket.

As for the antiquarian versus second-hand argument, the meaning of the word is sufficiently vague that I suppose Pumpherston could get away with calling himself an antiquarian dealer since he is 'dealing in, or interested in old or rare books.' Generally, though, antiquarian tends to imply an age of well over a hundred years, and of sufficient interest and quality to have significant value. A cheap hundred-year-old church hymnbook might technically qualify as antiquarian, but few dealers would ever attempt to pass it off as such.

WEDNESDAY, 1 JULY

Online orders: 3
Orders found: 1

Flo in. Callum came in to help the plumber, who apparently talked all day about local gossip and fitted two pipes, which Callum assured me should have taken about half an hour. Still, a small step further forward with the plumbing.

Anne Barclay turned up to collect the marquee (which I bought a few years ago under the deluded notion that I might have a fortieth birthday party) for Relay for Life. Anne runs the Wigtown Book Festival and is a stalwart, working tirelessly organising all manner of things, including the cancer fundraiser Relay.

In the afternoon I drove to Edinburgh with Anna to go to the Queen's garden party at Holyrood Palace. It was packed, and we bumped into quite a few people we knew. Anna had prepared a speech in case the Queen decided to talk to her, but considering the 8,000 other people there, it came as no surprise that she wasn't picked to be engaged in conversation. Anna's version of reality is very much that of a romantic American who has watched too many

Ealing comedies. I think in her imagination the Queen regularly has people like us around for tea parties.

We drove home via Prestwick airport to pick up Emanuela, the Italian woman who has volunteered to work in the shop for the summer. Prestwick is not known for its glamour. Even its slogan ('Pure dead brilliant') hardly evokes the sophisticated world of international air travel. I've often ruminated on the wisdom of the person who signed off on an airport using the word 'dead' in its marketing brand. Emanuela cut rather a stylish dash among the denizens of the Arrivals lounge, quite tall and slim, and well dressed. She talked all the way home, but I barely understood a word she said. Her written English is considerably better than her spoken English, which—while it may well have been perfect—was rendered in an accent so strong as to make it almost unintelligible. The 'ghost vowel' that is characteristic of many Italians speaking English is certainly present in Emanuela's version, so everything is prefixed and suffixed with the letter 'a.' We arrived home at about 7 p.m., with Anna visibly unhappy that there's another woman in the house (the bothy, predictably, isn't ready yet). Unlike Emanuela, she was completely silent for the entire journey back from Prestwick, and her usual sunny disposition and delight in everything around her seemed cloaked in a heavy cloud.

Till Total £108.20
22 Customers

THURSDAY, 2 JULY

Online orders: 2
Orders found: 1

There seems to be a problem with Amazon's FBA marketplace. We've had no orders for some time now. Flo emailed them, and managed to have it working again by the end of the day.

Emanuela appeared at 9 a.m. from the spare room, so I showed her around the shop and set her to tidy the shelves and familiarise herself with the layout. This was the first job John Carter gave me when I worked for him in the weeks before I took over the shop, and undeniably one of the most useful, as knowing where each section and subject is will enable you to answer 80 per cent of customer questions, but I have no idea how this is going to work with Emanuela's spoken English. Every time I say anything to her she cranes her neck and looks at me like a turkey through her incredibly thick glasses, and says 'Sorry?' Usually three or four repetitions will eventually result in some form of understanding. She also insists on pronouncing my name as 'Shone,' and describes her way of speaking as 'Chinese English.' It's almost like a poor parody of some politically incorrect comedian from the 1970s impersonating an Italian.

Language isn't my forte, so it would be unfair of me to criticise Emanuela for her embryonic English, although it often results in considerable amusement. When I first went to Wigtown Primary School at the age of four, I'd grown up on a farm with an English father and an Irish mother, and although I had friends (my mother set up the Wigtown Playgroup for pre-school children for this very reason), I had yet to be fully exposed to the Wigtownshire dialect. When I went to school, everyone seemed to know one another, and I could barely understand anything anyone said. As I progressed through Wigtown Primary I often felt that I spoke two languages. Even the words for 'one' and 'two,' pretty fundamental to an understanding of any language, are different: in Wigtownshire they're 'yin' and 'twa.' My parents always found it highly entertaining when they heard me speaking to my friends as a child.

Mark, the plasterer, turned up at 7 p.m. and finished plastering the bothy. Once that's dry I will get to work painting it a.s.a.p. and Emanuela can move into it, assuming the plumber turns up to finish the job. Shortly afterwards I was in the kitchen with Emanuela when *The Archers* came on the radio. Her ears pricked up and she listened with rapt attention. After the closing theme tune she asked, 'What dis? A comedy?'

Till Total £322.48
22 Customers

FRIDAY, 3 JULY

Online orders: 1
Orders found: 1

Nicky was in today. After she'd found the solitary order, she tracked down three of the orders that Flo had been unable to locate earlier in the week. She gave Emanuela a guided tour of the shop, which—I'm guessing—contained useful tips like 'The boss likes it if you leave books in piles all over the floor' and 'If you cannae fit the book on the shelf in the right section just find a space in another section.' She didn't seem her usual ebullient self, though. I wonder if she feels her job is under threat from Emanuela.

The Samye Ling people (who drop off unwanted books from the library of the Tibetan retreat in Dumfriesshire) dropped off four boxes, including one that contained nothing but books about incest—both grim survivors' tales and psychology books on the subject of sexual abuse. I'm not sure how big a market there is for that in the shop.

It was a sunny day, so I made Pimm's for Nicky and Emanuela, which we drank in the shop before closing up. Emanuela guzzled hers in a couple of large draughts, declaring that it was her first ever Pimm's, and that it was 'a-very-a good-a.'

Till Total £131.99
11 Customers

SATURDAY, 4 JULY

Online orders: 4
Orders found: 3

A dull day and a leaden sky.

Emanuela seems to be settling in well and is working hard, although she insists on wearing white gloves when she's handling the books. I'm not sure Nicky likes her, but Emanuela seems blissfully unaware of Nicky's opprobrium.

After work I cooked supper for Emanuela, who despite her slim figure wolfed down about three times what I ate. Like the Pimm's, she told me that it was 'a-very-a good-a' before disappearing up to her room for the rest of the evening.

Till Total £159.99
23 Customers

MONDAY, 6 JULY

Online orders: 10
Orders found: 9

When I came downstairs this morning, Emanuela was sitting in the kitchen wearing what appeared to be an enormous turban. In fact, it was just a towel. She explained that she has to keep it on for an hour after she washes her hair.

Callum came around to work on the bothy. No Flo—she's gone to Paris for the week with her mother. Emanuela volunteered to take charge of the front of the shop. At least, I think that's what she said.

There was no power in the circuit that runs to the bothy. Apparently it's been like that since the electrician came to do the wiring for the new pellet boiler, so I called Ronnie, the electrician, who always comes at the drop of a hat, and who appeared within moments and sorted it all out.

After work I went to the Unicorn Chinese restaurant in Newton Stewart with some old friends, Anne and David. Anne used to be the chair of the Wigtown Book Festival, and I've known her all my life. We got back at about eleven and David and I stayed up and talked about fishing and cricket until about 1 a.m. Emanuela looked bored, so I offered to explain the rules of cricket to her. She looked disapprovingly at me over the top of her exceptionally thick glasses and said an emphatic 'a-no-a, fank you.'

Till Total £333.81
24 Customers

TUESDAY, 7 JULY

Online orders: 3
Orders found: 3

One of today's orders was for a book called *R. F. D. Country! Mailboxes and Post Offices of Rural America*. Inside the front cover was a photograph of the authors, possibly the two geekiest-looking specimens I've ever seen.

As I was tidying the shelves, I spotted a copy of *Lucky Jim* by Kingsley Amis in the Penguin section and put it in the snug to read later.

After lunch I nervously left Emanuela in charge of the shop and went to the river. This is one of my favourite places in Galloway, and the lower stretches of the Luce meander lazily around the soft landscape of the glen before spilling into the sea. Tree-lined and tranquil, it is a place I've known for almost my entire life. My father first took me fishing when I was two years old, and I caught a small trout (with his help). From that moment, apparently, it was all I wanted to do, to the point at which whenever I saw him throwing his fishing gear into his car, I would become agitated and insist on going with him. Today I was fishing the pool in which I caught my first salmon, and I bagged a sea trout of about 3lb. Anna (who is staying with Finn and Ella at the moment) came over and we ate it for supper. Emanuela looked horrified at the sight of the dead fish, pointing to its head, saying 'a-poor-a feesh-a' several times, before devouring about half of it.

Till Total £325.53
35 Customers

WEDNESDAY, 8 JULY

Online orders: 3
Orders found: 3

Flo was in, back from her trip to Paris, so this morning I took Emanuela to the post office to show her where to leave the bags with the online orders, and to meet Wilma, the wonderful woman who works there. On the way back Emanuela pronounced, 'Wow, thees are amazing. It not just a post-a office. It sell-a everyfink.' As we were passing the chemist, there was a man outside telling his poodle that no, he couldn't go in there because dogs aren't allowed. But he's still a very good boy, apparently. Emanuela petted the poodle in Italian.

Later in the afternoon a customer brought in eleven boxes of completely unsellable books: Chambers encyclopaedias with spines sellotaped on, tatty Dick Francis and Jeffrey Archer paperbacks, Harmsworth Self-Educators, book club editions of John Galsworthy and so on. Of the eleven boxes, I managed to pick out about twenty books that might, at a push, sell in the shop.

At about 4 p.m. I went to the river for an hour, but caught nothing. After work Anna and I went to Rigg Bay to look for a piece of driftwood to adapt as a newel post for the bothy and found a superb piece of ash around which an ivy plant had snaked its way.

When I returned to the house at about 7 p.m., Emanuela was resplendent in her turban once again. When I asked her what time she'd like to eat, she replied 'alf an hour. I go upstairs and wash-a me legs first.' I thought it best not to inquire further.

Till Total £233.47
20 Customers

THURSDAY, 9 JULY

Online orders: 2
Orders found: 2

As I was checking the orders, I found a letter addressed to someone with the unfortunate name of Henry H. Crapo inside the front cover of one of them.

After work Emanuela disappeared off to the co-op, returning about an hour later with a faraway look on her face. When I asked her where she'd been, she told me 'The co-op. How I love de co-op. De people is so friendly, and it have everyfink. I spend one hour in there every day from now on.'

Till Total £196.80
20 Customers

FRIDAY, 10 JULY

Online orders: 2
Orders found: 2

Nicky was in. Her heart-throb from the Jehovah's Witnesses is going to be in the area this weekend, giving a talk at the Stranraer Kingdom Hall.

> Nicky: I need to lose two stone in two days.
> Me: How are you going to do that?
> Nicky: Well, I've shaved my legs. That's lost me four pounds.
> Me: What are you going to wear when you meet him?
> Nicky: I'm going for a 1972 Polish communist look.

We decided that the best solution for Nicky losing two stone in two days is to amputate something. We were all in agreement that it should be her head, as this solves the problem of how to style her hair at the same time.

In the afternoon I went to Robbie Murphie's funeral with Anna and Callum. Huge crowd. His daughter Christie spoke very movingly of him.

Till Total £270.58
31 Customers

SATURDAY, 11 JULY

Online orders: 1
Orders found: 1

Nicky was in on time.

Sunny day and the African Drumming Group was in the gardens all morning, lending an exotic tone to the town. They're based in the west of the county, and largely made up of women, although Sandy the tattooed pagan was a member for a while. He took considerable delight in telling me that he'd been 'drummed out.' They usually come to Wigtown during the festival or, if the mood takes them, at other times in the spring and summer.

A man in bleached shorts with white hair came in and talked at Emanuela for half an hour—'There's a big tree in Greece which has money growing on it and people just pick it off the tree when they want it ... same problem with the SNP, it's a ferocious culture, now here's a funny story, in the Normandy landings ...'—all this punctuated with some hip thrusts and dancing in his sock-and-sandal combo, and doing proper growling sounds into her face. The poor girl had no idea what he was talking about. Perhaps that was a blessing.

Nicky sold a map for £180 to a man who she decided (for reasons best known to herself) was a born-again Christian: 'They're mental, they folk.' She and Emanuela seem to be getting on a little bit better. Emanuela's English—while infinitely better than my handful of Italian words—is causing a few communication problems with customers, and her white gloves are not quite as clean as they were on her first day.

After work I made a short video in the garden about how to upgrade your Kindle to a Kindle Fire. It involved half a gallon of petrol and a box of matches.

Till Total £546.46
30 Customers

MONDAY, 13 JULY

Online orders: 7
Orders found: 6

Flo and Emanuela were both in the shop today. I left instructions for them to tidy the place up and list any fresh stock on Monsoon, then headed off at 9 a.m. for Yetholm (in the Borders, about three hours away) to look at a military history collection, and then on to a private library in Melrose. The Yetholm collection was a lead from my friend Stuart Kelly and belonged to a man who works in the Middle East who was disposing of his late father's collection. I offered him £350 for the books. As I opened the back door of the van to load the boxes of books, a tin of emulsion that I'd bought to paint the bothy kitchen fell out onto the driveway and cracked open, spilling paint all over the place. Thankfully, he was very understanding.

The place in Melrose was an enormous town house; the people selling the books were moving to a smaller house and lacked the space to accommodate the library. He had been involved in setting up the Melrose Book Festival. The books were piled on top of a full-size billiards table, and I had to walk through several rooms and past an indoor swimming-pool to get to them. I only wanted about one third of the library, but since they were moving house, they asked if I could take them all. Thankfully there was a team of three furniture removers packing the contents of the house up, so they kindly helped me lug the boxes to the van. I paid £600 for the books I wanted, which included a few interesting antiquarian titles.

After a fairly exhausting day I spent the night with friends near Peebles, as I have to look at another library in a nearby house in the morning.

Till Total £253.50
48 Customers

TUESDAY, 14 JULY

Online orders: 3
Orders found: 3

At 8.30 a.m. I received a telephone call from the person I was supposed to be seeing this morning to say that he'd been called away unexpectedly, and could we postpone, so I drove home, and was back in time for lunch, only to find that Flo and Emanuela had strewn books and boxes throughout the shop in a way that would have made even Nicky blush.

After work I went for a walk with Emanuela to show her a bit of the area. As we were walking past a field of cows, she suddenly stopped and grabbed my arm. When I asked what was wrong, she pointed at a nearby cow (on the other side of a dry stone dyke) and said, 'The cow-a he is look at me. Look, look his eye! He 'ate me!' I tried to explain to her that the cow didn't hate her, but she has managed to convince herself that it's not just cows, but all animals that 'ate her.

Till Total £259.49
29 Customers

WEDNESDAY, 15 JULY

Online orders: 1
Orders found: 1

Flo was in today. She parcelled up the random books, approximately 150 of them. While she was packing them up, she told me that she'd 'had a dream when I was in Paris that you had put a hidden camera behind the computer and uploaded a video of me asleep at work.' Ah, the high calibre of this summer's staff.

Owing to lack of space in the shop, I had to drop off most of the books from the Melrose library at Finn's. I told him that he can have most of them as stock for The Open Book if he so desires.

In the evening I made a huge pot of parsnip and apple soup for supper (and to last for lunch for the rest of the week). Emanuela appeared in the kitchen at about 8 p.m. and asked what it was, so I told her, to which she replied, 'What is bastarding apple soup?' I told her to help herself, then went into the garden to pick strawberries. When I came back twenty minutes later, she was sitting in a chair grinning. The pot of soup was completely empty.

Got to the chapter in *Lucky Jim* where Welch has a party in his house and Dixon stays overnight. I haven't laughed aloud at a piece of writing so much in a long time, particularly the moment when the pompous Professor Welch offers Dixon a drink: 'In a moment he'd taken a bottle of port from among the sherry, beer, and cider which filled half a shelf inside. It was from this very bottle that Welch had, the previous evening, poured Dixon the smallest drink he'd ever been seriously offered.'

Till Total £172.49
20 Customers

THURSDAY, 16 JULY

Online orders: 5
Orders found: 5

Unusually, there was no sign of Emanuela when I opened the shop. She appeared, half an hour later, a bit flustered and apologising that she was late because 'I have to put-a in order-a the face.'

Norman Furnishings arrived at 11 a.m. to put the carpet down in the bothy.

After lunch I left Flo and Emanuela in charge and went to look at books in The Barony. The Barony is an agricultural college about 6 miles from Dumfries, and Karen, the librarian, calls me whenever they're having a clear-out. Mostly it's ex-library stock, and not particularly good, but occasionally there's something amongst it that makes the journey worthwhile. On the way there I was stuck at traffic lights near the turn-off to Glenkiln when Flo rang. Normally this only happens if there's an emergency, so I answered. A concert pianist had come to the shop to sell CDs of her music, which, from what I could gather, was accompanied by some children's storytelling. I dislike this sort of thing, so I told Flo to tell her that we don't sell CDs. Clearly not satisfied with this response, the concert pianist demanded to speak to me, so I told Flo to tell her that I couldn't, as I was driving. I could hear the concert pianist in the background saying, 'Tell him to pull over so that I can speak to him,' so I hung up.

Till Total £157
16 Customers

FRIDAY, 17 JULY

Online orders: 5
Orders found: 5

Nicky was in today, with some feta and spinach horrors that she'd raided from the Morrisons skip last night after her Kingdom Hall meeting.

Following a call earlier in the week I drove to Troon (65 miles away) to look at a maritime history collection. My suspicions were aroused by the presence of a yapping terrier and a man with a fluffy moustache and freshly ironed nylon trousers washing his car outside the house. Both the terrier and the car (and probably the moustache) were clearly fussed about and doted over. A woman in her sixties in a polyester skirt (which probably generated enough static electricity to power half of Troon every time she stood up from the sofa) explained that the collection belonged to her late brother. I went through them and made her an offer of £200 for about half of them. Her husband took a break from stroking the bonnet of his vomit-yellow Mondeo and came in to see what was what. After I'd explained the situation, he asked me to separate the books I wanted from those I didn't—something I'd normally have done at the start but she had requested that I didn't. After a couple of minutes, when I was about a quarter of the way through, he interrupted and said, 'For £200 we're not even in the same ball park.' Occasionally it happens that the seller wants more than I'm prepared to pay for a collection, but it's quite rare. Rarer still is that the seller lacks the capacity to articulate this politely and leave any room for discussion, but this was such an occasion, and I was happy to leave empty-handed and with £200 still in my wallet.

The new boiler has started making a whining noise, so something is clearly wrong with it.

Till Total £202.96
25 Customers

SATURDAY, 18 JULY

Online orders: 1
Orders found: 1

Nicky opened the shop. She had made some sort of concoction that involved chocolate fudge cake, cherry pie, strawberries and yoghurt. Apparently it was 'healthy' because of the fruit and yoghurt. I politely declined her kind invitation to try some.

Shortly before lunch a customer marched up to the counter and asked, 'Is there anyone around here who makes bookcases?'

> Me: We made our own, but most joiners will build you a bookcase if you ask them.
> Customer: But I'm looking for someone who specialises in them and makes them habitually.

After being told that there was nobody around here who 'makes them habitually,' he spent a good ten seconds attempting to leave the shop by repeatedly pushing against the door which you have to pull to open.

Till Total £310.47
33 Customers

MONDAY, 20 JULY

Online orders: 3
Orders found: 3

Flo spent most of the day labelling the Random Book Club parcels. We couldn't find the Royal Mail forty-eight-hour delivery stamp—three of us (me, Flo and Emanuela) spent about two hours looking for it (it's normally in a plastic box under the counter with all the other mail supplies)—so I took the boxes of parcels to the post office for Wilma to process instead. There were roughly 150 of them. RBC mailing usually works out at about £1.80 per book using the online mailing system we have on contract with Royal Mail. Sending them via the post office they averaged £2.20.

Flo's idiotic comment of the day: 'Do the Scottish islands count as overseas?'

Flo and Emanuela continued sorting through the boxes from Melrose. They got very excited when they found a set of *Golliwog* books that were selling online for about £40 each.

Janetta came to clean the shop at 3 p.m., as she does every Monday, and found the missing Royal Mail forty-eight-hour stamp within about five minutes of arriving.

During supper with Anna and Emanuela tonight, Emanuela started complaining about her various ailments. I commented that it was very unusual for someone a mere twenty-five years old to be so afflicted (bad knee, bad back, terrible eyesight), to which she replied, 'Yes, but I am eighty-five years old inside, like an old granny.' And in that moment her new nickname was born: 'Granny.'

Till Total £699.29
53 Customers

TUESDAY, 21 JULY

Online orders: 2
Orders found: 2

I left Flo and Granny (Emanuela) running the shop to go to the Borders to meet with another childhood friend, Tris, who kindly spent the day teaching me a type of cast that is useful on larger rivers, or where there are trees near the bank. It's known as the Spey cast. We met up on the River Tweed (about three hours' drive away). After fishing for a few hours I had tea with him and his wife, Delia, a good friend from my teenage years and former neighbour on the farm on which I grew up. She runs a café/gallery in Lilliesleaf, in the Borders. We compared the seasonality of our businesses and the similar trials we face with staffing costs and other things that you only really discover when you're running a small enterprise in rural Scotland. Back home at 9 p.m. to find that Flo had made a huge display of the *Golliwog* books. I took them down immediately. They are far from politically correct. In fact, it conflicts me enormously when I'm buying books and come across this sort of thing. They have value, both financial and historical, but who knows into whose hands they will fall: possibly those of someone with a curious historical interest in attitudes to skin colour or someone who wishes to use them in a contemporary context either to ridicule them or to raise issues of racial prejudice—or perhaps those of a racist. Certainly, I don't want visitors to the shop to be greeted with an enormous display of them.

Till Total £299.67
30 Customers

WEDNESDAY, 22 JULY

Online orders: 1
Orders found: 1

Only one order today. Flo spent the day listing books on FBA. She managed 120 yesterday, but among them were things that I don't imagine will ever sell for more than a penny on Amazon, but for which Monsoon is bringing up prices of £5 or £6, such as Edwina Currie's autobiography. I should probably sit down with Flo and explain this: Nicky intrinsically understands, probably from working in the shop for so long, but Flo will happily put a P. G. Wodehouse in the bin if Monsoon shows that it is available on Amazon for a penny, despite every one of his titles selling like hot cakes in the shop for £2 or £3, even in tatty paperbacks.

Isabel came in to do the accounts.

In the afternoon I showed Flo how to complete the FBA shipment and organise UPS to come and collect the eleven boxes of books she's now listed, so that they'll end up in Amazon's Dunfermline warehouse and hopefully start selling from there.

Granny has taken to doing a sort of mafia thing where she points at her own eyes, then at mine, then makes a cutting throat gesture when I do something she disapproves of. Mercifully, her boots have a large, hard heel, and she sounds like a marching army as she clomps around the shop, so I can hear her approaching well in advance and take evasive action. When I pointed this out to her, she replied, 'Oh yes, I am very elephant-a.'

Till Total £254.48
27 Customers

THURSDAY, 23 JULY

Online orders: 2
Orders found: 1

Flo was in again. She proudly announced that she's mastered a new facial expression, which she had clearly spent a good deal of time working on in front of a mirror last night. It's a cross between a scowl and a pout. Tried to come up with a name for it. So far it's either 'scout' or 'powl.' I asked for whose benefit she had been working on this charming new look, and she admitted that she has a 'secret' boyfriend.

Despite the fact that it was a warm, sunny day, Granny spent a good deal of it complaining about the temperature. She has decided that her eyesight is getting worse, and took off her glasses to demonstrate: 'Everyfink are just-a colours, no shapes.'

The UPS driver came at noon to pick up the eleven boxes to be delivered to the Amazon warehouse.

Will, my neighbour, called round to complain that the noise of the boiler is keeping him awake at night, so I emailed Solarae to see if Ashley could come and have a look at it.

This weekend is Wickerman, a music festival near Dundrennan (about 40 miles away). Zoe Bestel, a talented local singer/songwriter, is performing. The festival has been going for about fifteen years and attracts some pretty big names these days. Peter, Zoe's father, asked if he could borrow the van for the weekend, and picked it up just before I closed the shop. Flo's off there tomorrow for the weekend.

Till Total £275.80
39 Customers

FRIDAY, 24 JULY

Online orders: 0
Orders found: 0

Granny was pricing books up when she came across a book called *Mother of God: A History of the Virgin Mary*. The title page has—scrawled in pencil in what bears a suspiciously close resemblance to Nicky's handwriting—the words 'Mother of <u>Jesus</u>, not God.'

Granny and I had a discussion about the condition of second-hand books. From my perspective as a dealer, I like them to be in as good a condition as possible, but Granny has a different, and more interesting view. She told me, 'I like to read-a books-a which have been read by many, many people. I love-a the folded corners of books-a because it makes me wonder what caused the person to stop-a reading at this point? What-a happened? Did the cat need-a to be fed? Did the police-a knock on the door-a to tell you that your husband had been killed? Or did you just need-a to go for a piss? All of these-a things, all of them make you fink about-a the other people who have read-a this book.'

Till Total £254.99
26 Customers

SATURDAY, 25 JULY

Online orders: 2
Orders found: 2

Nicky's first comment of the day was 'Ooh, I got you a lovely pastry from the Morrisons skip. It's got Belgian chocolate and caramelised sea salt.'

Me: You ate it on the way in, didn't you?
Nicky: Aye.

Telephone call mid-morning from Davy Brown reminding me that I'd agreed to lend him the van on Monday morning. I'd forgotten all about it. Peter Bestel is at the Wickerman festival with it. Hopefully it will be back by Monday morning.

It was a glorious day, so after lunch I left Nicky and Granny in the shop, and cycled to New Luce, round trip of 55 miles.

Peter Bestel dropped the van off at 5 p.m., thankfully.

Till Total £174
22 Customers

MONDAY, 27 JULY

Online orders: 5
Orders found: 5

Anna is off on a short trip to Amsterdam to meet up with some of her friends. She dropped Granny off at Lockerbie so that she could go to Edinburgh for a few days of 'touristic.'

The first customers of the week were a family of five who spent an hour browsing, then left empty-handed, complaining that 'There's too much choice.'

Flo telephoned in sick. Apparently she's not well following a tequila bender at the Wickerman festival, so I called Nicky, who agreed to come in. In the old days the girls (students) would turn up regardless of how hungover, or even still drunk, they were. I'm hard pressed to remember a day when her predecessor, Sara Pearce, failed to turn up to work under some form of intoxication. I never thought that I'd miss her. I once came down into the shop after lunch to find that she had taken a photograph of herself, framed it and written 'Employee of the Month' on it. It was sitting proudly on the counter.

Old friend Chris Brown and his family came to the shop. They live in China, so we made a short video outside the shop with his daughter speaking in Mandarin, to appeal to the people in China who apparently love the *Reader's Delight* video. Lara, my friend Colin's daughter, came with them and stayed behind when they left: she's here for a week's work experience.

Till Total £527.45
45 Customers

TUESDAY, 28 JULY

Online orders: 2
Orders found: 2

Heavy rain overnight and into the day. Flo limped in just after 9 a.m., looking rough, so I went to the river and left her to show Lara the ropes.

When I returned at 3 p.m., I found the Irishman waiting there with seven boxes of books about trains and buses, so I gave him £140 for them.

Both Robert (plumber) and Callum were in today, working on the bothy.

Till Total £414.99
41 Customers

WEDNESDAY, 29 JULY

Online orders: 7
Orders found: 4

Glorious sunny day. Flo was in again, finally back to her usual scowling, pouting self. Callum was in to work on the bothy. Robert, the plumber, arrived at 9 a.m.

Flo and I sorted the books from The Barony and we loaded the forty-seven boxes of recycled and rejected stock into the van, and I drove it up to the recycling plant in Glasgow. After I'd dumped the books at the Smurfit Kappa plant, I headed straight back home. Arrived just after the shop had shut.

Ashley from Solarae telephoned to say that he'd had to replace the fan on the boiler that was keeping Will awake all night. Once he'd stripped it down, he discovered a decapitated blackbird wedged in the blades. It must have fallen down the flue.

Till Total £197
32 Customers

THURSDAY, 30 JULY

Online orders: 3
Orders found: 2

Robert, the plumber, was working on the hot water tank in the bothy. My brand new pellet boiler has a brand new fault; the water pressure in the buffer tank has dropped. Robert reluctantly admitted that it might be because he has been messing about with the plumbing.

Till Total £467
35 Customers

FRIDAY, 31 JULY

Online orders: 0
Orders found: 0

Nicky in this morning.

I discovered that Flo hadn't checked the Amazon Seller Central messages all week and we had multiple complaints, so I showed her how to access them and deal with each one. Most sellers live in perpetual fear of being suspended from Amazon, and it doesn't take much for them to—seemingly arbitrarily—kick you off.

Granny showed me her fingers, the tips of which (around the nails) were inflamed and swollen. She thinks it is from handling dusty books. Another ailment to add to her comprehensive list.

Till Total £212.69
23 Customers

AUGUST

I say that these old fellows are the very backbone of the book trade.
As they drop off one by one, like leaves from a tree, there is a gap
which no modern pushful young salesman can fill, and they leave a
memory that is a good deal more fragrant than the smelly hair-oil
of those Smart Alecs who come asking me for a job in the confident
tone of one who is quite prepared to teach me my own business. I
salute old McKerrow and his colleagues as they pass from our midst.

Augustus Muir, *The Intimate Thoughts of John Baxter, Bookseller*

Old McKerrow and his colleagues have largely passed from our
midst, but a few of them remain. What they've been replaced
by, though, is not Smart Alecs, slick with smelly hair oil, but a
faceless behemoth that has sucked the humanity out of second-
hand (and new) bookselling. The backbone of the book trade of
which Muir speaks is all but gone, and the business is in danger of
becoming an invertebrate. I write this just a few hours after an old
friend from Edinburgh dropped in to say hello with her elderly
father. He wandered through the shop with a look of nostalgia,
occasionally touching a book, and looking wistfully around with
the amazement of a child who has entered a sweetshop for the
first time. As they were leaving to go for lunch with some mutual
friends, he came to the counter and said: 'You know, Edinburgh
used to be filled with places like this. I spent my life wandering
about them and building up my library. I bought a sixteenth-
century copy of Holinshed's *Chronicle*—you have a later edition,
I see—in a bookshop in Leith in the 1940s. I remember it clearly.
They're all gone now, all but a small handful.'

Collecting books was clearly an important part of his life, and
without bookshops there is little joy to be found in this pursuit.
The serendipity of finding something you didn't know even
existed, or asking a bookseller what they could recommend on a

particular subject, isn't really possible online yet, although I expect it will come. A couple of years ago I approached Napier University with an idea for that very thing; a 3D model of the shop through which avatars could wander, controlled by online customers, and look at the actual stock on the shelves and even interact with one another. They told me that it would require technology that has yet to be developed. In a way I'm glad it isn't there yet, but I doubt if it will be long before it is. Still, the smell, the atmosphere and the human interaction will remain the exclusive preserve of bricks-and-mortar bookshops. Perhaps, like vinyl and 35mm film, there might be a small revival, enough to keep a few of us afloat for a bit longer.

SATURDAY, 1 AUGUST

Online orders: 2
Orders found: 2

Nicky in. The first thing she did was to hoist her sandalled foot onto the counter and show me her toe, onto which she had dropped a large piece of timber. The little toe was, in fairness, black and blue. Shortly afterwards, this was her Facebook update on the shop's page:

> Nicky here!
> This morning's ding-dong went like this … 'Why have you priced up that huge box of maps & put them neatly on the shelves? and why do you keep promoting "Tripe" & "Rockets," the customers are buying loads of copies and who cares if you've broken your toes, just work faster.'

Telephone call at 10 a.m. from Solarae. Rob, the boss, told me how to reset the boiler, which I did. It promptly overheated and cut out again.

In the afternoon I went to the post office to pick up a copy of *The Guardian* and discovered from the girls there that there's a rumour about the nearby Bladnoch Distillery, which went into liquidation last year (the most southerly distillery in Scotland, and consequently the most southerly Scotch distillery in the world), has been bought by an Australian millionaire.

Granny appeared wearing a new pair of white archival gloves which she claimed would protect her swollen fingers from the ravages of handling books. When I told her that she looked like Michael Jackson, she called me a 'fucking bastard.'

Till Total £187.93
38 Customers

MONDAY, 2 AUGUST

Online orders: 4
Orders found: 2

Flo in, half asleep and more cross than usual.

Drove to Gatehouse (20 miles) after lunch, dropping Granny off at Newton Stewart on the way. She wanted to go for a walk. Headed on to look at books in a house in the grounds of the Cally Palace Hotel—an old lady who is moving into sheltered housing. This is frequently how I acquire stock, and always a salutary reminder of one's own mortality. There is a depressing sense of resignation that this really is the final chapter when an elderly person takes that step, although in this case the woman appeared to be looking forward to it. I took three boxes of mixed stock and gave her £100.

Captain has a nemesis who sneaks in through the cat-flap and eats his lunch. Today Granny heard them fighting downstairs. I probably shouldn't mention it to Anna, as it will only further contribute to her already extensive bundle of neuroses.

Granny got home at 6 p.m.

Till Total £199.78
21 Customers

TUESDAY, 3 AUGUST

Online orders: 1
Orders found: 0

Flo was in today. She worked hard yesterday, so I thought I'd start the day with some motivational words of encouragement: 'Thanks, Flo—you've sorted through a lot of books. Well done.' Flo, after a stunned silence, replied, 'Can I record you saying that?'

Shortly afterwards, a young woman pushing a pram said, 'I'm looking for books about tapestry, but not your fancy modern sort of thing. Good, old-fashioned tapestry.'

As Flo and I were sorting through fresh stock, I found another copy of *Famous Last Words*. My favourite so far is H. G. Wells to his nurse: 'Go away: I'm all right.'

I went for another walk after work with Granny, and as we passed the field of cows again (Galloway cattle, mostly heifers), one of them had its head over the dyke and was munching on some grass from the verge, so I walked over to it and began to scratch its head. Granny looked terrified and started shouting, 'What are you do! Pay attention, a-Shone!' so I assured her that Galloways are good-natured creatures and that she should come over and see, so she tentatively approached and in no time was scratching its head and speaking to it in Italian. Afterwards I asked her if she still thought the cows hate her. She replied, 'Oh yes, all of them apart from this one. When they look me, they say with their angry eyes "Piss off, this is my field."'

When we got home, she disappeared upstairs to wash her legs and hair, and came down (as usual) with her turban on while I cooked supper for her and Lara.

Till Total £390.89
36 Customers

WEDNESDAY, 5 AUGUST

Online orders: 1
Orders found: 0

Wigtown agricultural show day. The rain was torrential all day. Granny and Lara filmed the cattle; I filmed the sheep, then left at 3 p.m. and drove to Lairg (six hours' drive) to go fishing with some friends. Took *The New Confessions* with me.

Till Total £528.22
52 Customers

THURSDAY, 6 AUGUST

Online orders: 2
Orders found: 1

Fishing. Flo and Granny were in charge of the shop.

Till Total £480
36 Customers

FRIDAY, 7 AUGUST

Online orders: 3
Orders found: 3

Fishing. After a boozy supper I sat by the fire and read *The New Confessions* for a while. Todd is now a prisoner-of-war, and a German guard (Karl-Heinz) is covertly supplying him with pages from Rousseau's *Confessions* in exchange for furtive kisses. Boyd perfectly captures the passion of the voracious reader with this paragraph:

> Karl-Heinz 'fed' me the entire book over the next seven weeks. The metaphor is exact. The thin wads of pages were like crucial scraps of nutrition. I devoured them. I masticated, swallowed and digested that book. I cracked its bones and

sipped its marrow; every fibre of meat, every cartilaginous module of gristle was dined on with gourmandising fervour.

It later transpires that he traded his Red Cross parcels with Karl-Heinz for the second half of the book, saying 'I gave away my food for a book.' In the shop I have a quotation from Erasmus painted on a wall which reads 'Whenever I have money I buy books. Whatever is left I spend on food and clothes.'

Till Total £114.94

10 Customers

SATURDAY, 8 AUGUST

Online orders: 1

Orders found: 1

Fished the Oykel all day.

Till Total £349.89

34 Customers

MONDAY, 10 AUGUST

Online orders: 1

Orders found: 0

Flo and Granny packed the books for the next Random Book Club despatch this morning. Granny announced that it is her favourite job 'to put the book-a in the confection.'

I drove back from Lairg yesterday in the driving rain. This morning, as I was going through the mail that had piled up in my absence, I found a parcel containing a beautiful book that someone had sent me. It was entirely in Chinese apart from the title on the jacket, which was in English. It was called *Wanderlust for Books*, and it contained several photographs of my shop. It was accompanied by a postcard which read:

Dear Mr Bythell,

I'm Rebecca Lee (in Chinese my name should be Ya-Chen-Lee). I'm a Taiwanese girl who visited Wigtown and your lovely bookstore last summer. Your bookstore and Random Book Club inspired me a lot. After I went back to Taiwan, in order to promote book town concept and memorise my journey of book town culture I wrote my trip down and then published it. I send you a copy of my book, though you may not understand Chinese, but there are some photos of your shop, hope you'll like it. Sincerely yours, Rebecca. 2015-7-30

Our notoriety in the Orient continues to grow.

Once they'd finished packing random books, Flo and Granny cleared the remainder of the boxes from the Barony deal, and we received another delivery of books from Samye Ling, for which I'll send them a cheque for £30.

While Granny was working at the counter, a customer approached her and said 'Uniforms.' Nothing else. She was understandably confused, and trotted out her standard response of 'Sorry?' several times until the matter was cleared up slightly.

Before she left, Flo told me that 'a funny wee man came in when you were away swanning about in the Highlands. I've seen him before, but he never says anything, even when I chat to him when he's paying for books. I've made it my mission to try to have a conversation with him.' Very little further inquiry was required before we had established the identity of the mysterious character as Mole-Man.

Till Total £454.51
36 Customers

TUESDAY, 11 AUGUST

Online orders: 1
Orders found: 0

Flo in shortly after 9 a.m.

After lunch I drove to Port William to look at a private library. A very charming Northern Irish woman showed me around with her husband and her brother. The house had belonged to their parents, and it was completely full of clutter, including thousands of books, nearly all of which were on Christian theology. I picked a few boxes' worth and gave them £250. They were very kind about it but clearly disappointed. After further conversation it turned out that they'd been valued fifteen years ago at £1,200. When I explained that the Internet had driven book prices down to an almost unsustainable level, they looked both sympathetic and understanding. Her brother even helped me carry the boxes to the van, an occurrence that is surprisingly rare. Their parents, it turns out, had been missionaries and travelled all over the world.

Email from Eliot at five o'clock asking if he could stay tomorrow night. All the bedrooms are occupied, so it's a full house, with Catriona, Edward (Festival Company trustees who are here for a meeting and need a bed) and Granny, so I made up the sofa bed in the snug for him.

Last week we had two Amazon orders for books we couldn't find. I emailed a grovelling apology to each customer and refunded them. Here's the feedback:

> Customer 1, 4 stars: 'Received refund due to non-delivery of item. Settled amicably with seller.'
> Customer 2, 1 star: 'Turned out books not available for sale so order cancelled by supplier not happy at all.'

Closed the shop and went to Rigg Bay for a dip in the sea. It's warm enough to stay in for about half an hour now, and if you don't splash about too much, you can see the concentric circles formed by the feeding mullet on the surface of the water all around you.

Once, when I was much younger and barbecues on the beach were a regular feature of the summer, a group of us decided to spend the night there and, during a midnight swim, were delighted to find that the agitated water lit up around us with phosphorescence.

Till Total £360.81
39 Customers

WEDNESDAY, 12 AUGUST

Online orders: 3
Orders found: 3

Flo and Granny opened the shop. Granny's campaign to organise every element of the shop rigorously has now reached the Shakespeare section, which she has decided to sub-categorise into biography, criticism, collected works and single plays. New members of staff are almost always obsessed with over-categorisation. When Flo started working, she decided to subdivide the psychology section, which consists of two shelves. There were labels everywhere from FEMINISM to FREUD to EDUCATIONAL PSYCHOLOGY, to the point that she might as well have written a label for every single book on the shelf. When I explained that customers are intelligent enough to work their way through a couple of hundred books without the need for a mess of labels to distract them, she looked a bit wounded, so I didn't mention it again.

Jeff the minister appeared at 2 p.m., just as Anna and I were comparing the role of guilt in Catholicism and Judaism. Jeff had been unaware that Anna is Jewish, and when she told him he announced, 'Oh! My boss is one of your people!'

Eliot arrived at four o'clock. He, Catriona and Edward stayed. At midnight Anna drove us all to the stone circle at Torhouse, where we watched the Perseid meteor shower against a clear sky. Torhouse is a Bronze Age configuration of granite boulders, about 4 miles west of Wigtown. It's a beautiful place, with views down across the Bladnoch valley, and surrounded by drumlins and copses of trees.

Till Total £241.50
25 Customers

THURSDAY, 13 AUGUST

Online orders: 2
Orders found: 2

Finished *Lucky Jim*. Flo in today, so I hid, and then went to have my hair cut.

Till Total £320.37
26 Customers

FRIDAY, 14 AUGUST

Online orders: 2
Orders found: 1

Nicky arrived at 9 a.m., and the moment she spotted my haircut she started laughing uncontrollably, telling me, 'You look like a big poodle!' Once she'd wiped the tears from her eyes, she shared her news, which was that her Jehovah's Witness conference had been picketed by born-again Christians. When I asked her why, she replied, 'They've got nothing better to do.'

Callum was in all day, working in the bothy.

I took Granny to lunch at the Steam Packet. She spent the entire time talking about Eliot. 'Why he stamp-a around everywhere? Why he slam-a de doors? Why he in de bath all morning?'

Two orders this morning: one £4, the other £94. Typically, we couldn't find the £94 order.

When Granny and I got back from lunch, Flo passed on a message to call someone called Jane in Castle Douglas, but I couldn't work out from her writing whether the number ended in a 4 or a 9, so dialled both. Both were wrong numbers. This is the fourth time that she's taken a message and managed to write down the number incorrectly. I just hope it wasn't anything too important.

Nicky kept the shop open for twenty extra minutes because a man was browsing. He came to the counter with a pile of books, total price £47, and demanded them for £40. He left empty-handed when Nicky decided that £42 was as low as she could go. Once the door had closed behind him with a dull thud, Granny announced 'We need-a again.' After much repetition and head-scratching, it transpired that she was saying 'we need a gun'—presumably for such customers.

Till Total £292.99
39 Customers

SATURDAY, 15 AUGUST

Online orders: 0
Orders found: 0

Eliot was in the bath from 8.30 to 9 a.m. again.

Nicky was in today, and it was another beautiful day, so I went for lunch in the Isle of Whithorn again, this time with Anna. On the drive home she told me—with considerable sadness—that she's moving back to America at the end of the month. I wonder whether, even though we have established a very strong friendship, it might not be enough for her to want to stay in Wigtown now that the relationship is truly over.

Christian, a Festival Company trustee, dropped off some books that he had repaired for me, including a first edition of *Peter Pan in Kensington Gardens* which came from Samye Ling. On his retirement from the Citizens Theatre in Glasgow, he decided to take up bookbinding to keep busy. He's extremely good at it, and very reasonable on price, which means that when I'm buying, I can afford to buy valuable books in poor condition, factor in the repair cost and still leave a margin for profit.

Nicky's Facebook update for the shop:

Nicky here! Oh it is indeed, great to be back!

So far it's a tie for Today's Prize Customer.

1—'That's £2.50 please' ... 'Can i pay in American dollars?'

2—'Could you hide that behind the counter' (which often happens when customers want to buy a book as a surprise) ... 'my son wants it but i don't want to buy it for him.

You decide! Mind you there's 4 hours still to go ...

Callum and Sigrid came for supper. Sigrid is Callum's new girl-friend (he and Petra having separated), a Dutch woman who he met on the Camino de Santiago de Compostela.

Till Total £197
15 Customers

MONDAY, 17 AUGUST

Online orders: 1
Orders found: 1

I've dug out the blackboard from the cellar and instructed Flo to write something amusing and witty on it and put it on the pavement in front of the shop. Her effort for today is:

FAQs

1 'Can I take a picture of the Kindle?'
Of course.
2 'Are all your books catalogued?'
No, we're too lazy.
3 'Can we bring our dog in?'
Yes, but only if we can pet it.
4 'What's that smell?'
...
5 'Do you have any children's books?'
Yes, they're next to that sign that
says 'Children's Books.'
6 'Is Shaun here?'
Definitely not/probably not/he's hiding.

Till Total £195.45
15 Customers

TUESDAY, 18 AUGUST

Online orders: o
Orders found: o

It was a beautiful sunny day. Anna climbed the Merrick, the highest hill in the south-west (843m), with two friends. Anna's love of Galloway is infectious, and she's probably done more single-handedly than VisitScotland to encourage tourists to come here in the years that she's lived here. Her book alone noticeably increased footfall in the shop.

Flo was in, and I had to look at books in a house in Gelston (about 40 miles east of Wigtown). I took Granny so that she could see what the buying side of the business is like. It was another small bungalow: this time an elderly couple who were moving somewhere even smaller, nearer Dumfries, so that they could be closer to the region's main hospital as they became older. We took five boxes of pretty average stock and paid them £130. Granny was in her element, in the company of people who were roughly the same age as she feels inside, and spent the entire time comparing ailments and fragility with them. By the end of the conversation they must have felt that they were in relatively rude health when compared with her.

I asked Granny to do the blackboard messages today, which resulted in this rather bizarre message:

**PLEASE, DON'T EAT THE BOOKS.
(WE LOVE THE COVERS)**

At 1 p.m. a huge stone fell from the chimney stack on one of the gables that I share with my neighbour and crashed through their roof, so I telephoned a local builder and left a message. Mercifully nobody was killed, or even hurt. It must have weighed a quarter of a ton.

Ken Barlow, an occasional customer and partially successful autobiographer, brought in two boxes of fishing books. I told him that I'd get back to him this week.

Till Total £369.49
35 Customers

WEDNESDAY, 19 AUGUST

Online orders: 1
Orders found: 1

Granny appeared at breakfast time looking for a plaster for a cut on her face. Anna had popped round to pick up her mail, and was in the kitchen when Granny appeared. She found one and gave it to her, assuming that she'd squeezed a spot or something. She told Anna that she'd cut herself shaving. The horror must have been clearly visible on Anna's face, as she continued to tell her that in Italy it is common for women to shave. God bless national stereotypes when they turn out to be correct. She told Anna that the cut had happened when she 'was put in order the face.'

Went for a boozy lunch with Carol-Ann and Anna at The Open Book which Anna is running this week. They'd decided to crack open a bottle of cava at noon and get some snacks from the co-op.

No reply from the builder about the chimney, so I phoned another builder and left a message on his voicemail. I'm keen to get someone to have a look at it before further loose mortar breaks free and does further, potentially fatal, damage.

Till Total £529.52
45 Customers

THURSDAY, 20 AUGUST

Online orders: 1
Orders found: 1

Flo and Granny were in the shop, Granny still sporting the plaster on her chin.

Flo's contribution to the blackboard today was a chalk sketch of a scruffy man in shorts (clearly me) with a speech bubble that said, 'Write something that Facebook will like.'

An old woman came in with five boxes of sci-fi paperbacks. She didn't strike me as a sci-fi reader, so I asked whose they were. I regretted it immediately when she told me that they'd belonged to her son, who had committed suicide ten years ago. Only now did she feel as though she could finally bear to part with them. I apologised for having asked, and gave her £100 for them.

Ashley arrived at 11 a.m. and managed to get the boiler working again.

In the afternoon I drove to a house in Carronbridge (about 40 miles away) to buy books. Two extremely well-spoken women ('We're in Debrett's, you know') were clearing their late parents' house, a large Victorian villa in gorgeous grounds. Very good shooting and fishing collection, including some by BB (always sellable), some Thorburn illustrated books and one by Malloch, the master of salmon fishing in the early twentieth century, as well as some other interesting Victorian material. They seemed happy with my offer of £750 for five boxes.

No reply from either builder about the lump of granite that fell from the chimney.

Till Total £325.95
31 Customers

FRIDAY, 21 AUGUST

Online orders: 1
Orders found: 1

Nicky brought in a treat for Foodie Friday. This time it was two chocolate éclairs, but the chocolate had either melted off them or she'd licked it off them on her way in. Either way, I wasn't going to take any chances.

This morning I discovered—to my horror—that a customer had moved Ken Barlow's boxes of fishing books into the pile to be listed on FBA, and that Flo hadn't noticed and listed them and sent them off to Dunfermline before I'd had a chance to discuss a price with him. This is never a good position to find yourself in. If he wants the books back, it's almost impossible to recover them from Amazon.

This is the third day in a row with just one order. Something's up with Amazon, Abe or Monsoon.

Nicky has been making a dress for Rebecca Plunkett's wedding reception tomorrow night. Rebecca is the eldest daughter of Mary and Wilson, friends who live in nearby Newton Stewart. Their middle daughter, Charlotte, worked in the shop one summer. Rebecca's getting married on the farm where Nicky has her cottage, and Nicky has very kindly offered to have me, Anna, Callum and Sigrid to stay for the night. She's stitched a pair of curtains together to make her outfit for the wedding—'I had to use the ones from the bay window. The others were too small.'

On the way to the post office I bumped into Wigtown resident Stuart McLean, the brains behind The Dark Outside, who reminded me that I still haven't submitted my piece of audio for this year's event. I'm one of a handful of people who have produced a piece for it every year. The Dark Outside is Stuart's brainchild. A few years ago he had the notion to produce something that is the opposite of the infinitely copyable, shareable and distributable world that digital music has become, so he invited people in the music industry to record an entirely new piece of music (or any sort of audio) and send it to him, then destroy the original audio file. Stuart, with the only copies of these recordings, then set up an FM transmitter in the Galloway Hills and broadcast twelve hours of this previously unheard material to anyone with an FM radio who cared to tune in, within a 4-mile radius of the transmitter, before destroying his copies of the files. To quote his website: 'The Dark Outside FM radio broadcast can only be heard by travelling to the site with a radio, there is no streaming or recording and all files are deleted after being played.'

The place he broadcasts from is the top of a hill with a monument to a man called Alexander Murray, a self-taught shepherd's son who became Professor of Oriental Languages at Edinburgh University in 1811. The view from Murray's Monument is glorious, and although it is only a few miles from the rolling, green, fertile landscape of the Machars, the difference is extraordinary. It is surrounded by rough, wild hills—uncultivated and populated by goats and red deer. Waterfalls and thundering burns cut through the granite wilderness. It is like another country, so different is it. It has the grandeur of the Highlands but not the coach-loads of tourists. It is almost unpopulated for hundreds of square miles, and the road below the hill on which the monument sits—the Queen's Way—is so called because Queen Victoria apparently described it as the most beautiful route in Scotland.

Kevin—my tenant who rents the house in the back garden—asked to borrow a ladder. While he was on the phone, I told him about the chimney problem and he gave me the number of a builder friend of his, so I called him up; he replied straight away and is coming to look at the problem on Monday.

Ken Barlow came in to discuss a price for his fishing books. I told him that I didn't want many of them but was happy to give him £40 for those I wanted. He asked to see which books I was interested in so that he could take the rest home. When I told him that I couldn't find them he was pretty annoyed and told me that he'd come in next week. My calculated gamble that he'd just take the money and ask if he could leave the rest failed.

Till Total £270.96
30 Customers

SATURDAY, 22 AUGUST

Online orders: 0
Orders found: 0

No orders today. Checked Monsoon, and it seems to be working OK.

Telephone call from Ken Barlow. Granny took it and left the following message: 'Ken Barlow rang. He VERY ANGRY!!!'

Nicky took the day off to work on making her dress for the wedding reception tonight, so Granny and I worked the day between us.

In the evening I drove to Rebecca's wedding reception. We all drank a lot and danced a lot.

Till Total £214.68
22 Customers

SUNDAY, 23 AUGUST

We awoke in Nicky's hovel, the sun was streaming in, and the view across Luce Bay was stunning. We all sat outside in front of the house and ate breakfast and drank tea and coffee. It was as idyllic a situation as I can remember in a long time.

MONDAY, 24 AUGUST

Online orders: 3
Orders found: 3

Flo in. Her blackboard for the day consisted of a chalk sketch of a battery with a low power warning, and the words 'Real books never die' above it.

Callum and Tracy appeared at 11 a.m. for a cup of tea.

Granny hurt her knee lifting books. She complained that it was swollen, but it looked pretty normal to me. She asked me if the chemist sold mud packs, so I told her that I would get her some mud from the estuary if that was what she wanted. She looked delighted, and said that she hoped that it wouldn't 'distoorb' my day too much.

The builder who I'd called last week telephoned to say that he'd be round at 3 p.m., and—to my amazement—turned up at 3 p.m.

As Flo was putting a book on a shelf, a customer farted in front of her. He looked at her, apologised, then let rip with a second blast and carried on browsing.

Anna invited several friends around for supper and to watch a film, so I set up the projector and we watched *Oh Brother, Where Art Thou?* Tracy stayed over.

Till Total £300.47
24 Customers

TUESDAY, 25 AUGUST

Online orders: 1
Orders found: 1

Flo in at 9 a.m.

The builder came round again at 1 p.m. to say that he and his business partner, Sean, would be around tomorrow morning to make sure that the chimney stack was safe.

Granny spent the day 'putting in order' the hardback section before stopping for lunch, during which she managed to spill tea on her laptop, which has now stopped working.

After closing time I telephoned Ken Barlow and told him what had happened with his books being inadvertently sent to FBA. I offered to replace everything on his list, or give him £150 rather than the £40 I had originally offered. After some negotiation we agreed on the latter solution.

Granny, as a thank-you for me offering to go to the harbour and digging up some mud, bought me a treat from the butcher's. She told me that it took them a considerable amount of time to work out what she was asking for, and eventually all three of the staff (Stephen, Jack and Nancy) got involved in the discussion until they worked out that a 'shoshageroll' was in fact a sausage roll.

Till Total £276.48
19 Customers

WEDNESDAY, 26 AUGUST

Online orders: 1
Orders found: 1

Flo in. Blackboard for the day was a quotation from *As You Like It*, accompanied by a fairly competent chalk sketch of Shakespeare saying, 'I like this place and willingly could waste time in it.'

John and Sean, the builders, appeared at 9.10 a.m. with the scaffolder to have a look at the chimney. Sean clambered out of my bedroom window and up the roof and made sure that nothing else was likely to fall off. Thankfully, it wasn't. After they'd gone, a young man with a splendid quiff came in with three Ian Fleming firsts, including a *Dr No* without a jacket. Gave him £150.

This afternoon I drove to Newton Stewart to the opticians, only to be told that my appointment is tomorrow. Irrefutable evidence that I need new glasses. I took Granny with me—since I hadn't got round to digging up clay from the estuary yet, she was looking for some sort of poultice to put on her knee to relieve the swelling. She went to both chemists and several other unlikely places and, unsurprisingly, failed to find it. Apparently 'it normal in Italy.'

After I'd dropped her back at the shop, I went to the river and caught a 6lb. salmon, which I returned. (This has become the norm—when I was young, we kept almost everything we caught, except the fish at the end of the season, whose condition had deteriorated.) The river, on a warm day at this time of year, is the most relaxing place, with no sounds other than the breeze on the leaves of the trees, the gentle lapping of the water and the birdsong. It's the perfect antidote to everything. The autumnal colours are still a way off, but hints of them are starting to appear.

Granny cooked supper for Anna and me. Her odd dietary fussiness was manifestly obvious in her offerings: pizza on some sort of wholefood base which tasted of cardboard and had no cheese; raw courgettes; and a bizarre bowl containing roasted pumpkin with segments of orange and bits of cinnamon stick. None of it was to my taste. In fact, it was almost as though she'd been blindfolded when she was preparing it, and just randomly grabbed ingredients from the fridge and the cupboard. When she's being cooked for, Granny's appetite is voracious and not discerning in the least, but when she cooks for herself, she is meticulously fussy about using ingredients with no fat, oil or butter.

Till Total £612.89
45 Customers

THURSDAY, 27 AUGUST

Online orders: 2
Orders found: 2

Flo's blackboard for the day:

> Money can't buy happiness, BUT it can buy books (which is basically the same thing).

No orders from Abe for nearly a month, so I emailed Monsoon to check that our database is uploading properly.

Granny's laptop still hasn't come back to life, so she's taken to using the computer in the shop and now, whenever I log on to Facebook, I'm met with the Italian version.

Spent the morning digging a trench in the garden for the sewage pipe for the bothy, in the horizontal rain. I need to get the thing done and the garden reinstated at least two weeks before the festival, which is now less than a month away. Also, the shop has been a mess since we relocated most of the stock that had been in the bothy and dumped it on the floor of the railway room. We really need to get that organised before the festival too, so Granny brought it all into the front room, and Flo checked it and listed what was viable on FBA and boxed it for sending away. The rest we boxed to send to the recycling plant in Glasgow. Flo, to her credit, has listed several hundred books over the past few weeks. Much as I hate to do it, it does solve the problem of space for storing books, and the books—out of our hair—appear to sell more quickly than the stock we list on Amazon that remains in the shop.

We still haven't started going through the boxes from the house in Carronbridge, for which I paid £750. Nicky can start listing them for sale in the shop tomorrow morning.

Till Total £525.89
42 Customers

FRIDAY, 28 AUGUST

Online orders: 2
Orders found: 1

Nicky, Callum and Robert were all in today.

Nicky proudly thrust a packet of Caramel Digestives in my face the moment she arrived. 'Look what I found in the Morrisons skip—aye, they've melted together, but they'll still be delicious.'

Granny has been continuously complaining about her knee, so I took her down to the harbour with a bucket and spade so that she could collect enough mud to treat it.

I was digging a hole in the garden to put a post in so that I can extend the log shed to make space for the bags of pellets for the new boiler when Amy, who has asked if she can run a wine bar in the downstairs of Lochancroft (formerly our warehouse, and now where Nicky sleeps when she decides to stay overnight), appeared with her baby. Amy's a young woman who's married to a friend a few years younger than I am. She's from down south, but seems to have adapted remarkably well to Galloway. We went over and looked around and discussed various options, including access. If we decide to make the access via the garden, then I have a colossal amount of clearing up to do before the festival. Eliot has also asked if we can set up a pop-up restaurant in a marquee in the garden (*en route* to the wine bar) during the festival. I must check the dates to see when it starts, but it is some time in the end of September so I'd better get my skates on, particularly since Flo finishes at the end of next week and Granny is going to be running The Open Book, so I'll be on my own in the shop for most of the week.

At 3 p.m. the UPS courier arrived to collect fourteen more boxes of stock (which Flo has listed on FBA) and take them to the Amazon warehouse in Dunfermline.

Granny told me that—among her numerous ailments—she suffers from lower back pain, so I told her that I do too, and that I have exercises which the physiotherapist gave me. I've been very lazy about doing them, which—if I'm being honest—means that I haven't done them at all. She told me that from Monday onwards we are going to do them together. She did the mafia pointing and throat cutting thing again which means, apparently, that I have no choice. I called her 'Mussolini.' She called me a 'fucking bastard.'

Made a list of jobs to do before the festival:

Clear the books from the floor of the garden room and railway room, list them on FBA and get the boxes shipped and out of the way

Clear the blocks from the garden and all the rubbish from the bothy

Finish the bothy (about a week's worth of painting and cleaning)

Get the new stock from the past few deals priced up and on the shelves

Get the big room organised for the Writers' Retreat

Move Emily's things for Lochancroft/Festival Café to make way for Amy's wine bar

Put up signs for Amy's wine bar

Move the garden path from the front of the bothy and seed the lawn

Get the speakers working in the railway room and the Scottish room

Get rooms ready for Stuart Kelly and Robert Twigger, who are staying during the festival

Replace the balcony door on the flat on Lochancroft Lane

Level the top garden so that the pop-up restaurant marquee can go up

Make new shelf labels for the subjects which we've relocated from the bothy

Edit Wigtown Show video

Edit Whithorn video for Julia Muir Watt

Organise books for next Random Book Club mail-out

Make insurance claim for the damage caused by the chimney

Repair the chimney

Make cover to protect the new boiler

Make step for front door of the shop

Paint bench in garden

Erect marquee in garden for pop-up restaurant

Take spare insulation to Callum's

Paint the shop floor

Paint the side door to the house

Replace all the batteries in the lights in the garden

Carol-Ann stayed the night. We cooked a meal between us: Nicky did the vegetables, Anna made brownies (her cooking is diabolical, but she's an excellent baker), and I made toad in the hole.

Thankfully Granny didn't contribute anything. We stayed up late and drank too much. Once everyone had finished their food, Granny ripped into the leftovers like a starving piranha and polished the entire lot off—it was about the same amount as we had eaten between us already.

Till Total £236.79

23 Customers

SATURDAY, 29 AUGUST

Online orders: 2

Orders found: 2

I awoke to the sound of cackling and the smell of burning from the kitchen, came downstairs to find Carol-Ann buttering a charred lump of toast and Nicky eating the leftover brownies, while Granny was making some vile concoction involving soya milk, wheatgerm powder and a banana. Anna, meanwhile, was eating a lump of the melted caramel digestive thing that Nicky had brought in yesterday for Foodie Friday. The chocolate had turned a shade of white that I would normally associate with poisonous mushrooms.

Callum in. Robert in. Robert left at 11 a.m. on an emergency call, but returned at 2 p.m., then left again at four.

The Saturday market which happens in Wigtown during the summer occasionally hires a piper to play some tunes for an hour, and today was such a day. As I was packing to go to Edinburgh, I was thinking of Anna, and how devastating it must be for her to be leaving the place and people she loves so much. At 3 p.m. the piper played 'Will ye no come back again.' As the spectre of her impending departure looms ever closer, I'm questioning whether this is the right thing to be doing. I'm forty-four and want a family. She's thirty-two and, despite our differences, there's far more that unites us than divides us.

With every year that passes, I see my friends with their children—who I've known since they were babies—sending them off to university, or to lives of their own, and I see the chances of me having a family of my own slip slowly out of my grasp. The vision of children grows more hazy with the passage of time. Now the children I had hoped for are almost invisible: not just ghosts, but the shadows of ghosts. Like Rosie Probert in *Under Milk Wood*, they seem to be 'going into the darkness of the darkness forever.'

Anna and I left Wigtown for Edinburgh at about 1.30 p.m. We stopped for her to say goodbye to my parents and arrived at my sister Lulu's at about 5.30. Lulu had invited Vikki, my other sister, and her husband, Alex, over for supper with two of their children, Rosie and Lily. Lulu's schoolfriend Meach and her fiancé Ben came too. After a fairly staid start, we ended up drinking, dancing and singing until 5.30 a.m.

Till Total £436.14
45 Customers

SUNDAY, 30 AUGUST

Online orders:
Orders found:

Awoke at about 2 p.m. feeling considerably better than I had expected. Anna and I wandered about Edinburgh, saw a few fringe street performances and had a very late lunch in the Grassmarket. We got back to Lulu's at about 7 p.m.

MONDAY, 31 AUGUST

Online orders: 1
Orders found: 1

Flo opened the shop, and I drove Anna from Edinburgh to Glasgow airport to catch a flight to Dublin, and then on to Boston. We had breakfast together in the airport at 8.45 a.m., during which my appetite was considerably suppressed by the sight of the man at the next table—a short, fat man who insisted on sitting with his tightly nylon-trouser-clad legs wide open facing me so that I was exposed to the vision of his belly/genitals wobbling with anticipation as he spooned his full Scottish breakfast into the gaping maw below his walrus moustache.

It was a very tearful farewell for both of us. Before she went through the interminable maze of security checks, I gave her a letter that I had written on Friday in which (I hope) I managed to articulate my feeble apologies for being unable to commit to a relationship, and my appreciation of her as the most giving, kind and wonderful person it has ever been my good fortune to have met.

I drove back on the Nick of the Balloch road—a 20-mile single-track hill road—only to get to Glentrool to discover that the road had been closed for resurfacing, and that I had to turn back and drive all the way back to Maybole and come back on another road.

Till Total £156
12 Customers

SEPTEMBER

Some customers are talkative; some are dour and silent. It is the talkers I guard against. They will hold you with a glittering eye for half an hour, sometimes longer, and care nothing that three other folk are waiting to be served. After a little practice, it is easy to spot these garrulous bodies. They come in with an expectant smirk, full of bonhomie, smacking their lips for a fine long crack. With this kind I always stick to business. At the first responsive snicker, or even nod, my button-hole is gripped between firm finger and thumb. They are friendly bodies, these talkers. They are the kind that used to throng bookshops in the old days when such places were a howff for book-lovers.

Augustus Muir, *The Intimate Thoughts of John Baxter, Bookseller*

Baxter is remarkably accurate in his descriptions of customer behaviour. The talkative types he introduces here still haunt bookshops today, and I doubt whether any other business receives the benefit of their wisdom in such prolixity. It's hard to say why we who work in bookshops are the victims of these people. In some circumstances it would be interesting to hear someone talking about nuclear reactors for forty-five minutes, but those circumstances are not when you're at work, and you're looking around you at boxes of books that need to be emptied, the books priced and put on the shelves, or piles of books that need to be listed online, or other customers who require assistance. We have a few of these, though not too many, but there is one in particular who causes my heart to sink whenever he appears in the shop. In the interests of diplomacy I ought not to reveal too much about his identity as he lives locally, but I have spent many a long hour trapped behind the counter, listening to his thoughts about Scottish independence (against), gay marriage (against), immigration (against) and large multinationals (very much in favour), as well as a host of other subjects. On one occasion he bought a book for £2.50. I think in future I'm going to charge him by the minute for the amount of my time he wastes during the working day.

Baxter's tactic of remaining stoutly indifferent to this type of person is occasionally effective, but infrequently. More often than not they are not looking for a discussion, or an argument; the affair is entirely a soliloquy and your attention is only required to make the occasion look less self-indulgent to any unfortunate onlookers. There's very little that can be done to stop them, although recently I've taken to discreetly dialling the shop landline from my mobile phone and answering it, pretending to be dealing with a customer return or some such thing to break the monotony. It almost inevitably continues the moment I hang up on myself.

Sandy the tattooed pagan is a master of conversation. He is always interesting, engaging and witty. I often find him in the shop in animated dialogue with complete strangers. His finest gift, though, is timing. He knows exactly how long to chat without being intrusive, which is why it is always a pleasure to see him.

TUESDAY, 1 SEPTEMBER

Online orders: 1
Orders found: 1

Flo was in today. Her blackboard effort this morning:

SPECIAL OFFFER—you give us
money and we give you books!

I made a deal with Flo that once she finishes work (Thursday) I'll give her £5 for every blackboard idea she comes up with that gets more than twenty shares on Facebook, but she's not allowed to get her friends to share them. Today's one was shared forty-nine times in the first hour of posting on Facebook. Yesterday's was shared sixty-five times.

Granny reminded me that we'd agreed to do the back exercises that the physio had given me. We both decided that the whole experience would be considerably improved by a gin and tonic, so I prepared a fairly strong one for each of us. Granny asked me, shortly after she'd finished it, 'Was there any gin in that? It taste like water.' Shortly afterwards she disappeared upstairs to wash her legs.

After work I painted the side access door into the garden. I've messaged Willie Wright, a local man who does odd jobs for me from time to time, to see if he can help me shift the remaining rubble tomorrow morning. Willie is a well-known figure about Wigtown. He spends a good deal of time walking up and down the street, looking as though he has something very important to attend to, and with an impressive sense of purpose, but generally he's just going between the co-op and his house.

Till Total £239.22
23 Customers

WEDNESDAY, 2 SEPTEMBER

Online orders: 1
Orders found: 1

Flo in. Set her to work listing the sci-fi titles on FBA.

Granny came down at 9.15 a.m. and did her mafia pointing thing at me, and said, 'a-Shone, last night I go for a piss at 3 a.m. and I hearing a funny noise-a. I finking-a "What thees? An animal?" Then I realise that it is you snorking. It was very loud-a.'

My father appeared at 11 a.m. to discuss fishing, and whether or not he's going to take a rod on the River Luce next year. It will be a sad day, the day he gives up the Luce. He's been fishing the river for over forty years.

As has become the norm now, after work I did my back exercises with Granny. Tonight she wolfed down her G&T in seven seconds. She's getting faster.

Finished painting the side door to the garden after I'd closed the shop.

Till Total £145.49
10 Customers

THURSDAY, 3 SEPTEMBER

Online orders: 1
Orders found: 0

Callum and Robert arrived at 9 a.m., Flo was slightly later, but as it was her last day there seemed little point in mentioning it. Not that it ever made the slightest difference when I mentioned it before.

This morning I drove to Newton Stewart to collect two new pairs of glasses, fitted to my new prescription. One pair is a bit trendy, the other very similar to the pair I have worn for the past twenty years. I showed them to Granny, who told me that I look like a hipster in the trendy pair. They will never see the light of day again. While I was in Newton Stewart, I picked up paint for the door of the bothy and a lock for the side door. Claire in Home Hardware told me that her daughter had forced her to watch our rap video, 'Readers' Delight.' She was less than impressed.

On my way home I picked up the laptop from my parents. I bought it for them two years ago, but now that they both have iPads they never use it, so I'm going to give it to Granny, since hers conked out when she spilled tea on it. Wore my new glasses all afternoon and ended up with a dreadful headache and the feeling that I'd taken a huge dose of LSD.

I attempted to hug Flo as she was leaving at the end of the day, and thank her for her (relatively) hard work, but she pushed me away.

Granny and I did our back exercises at 6 p.m., as usual. As I prised myself from the floor, creaking and moaning, I complained that being in my forties was depressing. She replied, 'No, Shaun, forty is the new thirteen.' Tonight's G&T lasted—I would guess—two seconds. It's almost as though she's in training for some sort of competition.

Spent the evening painting in the bothy. Finished at 9 p.m.

Till Total £125.50
8 Customers

FRIDAY, 4 SEPTEMBER

Online orders: 1
Orders found: 0

Nicky brought in oatcakes, cheese and pickle, all pillaged from the Morrisons skip. Granny ate them all before lunchtime.

Dennis—a former employee of The Bookshop (before my time) and fellow fisherman who is always keen to pick up odd jobs whenever he can—arrived at 10 a.m., and we loaded the trailer with rubble from the bothy, then dumped it in Bob's field. We loaded a second trailer and were going to take it to the dump, but Nicky started scavenging through it and asked if she could have all the off-cuts of timber, so instead we drove to Auchenmalg and dumped it in a pile outside her hovel. On the way home we dropped the trailer back at Callum's.

The garden is starting to look like it might be almost present-able by the time of the festival. During the drive to Nicky's, Dennis regaled me with tall tales. He is well known in Wigtown for these, which inevitably end with an account of a fight in which the odds are stacked against him, and which he wins through a combination of cunning and brute strength. Today I heard the story of a friend of his who fell 170 feet and broke his back, but stood up, dusted himself off and went back to work, and of the year in which he lost twenty-seven teeth in an assortment of punch-ups, how he escaped from a police van after he was arrested and how he punched the headmaster of his primary school. Even before he lost his teeth, he was completely incomprehensible, but since he had the last few removed, he might as well be speaking Swahili.

Granny came outside and said, 'I sorry for distoorb you, but a-can I a-tidy up the Railway Room?' It has become completely chaotic, so I happily agreed. By 3 p.m. she had cleaned and reorganized every shelf, and the place looked immaculate. At four she pointed out that despite buying two new pairs of glasses, I had reverted to wearing my old pair. I honestly have no idea how that happened. I must have taken the wrong pair from the case when I went to bed.

Till Total £357.29
20 Customers

SATURDAY, 5 SEPTEMBER

Online orders: 1
Orders found: 1

Nicky in. Sunny and warm, now that the wind is coming from the west again.

Online sales seem to have dwindled from a small stream to a trickle.

Dennis came in again, so I set him to digging the turf for the new path outside the bothy. At 11 a.m. I drove to Penkiln Sawmill to pick up some materials and order some timber and gravel so that the path will be ready before the festival. Also, the bag of sand outside the shop which has been there since we started work on the bothy is finally nearly empty. Every time I look at it I think of what Robbie Murphie said about it becoming part of the street furniture.

Granny did the blackboard sign for the day. I realised that she's been here for two months and has barely seen anywhere in the area, so I took the afternoon off to drive her to St Medan's, an ancient church and graveyard (she's obsessed with graveyards), and a beautiful sandy beach. 'This beautiful, the water-a, it beautiful, not like the water-a in Italy.'

Got back at 7 p.m. and did the back exercises with Granny (her G&T almost lasted a full minute before she'd hoofed it), then cooked supper, then went out to paint the bothy. Finished at 10.20.

Till Total £249.45
12 Customers

MONDAY, 7 SEPTEMBER

Online orders: 2
Orders found: 2

Granny opened the shop. Parents came for coffee at 11 a.m. and we discussed the possibility of them buying another property in the town and setting up a Writers' Workshop residency. This, unsurprisingly, was Anna's idea.

I told Granny—in jest—that she couldn't have a lunch break. She called me a 'shitty fucking bastard,' then told me that I'd been 'snorking' again last night. We decided that it was probably a good idea to tidy up the science fiction section of the shop before the festival, so we set about that. I'd never really considered myself a fan of the genre but, sorting the books out, I was surprised by how many of them I'd read: all of Douglas Adams, most of Harry Harrison's Stainless Steel Rat series, some Isaac Asimov, Terry Pratchett, John Wyndham, mostly read as a teenager.

Dennis and Robert, the plumber, were in today. They both have the capacity to talk for hours on end, so neither of them achieved a great deal.

Picked up £160 in pound coins and 50p pieces from the bank in readiness for the festival. Running out of change during the busiest week of the year is not what you want to happen.

This morning's post included, among the bills, a beautiful letter from Anna.

Till Total £326.40
17 Customers

TUESDAY, 8 SEPTEMBER

Online orders: 4
Orders found: 4

Granny began her stint at The Open Book today, meaning that I was on my own in the shop for the first time in months, so it was left to me to do the daily blackboard:

> You have just walked past a bookshop.
> Is there something wrong with you!

Posted it on Facebook at 11 a.m. Much to my surprise, within a few minutes it had been shared twenty times. By the end of the day it had been shared over 1,400 times, the record for anything ever posted on the shop's Facebook page.

Robert came in, and asked me if I could make a mount for the radiator for the bathroom in the bothy.

Anne Barclay, festival manager, appeared around midday with the interns for this year's festival, Beth and Lindsey. She asked if I could organise some books for them all to hold for a photo shoot on Thursday.

Telephone call at lunchtime from Stuart Kelly to confirm that he's staying here during the festival, and asking if there's a spare room for a friend of his on the second weekend.

The Penkiln Sawmill lorry arrived at 2 p.m. with materials for the new pellet shed and the gravel to finish the path through the garden. This all needs to be done before the festival, which is now just over a fortnight away.

Till Total £256.95
14 Customers

WEDNESDAY, 9 SEPTEMBER

Online orders: 3
Orders found: 3

I could hear the signature 'clack clack clack' of Granny's hard-heeled boots as I came down to open the shop at 9 a.m. She'd opened up early, so I took over and she left for The Open Book.

Stuart McLean returned to trawl his way through the remaining boxes of sci-fi. By the end of the day I'd had three emails from friends he'd contacted to tell them about the collection, and had sold £70 worth of them thanks to him.

In today's post was a letter from Mrs Phillips ('I'm ninety-two and blind' was how she began every phone call when she used to ring the shop, although by now she must be ninety-four and blind), simply addressed to 'Shaun, The Bookshop, Wigtown.' Mrs Phillips is utterly wonderful. She constantly sends me requests for books that she thinks her great-grandchildren ought to read. Particularly endearing is her sign-off for her correspondence, which is simply 'Phillips.'

Customer in the shop at 5.10 p.m. (we close at 5 p.m.) asked Granny, 'What time do you close?'

Emanuela: We are closed. We close at 5 p.m.
Customer: Oh.

Ten minutes later I spotted him still there and told him that we were closed. A further ten minutes later he finally left without buying anything.

With the colder weather approaching, I decided to cook a casserole for tomorrow. I told Granny that I would be away for most of the day and she'd be alone in the shop. (The Open Book is being covered by a volunteer.) She called me a 'fucking piece of shit-a.' She seems to have overcome the timorousness that characterised her first few weeks.

Till Total £203.48
21 Customers

THURSDAY, 10 SEPTEMBER

Online orders: 1
Orders found: 1

Gorgeous, sunny day. Granny in. Only one order, so Abe has clearly yet to give us the OK to upload our database. I spent the first hour of the day showing Granny how to list books on FBA, and set her to work on the enormous pile of sci-fi boxes that Flo had made a start on. While I was explaining the process, she made several references to Flo, calling her 'the Flo.'

There was a letter from the builder in the post today; the estimate for the repair to the chimney is £7,500. I must email it to the insurance company a.s.a.p. It's unlikely that I'll get the repair done before the festival now, even if the insurance company decides to make a contribution towards it, which seems unlikely following the last telephone call with them about it.

Left the shop at 11.30 and drove to Clydebank to look at a book collection. It had belonged to a man who died last year. His widow was selling his collection of books on the American Civil War. I arrived slightly late to find the widow, her daughter and her grandson all sitting in the tiny room in which the collection was shelved. I introduced myself, then started working my way through the books, making piles on the floor; all the while they sat there in silence, staring at me. This rarely happens, as people tend to leave you to go through their books unscrutinised while they continue with whatever business they generally conduct throughout the day. It's quite disconcerting to know that six eyes are monitoring your every move. After I'd made a pile of about forty books, the daughter asked me to give them an idea of what they could expect me to offer for the books I'd already removed, so I told them that the paperbacks (all in mint condition) would be roughly £1 each—some more, some less, but that would be the average—and the hardbacks would range from £2 each to £20 each, depending on scarcity, condition, subject matter and demand. They seemed relieved, then the widow told me that another dealer had already been to look at the collection, and offered them 50p a book for the whole lot. Not wishing to make an enemy of the absent, unnamed dealer, I explained that the second-hand book trade is in turmoil, and that we all have different pricing strategies and buying rates. The widow replied that she had 'told him to get out' as soon as he'd made the offer. It was a fairly good collection, and the condition was near fine in almost every case, so I selected seven boxes' worth and offered them £365. They accepted immediately, so I boxed them up, wrote her a cheque, then left. American Civil War books sell quite well in the shop, and it's always good to acquire the collection of someone who knew exactly what he was buying when he put the library together.

Back home at 5.30 p.m., so I heated up the casserole I'd cooked last night for supper. Granny and I sat down to eat it at 8 p.m. At about 8.30 I went out to do more work on the bothy. When I got back in at ten, I discovered that Granny had once again eaten the entire casserole. I had anticipated that it would last me until Sunday, but on the strength of experience I probably ought to have guessed that she'd devour the entire thing. When I mentioned it to her, she replied, 'Fuck off, fucking bastard.' The cursing side of her English vocabulary has considerably expanded since she arrived.

Bed at 4.30 a.m. after a late Skype with Anna, who seems

resigned to settling back in America, although she clearly feels that Scotland is her spiritual home.

Till Total £257.88
26 Customers

FRIDAY, 11 SEPTEMBER

Online orders: 1
Orders found: 1

Nicky shuffled in just after 9 a.m. She started the day with a hectoring lecture about evolution and what a ridiculous concept it is. After only three hours' sleep, I wasn't really in the mood.

It was a windy day, but sunny. At 11.30 three people from the National Theatre of Scotland arrived in the shop for a photo shoot as part of the pre-festival publicity.

Granny was in The Open Book, and shortly after she'd left to open it, Anna emailed me from America to tell me that she'd been interviewed on Radio New Zealand about it, so I went online and listened to it. She was extremely impressive, except when she attributed *Ring of Bright Water* to John Buchan rather than Gavin Maxwell.

Once Nicky had settled down from her evolutionary rant, I drove to the dump in Whithorn (12 miles away) with some waste materials from the bothy.

Bum-Bag Dave came in mid-afternoon, presumably doing his usual circuit on the bus. Now that he has a bus pass he makes the very most of it, and seems to go from one public library to the next using free public transport. He spent about ten minutes in the shop, with various watches, phones and other things beeping frequently, as they always do. As he left, he told me that he was going to go and see who was running The Open Book, so I quickly called Granny to warn her. When she came back at 4.30 having closed the shop, she asked me, 'Who this man with all the bags? He is a *clochard*?' Once we'd established that he was not a homeless man,

I explained that we call him Bum-Bag Dave, to which she replied, 'His name is Big Bad Dave?'

Till Total £212.40
17 Customers

SATURDAY, 12 SEPTEMBER

Online orders: 2
Orders found: 1

Awoke to the smell of baking and went downstairs to discover Granny making muffins with beer and bacon. She gave me strict instructions to eat them all. Despite the promising sound of the ingredients, they were utterly revolting.

Nicky came in at 9.10 a.m. I felt rotten, so went back to bed for a couple of hours after she'd arrived, but not before I had asked her to price up the boxes of fishing books from the Carronbridge deal, but she decided that her time would be better spent checking books that are already on the shelves and have already been listed.

Telephone call after lunch from Ian, a fellow bookseller from Hull, asking me if I've ever been reported to Amazon for selling a 'banned book.' Apparently they'd been in touch to rebuke him for selling a history of the Second World War that had a swastika on the cover (almost all books about the Second World War have a swastika on the cover). When he asked them for a list of banned books, they told him that there was no such list, and that they react when notified by a complaint from a customer. Ian—quite fairly— asked them how booksellers could be expected to know what is going to cause offence and to whom, to which they appeared to have no answer.

Ian is a book dealer, and has been for about thirty years. He ran a successful bookshop in Hull until Oxfam opened a shop next door to him a few years ago. He extracted a promise from their management that it would not become a charity bookshop, but it did, and with volunteer staff, books donated for free, rate and rent concessions and no tax to pay, there was only ever going to be one consequence. Ian, who paid his staff, paid for his books, paid tax, paid rates and paid full rent could not possibly compete and had to close his shop.

Went for a bath at 6 p.m. and asked Granny if she needed to use the bathroom before I dived in. She replied that she likes to have a bath early in the morning because she enjoys a long soak and likes to make herself look nice before facing the world—'I am very-a slug in de baf.'

> Me: Do you know who else is a slug in the bath? Eliot.
> Granny: Yes, but Eliot look-a like a woman.

Till Total £296.49
18 Customers

MONDAY, 14 SEPTEMBER

Online orders: 3
Orders found: 3

Granny was in the shop today. Her turn to do the blackboard:

GUESS!
In this bookshop we sell:
- words
- paper
- dreams
- illusions
- grapefruits
- ho ... what?

I have no idea what she meant.

At 11 a.m. a customer arrived with a parrot (called Jacob) in a cage, which she left on the counter while she browsed. I tried to sell her a copy of *I Know Why the Caged Bird Sings*, but she quite wisely refused to engage with the whole thing. Granny was infatuated with the parrot, and spoke to it in Italian for about ten minutes, as if being locked in a tiny cage wasn't punishment enough for the poor creature.

Email from Laura at Byre Books reminding me that we have a meeting of the AWB on Wednesday evening at Beltie Books, at 5.30 p.m. After the death of her husband, Robbie, Fiona (Box of Frogs, the shop next door to mine) stood down as secretary. I volunteered to take her place, so I wrote the agenda for the meeting and emailed it to all the other members.

Till Total £170.46
18 Customers

TUESDAY, 15 SEPTEMBER

Online orders: 3
Orders found: 3

Granny was at The Open Book today, so I was stuck alone in the shop.

As I was opening up, I heard the unmistakable honking of geese and looked up to see a skein of about fifty or so flying low overhead. I can imagine, if you've never seen it before, that a low-flying skein of geese could be quite a startling sight. Once, walking to a friend's house in Wigtown at dusk, I saw a skein of several hundred—possibly even a thousand birds—flying in a nearly perfect V formation, all honking as they headed for the salt marsh for the night. The farm I grew up on had a wide area of salt marsh, so seeing them every winter wasn't anything unusual when I was a child, but after moving back here after five years of living in Bristol, witnessing their return in autumn made me appreciate quite what an extraordinary sight it really is.

There was a letter in today's post from the Inland Revenue about the new automatic enrolment to pension schemes for employees. I emailed them to check whether or not I fall into the exempt category because I only have part-time staff and received a reply that left me even more bewildered than I had been prior to its receipt:

The automatic enrolment legislation will affect all employers with at least one member of staff. If there is anyone employed who falls into the category below, then there will be a requirement to set up a pension scheme. If there is already an existing pension scheme (i.e. a stakeholder pension scheme) in place for those who meet the criteria, they can remain the pension scheme without being automatically enrolled in providing the scheme is a <u>qualifying</u> one.

- Aged 22–SPA

- Earning above £833 monthly or £192 weekly

If there is no one who falls into the category above, then there will still be automatic enrolment duties towards your member(s) of staff. You will need to write to these employees detailing their rights towards automatic enrolment and may need to set up a pension scheme (only if they request it).

Emailed them back requesting an explanation of SPA. Apparently it is State Pension Age.

Wilcy, the fish man, turned up at 10 a.m., so I bought some smoked haddock as I have promised to make Cullen Skink for Granny tonight. Wiley normally turns up on a Friday. He has a small white van, and drives various routes—a different one for every day of the week—selling fresh fish from the back of it. Not only is the quality of his fish vastly superior to supermarket-bought, the range is fantastic, and he comes to your door. Janetta, who keeps the shop and the house clean and tidy, was chatting recently about the days of her childhood on a farm, miles from the nearest shop. Back then farms employed a good many more people than they do now, and not very many people had cars. Many of those farms wouldn't be anywhere near the bus routes, and Janetta remembers that the butcher's van would do a farm run every week, and the grocer's and the baker's vans would visit twice a week. Many people would barely have any need to leave their farms for most of their lives. Even their clothes were supplied by hawkers who would go from farm to farm.

At 4 p.m. a customer asked, 'Do you have any books with pictures in them?' No more specifics were forthcoming.

Cooked Cullen Skink for supper, then worked in the bothy until 10 p.m. Sadly it will be finished and inhabitable too late for Granny to use it, but it might come in useful as a spare room during the festival.

Till Total £110
7 Customers

WEDNESDAY, 16 SEPTEMBER

Online orders: 3
Orders found: 3

Granny was in the shop today, as one of the volunteers is covering The Open Book.

Amy, who's going to be running the pop-up wine bar in our old warehouse at the end of the garden during the festival, came round with her father-in-law, Robin, to inspect the premises. I've known Robin since I was a child, and he and I enjoy being extremely rude to one another. I think Amy may have found it a little unsettling.

Three customers (two old women and an old man) were milling about the shop telling me about sets of Shakespeare and Waverley novels they want to sell when the old man announced that the reason they were here was because he'd read Anna's book about coming to live in Wigtown, *Three Things You Need to Know About Rockets*. Apparently he'd taken it out of his local library in Morecambe after reading Neil Armstrong's autobiography in an effort to learn more about rockets, only to discover that it has very little to do with rockets at all. Unperturbed, he read it anyway and enjoyed it, and gave a copy to his wife for her birthday, then decided to make the pilgrimage to Wigtown.

Back exercises with Granny at 6 p.m., as usual. Shortly afterwards, as I was cooking mince and tatties (introducing her to Scottish cuisine), I dropped an onion skin on the floor. We both bent down to pick it up, groaning in agony as our backs clicked and spasmed.

At 8.30 I remembered the AWB meeting that I was supposed to attend at Beltie Books three hours earlier as secretary for the first time. Too late. It would have been over by seven.

Eliot arrived. Did the washing up before bed and discovered that Granny had scarfed the remaining mince and tatties.

Till Total £338.81
30 Customers

THURSDAY, 17 SEPTEMBER

Online orders: 0
Orders found: 0

Came down for breakfast at 8.15 a.m. to find Granny in the kitchen, giggling about the fact that Eliot had been in the bathroom since eight o'clock, with the radio blaring. He has yet to re-tune the radio in the kitchen (permanently on Radio 4) to Radio 5 Live, which he normally does within an hour or so of arriving so that he can listen to a football match.

Maria arrived at 11 a.m. to discuss the catering arrangements for the festival. She's done the catering for the past few years in the Writers' Retreat during the festival. On the weekends it is particularly busy, and she usually has two girls to help her, mainly with waitressing and cleaning. Sometimes, when it's full of writers and visiting speakers, we all have to lend a hand to keep up with demand. Other times, when it's quiet, the girls sit silently in the kitchen, on Facebook or messaging on their phones.

Granny explained her unusual eating habits to me. Apparently a few years ago she went on a diet and lost a lot of weight. This involved only eating protein all week apart from one day, on which you can gorge on carbohydrates. The problem is that now, whenever she is presented with food containing carbohydrates, her natural instinct is to gorge, even though she's no longer on the diet.

I drove to the dump after lunch to drop off more rubbish from the bothy construction. The book festival starts next Friday, and the plumber hasn't finished yet. I called him and he assured me that he'll be here on Monday. Bought a haggis from Kenny, the butcher in Newton Stewart.

Granny spent the day listing the sci-fi collection on FBA.

Eliot appeared in the house at 7.30, when I was working in the bothy. Granny told me that he strolled into the kitchen, opened the fridge, took one look, made a face of bitter disappointment, took out a bottle of wine and poured himself a glass, then sat down and drank it. Apparently when she eventually managed to get into the bathroom in the morning to 'put in order the face,' she went to wash her hair and discovered that he'd used all her shampoo. She's gone from being amused by his antics to finding them irritating. Mercifully, he's oblivious to it. Granny came out to help me paint the bothy, possibly for a bit of peace and quiet.

Till Total £122.30
9 Customers

FRIDAY, 18 SEPTEMBER

Online orders: 3
Orders found: 3

Awoke at about 7.30 a.m. to the sound of doors slamming shut and someone talking very loudly. Got up to discover Eliot stomping about the place on the phone to his wife. Granny was in the kitchen, silently drinking her coffee and trying to read. As I put the kettle on, Eliot marched in and sat down, and continued his telephone conversation while riffling through some papers on the table, which included my life insurance policy, a letter from Anna and some overdue invoices. I caught Granny's eye. She looked furious. I went back to bed with a cup of tea and tripped over Eliot's shoes, which he'd kicked off and deposited in the doorway. Managed to salvage about a third of the tea; the rest went over the carpet.

Slept in until 8.30. Got up to find the bathroom locked and Eliot in there listening to the radio. He emerged at about 9.15.

I'm starting to realise how much I'm going to miss Granny when she leaves after the festival, not just for all the work she does, but because I've grown to like her, even if I can't understand a word she says. She's extremely entertaining. Yesterday evening, when we were painting the outside of the bothy, we were talking about mortality. She told me, 'I fink I will die when-a I was thirty years old.'

Till Total £375
21 Customers

SATURDAY, 19 SEPTEMBER

Online orders: 3
Orders found: 3

Nicky was in again today. She's very obliging in the run-up to the festival, and deals with the steadily increasing pressure with a level head. Her Facebook update for today:

> Shortlist for Today's Prize Customer …
> 1. Brings 2 mint books to counter, 'Just what I'm after,' then gives me 10 minutes of family connection to said book, when asked for £4 leaves it on counter because 'the original price is £2.50.'
> 2. 'Can i pay to have a piddle, hen?? 'Well, can i go out the back?' …, on his return 'That's lovely pipework you've got out there.
> 3. Customer stands tapping money on counter, watches me atop a very high, very shoogly ladder, when i come down. 'Where can i buy a lottery ticket—and what would you buy with your winning millions, eh? New white socks to match your grey jobby-catchers?'

Spent the day in the bothy, painting and tidying up. After supper, went over to Lochancroft—the old warehouse—where Amy is going to have her pop-up wine bar and painted the concrete floor there. Emily (a young artist who rents it as a studio) has moved all her things out for the duration of the festival, and Amy is going to start setting up on Monday.

Till Total £661.90
35 Customers

SUNDAY, 20 SEPTEMBER

Online orders:
Orders found:

Awoke to a clamour from the kitchen. Came downstairs to find Eliot filling every pot, pan and tray in the kitchen with food. He told me that he'd decided to invite some friends around for lunch. Lunch lasted from 1 p.m. to 6 p.m., and the interns turned up, as well as Finn and Ella. Eliot spent the entire meal checking his phone, texting and emailing. He's under a great deal of pressure in the run-up to the festival, and with over 200 events crammed into ten days, it's inevitable that he'll have to field texts and emails around the clock.

MONDAY, 21 SEPTEMBER

Online orders: 7
Orders found: 6

Awoke at 5 a.m. after very little sleep. Went back to bed after a cup of tea, but didn't sleep. Granny was in the kitchen reading when I got up. I asked her why she was up so early, and she replied that she always gets up at five o'clock.

At 9.15 I went to the bathroom to discover that the seat had broken off the loo. I'll have to repair it before the festival. It's the loo that is used by the Writers' Retreat. It has also taken to making a loud, groaning noise when it's flushed, which vibrates through every pipe in the house.

Drinks with Ben and Beth from The Bookshop Band in The Ploughman at 8 p.m., then painted windows for Amy's pop-up wine bar in the dark. Not sure how they'll look in the cold light of day.

Till Total £311.99
17 Customers

TUESDAY, 22 SEPTEMBER

Online orders: 5
Orders found: 3

Awoke at 5 a.m. and came downstairs to again find Granny drinking tea. Made myself a cup and chatted with her for ten minutes, then returned to bed. Granny's preferred subject matter for conversation tends towards the darker side of life; this morning it was death.

I spent the day painting the woodwork on the windows that I had made the mistake of attempting to finish last night in the dark. After that, I hung paintings in the bothy, fixed the loo seat for the Writers' Retreat, mowed the lawns and tried to organise the uplift of the sixteen boxes of sci-fi that Granny has listed on FBA. Granny, meanwhile, looked after the shop, clack-clack-clacking about in her hard-heeled boots.

At 4.30 I was struggling to put up the marquee in the garden for the pop-up restaurant that is on during the first weekend of the festival when Ben and Beth appeared. I was wrestling with the frame, trying to work out how to put it up, when they wandered in. Ben immediately offered to help, but I declined and instead seized the opportunity to have a break and offered them a cup of tea. While we were chatting in the kitchen, Eliot turned up and, after making him a cup of tea, I suggested that we look at the space and the marquee for the pop-up restaurant. The moment we got there, he looked disappointed that I hadn't finished erecting it and complained that he thought it would be far too small. It won't. It will be fine. Later, after the shop shut, I was struggling to put it up on my own when Granny appeared and offered to help. We put it up in about fifteen minutes.

At 6.15, as I was lying on the floor doing my back exercises, Eliot stomped into the kitchen, stepped straight over me and poured himself a large G&T.

After my back exercises I went out and carried on tidying up the garden, but by eight o'clock it was too dark to work, so I came in and began cooking. At about 8.15 Granny appeared and asked, 'I have time for wash my legs before to eat?'

Till Total £428.49
18 Customers

WEDNESDAY, 23 SEPTEMBER

Online orders: 5
Orders found: 3

Granny was in the shop all day.

The plumber showed up at 9.15 a.m. and told me that I need to find an electrician to wire up the hot water tank, so I called Ronnie.

Granny organised the postage for the RBC, a job I loathe. It will be strange when she's gone and I have to go back to being tied to the front of the shop.

Till Total £452.36
32 Customers

THURSDAY, 24 SEPTEMBER

Online orders: 3
Orders found: 2

Nicky was working in the shop today, a glorious, sunny day.

Wigtown Book Festival begins tomorrow, and next week I will be forty-five. Normally, despite autumn being the most depressing time of year for me, the excitement about town and in the shop on the day prior to the start of the festival is contagious, and there's a kind of energy around the place. The last day of the festival is the opposite; everyone is exhausted, the clear-up is ahead, followed by the cold, quiet, dark days of winter.

After lunch I drove to the dump in Newton Stewart once again, and dropped off a van load of books and cardboard boxes. Unfortunately there is no time to take them to Glasgow for recycling before the festival now. This won't be the last of my trips to the dump—the Writers' Retreat generates far more waste than the humble wheelie bin can accommodate, and I'm obliged to drive there regularly throughout the festival with bin liners full of paper plates, kitchen waste and lobster carcasses. The empty bottles go into boxes, and I recycle whatever I can.

Granny did a predictably bewildering blackboard this morning:

Without a book you look very confused.
Am I upside down?

Robert, the plumber, arrived at noon, and Ronnie, the electrician, arrived at 2 p.m. to wire up the hot water tank.

At four o'clock Maria arrived with all the drinks for the Writers' Retreat, so the kitchen is now full of food, about twenty cases of wine and equipment for the festival catering. During the festival my drawing room is converted into the Writers' Retreat, an area exclusive to visiting authors who are giving talks. We bring in Maria to take care of the catering, and writers are fed and plied with wine during their visit to Wigtown. Laurie, a former employee, is tasked with making sure that everything runs smoothly, which it never does (through no fault of hers). One year, one of our house guests had a bath on the morning of the first day of the festival and the bath drain started leaking the moment he pulled the plug. A torrent of water crashed through from the bathroom, soaking the electric cooker, which exploded with a bang. I had to telephone a friend and ask her to pick a new one up from Dumfries and bring it over with her. The surge in power when the cooker exploded damaged the wireless router, so we had no Internet, and later in the day the washing machine stopped working.

Carol-Ann phoned and asked if she can use the bothy during the festival, so I've said yes. I spent the evening out there putting the finishing touches to it: hanging curtains and putting handles on cupboards.

Anna arrived back in Wigtown. She's staying with Finn and Ella (friends who have a farm about 8 miles away). It's such a highlight of her social year, and she contributes enormously towards it both with ideas and with helping out whenever she's needed.

Till Total £568.48
20 Customers

FRIDAY, 25 SEPTEMBER

Online orders: 2
Orders found: 2

Nicky was in early this morning. Today is the first day of the festival, and the first festival guest to grace the Writers' Retreat was Mairi Hedderwick. Mairi writes and illustrates the Katie Morag books, much beloved by children, as well as many other books, mainly about the Scottish Islands. I first met her at the festival about ten years ago. She's been back several times since, and is a friend of my father's cousin, fellow artist Frances Walker.

Filled the log basket and lit the fire in the Retreat at 10 a.m. Filling the log basket is one of the many mundane tasks that keep me busy during the festival, but Robert Twigger—an author and a festival institution—often beats me to it, and when I come down in the morning, I find that he's been up before me and filled it.

Today Twigger set up a photographic studio in the snug (normally my only place of sanctuary during the festival). He's photographing writers holding a blackboard with their advice to the world written on it as part of the festival this year.

Laurie arrived at nine o'clock, Maria and Shona (one of Maria's helpers) at about ten. The Writers' Retreat opened at noon. The drawing room becomes this venue, and the kitchen is awash with dirty plates, loaded dishwashers and sinks, crates of orange juice, bottled water, paper plates, boiling kettles and the like for ten days from now. Slow to start, but by the end of the day it was busy, a foreshadowing of what tomorrow will be.

I cut back some foliage in the garden to clear the access to Amy's wine bar, took some chairs over for her and made some more signs to direct people there. Shifted the (now empty) bag of sand from the alleyway and cleared some space in front of the bothy. Amy opened the pop-up wine bar at 1 p.m.

Drove to Newton Stewart with yet another van load of rubbish for the dump. The woman who runs it (whom my father refers to as Attila the Hun) has become quite friendly following my frequent visits.

Two kegs of beer arrived at 11 a.m. Nicky has decided that the festival needs even more alcohol and ordered them on my credit card.

Pru (Eliot's wife) arrived at 5.30, and shortly afterwards Eliot appeared in the snug and asked for an iPhone charger as he's already lost his. 'I promise I won't steal it.' On average, he loses three phone chargers during each book festival.

Shortly afterwards Catriona (festival trustee) appeared and wandered into the kitchen and asked loudly—in front of everyone—'Why did you split up with Anna?'

Till Total £326.98
32 Customers

SATURDAY, 26 SEPTEMBER

Online orders: 0
Orders found: 0

I was in the kitchen moving some chairs when Finn came in with a huge Norwegian man in a lumberjack shirt. Finn introduced him as Lars Mytting, the author of a surprisingly popular book about wood-cutting and burning, called *Norwegian Wood*. He was completely charming.

Phill Jupitus came in at noon for lunch. I spent most of the morning setting up Simon Wroe's pop-up restaurant in the garden, running extension cables, moving gas cylinders, finding knives etc. for the meals he and Laura Mitchison prepared for guests at noon, 2.30 and 5 p.m., all of which were well attended and appeared to go well, despite Eliot's concerns about the size of the marquee.

In the evening we all went to 'Wigtown's Got Talent' in the big marquee—credit for which resides firmly with Anna. During the first festival that she was here for, after hours in the Writers' Retreat there were a dozen or so of us sitting around and chatting, when

Martin (my old housemate) announced that he could hammer a 4-inch nail up his nose. Anna immediately latched onto this, and asked if anyone else had any unusual skills. Before I knew it, she'd programmed an evening of entertainment with me, my sister Lulu and Twigger as judges. Eliot was so enchanted by it that he programmed it into the festival the following year, and now it's a mix of locals and visiting writers performing on the night.

Closed shop at 8 p.m. Bed at 1 a.m.

Till Total £829.98
84 Customers

SUNDAY, 27 SEPTEMBER

Online orders: 1
Orders found: 1

Woke up early and filled the log basket. Opened the shop at 9 a.m. in time to let Laurie in. Granny took over the shop shortly after I'd opened, so I went upstairs and lit the fire in the Retreat at 10 a.m.

Today's festival events began at 10 a.m. with the start of the Alastair Reid–athon, a tribute to the local man who achieved literary greatness and whose obituary was given full pages in all the broadsheets in the UK, despite his relative obscurity. He was the perfect example of a man whose genius was recognised in his lifetime, but who will be posthumously immortalised in the world of literature.

Following swiftly on the heels of Alastair's event was the oxymoronically titled Festival Fun Run, which began at 10.15 a.m. and which nobody I know attended.

As always, I spent the day firefighting and clearing up rubbish from the Retreat. Phill Jupitus and Charlotte Higgins were around, both of whom had another event today, as did Val McDermid. The Retreat was considerably less busy today than it was yesterday, but that's normal for Sundays during the festival.

I gave Granny a break for lunch at 12.30, and she headed up to the Retreat. Maria had made brownies, and they are like crack to Granny. She visibly salivates as soon as they appear, and it's a miracle that anyone else even gets a whiff of one, let alone a taste, when Granny's around.

After Simon and Laura had finished their second pop-up meal at around 3.30 p.m., I took the marquee down and put it back in the shed, then popped into Amy's wine bar, which was, to my astonishment, absolutely packed with people. It seems that between events, particularly on either side of a big name, people flock there for food and wine. Val McDermid finished at about 2.30 p.m., so I imagine that most of those present were there following her event.

Closed the shop at 7.30 so that Granny could go and watch *Deliverance*, which was on at the temporary cinema in the County Buildings.

Till Total £842.43
92 Customers

MONDAY, 28 SEPTEMBER

Online orders: 1
Orders found: 1

Opened the shop at 9 a.m., and my mother appeared at 10.30— exactly the same time as Ronnie, the electrician. If anyone can give my mother a run for her money on filling silence with chat, it is Ronnie. The two of them migrated straight to the kitchen, where Shona, Katie and Laurie were setting up, and plonked themselves on chairs and talked for an hour about Ronnie's motor-bike journey around the world.

At noon I drove to the Whithorn dump (or 'Civic Amenity Centre,' as it is euphemistically called on the council signpost) with twelve bin liners full of paper plates and decomposing food from the Writers' Retreat over the weekend, as well as the two polystyrene lobster coolers, which leaked stinking lobster juice all over the back of the van. The smell usually lingers for about a month after the festival.

Twigger took part in a discussion about Harper Lee's *Go Set a Watchman*. From his own account of the event, it was painfully obvious that he hadn't read it.

Allan Little, a BBC journalist whose roots are near Stranraer (20 miles away), and Vince Cable were among the guests in the Writers' Retreat for lunch. Met Vince's wife, who rather humbly refers to herself as 'Mrs Vince.'

Till Total £603.99
38 Customers

TUESDAY, 29 SEPTEMBER

Online orders: 2
Orders found: 1

Janetta in at 7 a.m. to clean the Writers' Retreat.

Isabel was in at 1 p.m. to do the accounts, and Granny covered the shop. One of the customers this morning demanded change (£17.50 from a £20 note) in English money. Granny didn't understand what he was talking about, so she came up to the kitchen where I was having a chat with Stuart and said, 'Sorry if I distoorb you, a very rude man is in the shop.' I went downstairs with her and dug out an English £5 and £10 and gave the man his change.

The Writers' Retreat was fairly quiet today, but I topped up the log basket and lit the fire just in case.

I had a flick through the programme for today's events and noticed that the first one was a visit to a tea plantation near Creetown, about 10 miles away, on the other side of Wigtown Bay.

Closed shop at 7.30 p.m. and headed over to The Ploughman for Stuart Kelly's Literary Pub Quiz, where I teamed up with Lee Randall, Twigger and Anna. With no help from me, we managed to come second.

Till Total £425.47
42 Customers

WEDNESDAY, 30 SEPTEMBER

Online orders: 2
Orders found: 2

Nicky was in today. Winter must be approaching because she was wearing a thick coat and her hat, which is a sort of trilby made of felt. This is my favourite of her winter outfits—I always point out that she just needs a pair of lederhosen and she could pass for a Tyrolean yodeller. She enjoys coming in during the festival, and inevitably ends up having a bizarre conversation with one or two of the authors, who probably leave Wigtown somewhat shell-shocked as a consequence. Captain appeared at the same time as Nicky. He dislikes the festival intensely, as the rearranged furniture confuses his navigation system, and there's always lots of noise and movement. He tends to hide in my bedroom for most of it, and Anna relocates his food supply to there.

Twigger had already lit the fire by the time I remembered to do it at 11 a.m.

David, who works for BBC Scotland and is running Radio Wigtown with Anne Brown, asked if I could record an interview with him and John Higgs in the Martyrs' Cell. It took about twenty-five minutes. I went into the Retreat afterwards for something to eat and found Liz Lochhead asleep in one of the armchairs by the fire, an open newspaper on her lap. She'd clearly nodded off reading it. Over lunch, as I was chatting to the historian Max Arthur about the ethics of using drones in warfare, I mentioned that I have a video drone. He perked up and asked if he could see it, so we drove down to the salt marsh and I flew it around for a while. He seemed unduly impressed.

At 3 p.m. Anna and I went to John Higgs's event about making sense of the twentieth century, an entertaining hour well spent. Someone left a copy of his book in the Writers' Retreat, so if it's still there at the end of the festival, I'll read it, although for many people, I suspect, going to events at literary festivals is an alternative to reading the book, rather than a supplement to it.

At the busiest time of the year the planning department decided to send a delegation to inspect the concrete book spirals. In their defence, they were extremely apologetic, and seemed very taken with the spirals.

Stuart, Twigger, Anna and I had supper with Simon Wroe and Laura in the kitchen. After we'd eaten, everyone started reciting their favourite poetry around the table. By bedtime, everyone was drunk and it had assumed an air of pretentiousness otherwise unheard of in the kitchen, and possibly the whole town.

I have—to this day—no idea where she came from, or how she got in, but at about 11 p.m. a small young German woman appeared and asked if she could stay for the night. Nobody had the slightest idea who she was, but I showed her to the bed in the shop and told her she was welcome to stay.

Till Total £489.83
37 Customers

OCTOBER

There is also the confidential customer. He walks in on tiptoe and talks to you in whispers. He blushes and looks around as if he were committing a crime. Probably he only wants Hume Brown's *History of Scotland*, but you'd think he had stepped into a police station to make a confession. You can do nothing with him: you cannot put him at his ease. He takes the parcel from you, and goes off with it like an apologetic thief. He is a contrast to the bluff, outspoken man who talks in a loud voice. This kind won't listen to what you say and bangs down his money as if he were driving a nail into the counter. Although he thinks he knows what he wants, he often doesn't. But there is no need to worry. Once he has bought a book, he has bought it and he'll never come back and admit his mistake.

Augustus Muir, *The Intimate Thoughts of John Baxter, Bookseller*

Without wishing to spend too much time stereotyping customers, I'm about to do precisely that. This second kind described by Baxter is sadly all too common. More often than not they will ask you a question and give you a window of silence in which to answer it, but the moment you open your mouth to do just that, they'll begin telling you why they asked you the question, or they'll repeat the question, or rephrase it. Whichever it is, you can guarantee that this will happen every time you open your mouth, and for several minutes at a time. I once had an Australian woman ask me where the gardening books were. I must have made ten attempts to answer, each of which was talked over until eventually I sat down and started listing books on the computer until she stopped talking.

This same type will, as Baxter points out, breezily ignore any contradiction to whatever they happen to be saying, and loudly talk over you as you explain that it was Edward Gibbon, not Evelyn Waugh, who wrote *The Decline and Fall of the Roman Empire*, or

247

that C. S. Forester, not E. M. Forster, wrote the *Hornblower* novels.

The transfer of payment also provides scope for a range of behaviours. There are customers who do, as Baxter points out, slap the money onto the counter in what appears to be a gesture of power (only men do this, in my experience), and others who will, with painfully slow deliberation, extract the coins from their wallets or purses and pile them onto the counter. Once finished, they will generally push them weakly towards you. And finally there are others who seem less afraid of physical contact, who will push the money into your upturned palm. Customers from anywhere south of Manchester tend to demand English notes in their change. Callum once told me that when he paid for tobacco in a petrol station in England with a Scottish £20 note the man behind the counter in the shop made a great show of holding it up to the light to check for a watermark, tutting all the while. When Callum received his change, which contained an English £10 note, he did the same thing.

In the fourteen years since I bought the shop, I've taken Isle of Man notes, Northern Irish notes, euros and even English notes, and I've never once had any of them rejected by the bank when I've lodged them, but for some reason businesses in England—and it gets worse the further south you go—don't like Scottish notes. Once, when I'd just left school, I was in London and needed to take a bus somewhere (I forget where). The fare was 45p, and when I handed him a Scottish £1 note, the bus driver refused to take it. I ended up writing him a cheque for the fare.

THURSDAY, 1 OCTOBER

Online orders: 2
Orders found: 2

Today was my forty-fifth birthday. Nicky was in, so I got up and made sure that everything was OK, lit the fire in the Writers' Retreat, then went back to bed for an hour as a birthday treat.

Every year my birthday falls in the middle of the festival, in the same way that when I was a child, it always fell shortly after going back to boarding-school. Probably because of that, the day assumes no importance for me. When I turned eight, I had been at boarding-school for a month. The school would provide a cake whenever it was a pupil's birthday. It was a confection of such revoltingness that it would probably now be in breach of health and safety regulations, but in comparison with the rest of the food offered to us by the cook, Mr Swiggs (a former prison cook who would chain-smoke over the pots of gruel he prepared), it was both nectar and ambrosia, and we fell upon it like vultures.

At 11 a.m. I drove to the Newton Stewart dump with the rubbish from the Retreat. While I was there I bumped into Hugh Mann, a retired antique dealer who I've known for years. We used to meet at the auction in Dumfries. We had a curious conversation about the 'Degenerate Artists' (as described by the Nazi Party)—Hugh thinks he's found an important collection of paintings, but Hugh often thinks this. On my way back from the dump I went for a swim in the River Luce and in the sea to mark the passing of another year. Normally I do this with Anna and some friends, but for some reason (possibly because I can no longer say that I'm in my early forties) I felt particularly morose this year and chose to do it alone.

At two o'clock my parents turned up with a cake (lemon meringue) with a candle that played a tinny 'Happy Birthday' tune which refused to stop, even when it was in my mother's bag after I'd threatened to smash it with a hammer. The author and doctor Gavin Francis (who's talking at the festival) witnessed my mother singing 'Happy Birthday' and producing my birth ID tag, baby booties and various other embarrassing things. For some reason, my mother is obsessed with the most horrendous tat: candles that play 'Happy Birthday' when you light them, Christmas decorations with motion sensors that start singing 'Jingle Bells' when you walk past them; anything that makes my sisters and me squirm she seems to adore. She had a fake Christmas pudding in the bathroom of their house at Christmas a few years ago which erupted into song just as you were about to sit on the loo. The number of visitors it surprised was clear from the number of times the words 'Jesus Christ!' could be heard shouted from the loo over the festive period.

For reasons that are probably obvious, in the past few years when I see my father on my birthday, I think of what he'd achieved when he was my age. When he turned forty-five, I was sixteen years old, and my sisters fourteen and ten. He'd married, moved from Somerset to Galloway with my mother, bought a farm and made enough money to send Vikki and me to boarding-school. I can't compare my own achievements favourably.

Peggy, manager of the Dundee Literary Festival and one of the fixtures of the Book Festival: a voracious reader and quick wit, and her partner Colin and Stuart gave me a bottle of Talisker, Twigger gave me a bottle of sake. Carol-Ann and Laurie each made me a birthday cake.

Closed the shop at 7.30 p.m.

Stuart's friends Rebecca and Olivia turned up at eight o'clock, and Stuart and Laurie cooked supper, supposedly for ten people: two chickens and some vegetables. About thirty people turned up. The lemon meringue cake was produced for pudding, and opinion was divided on it (it was revolting, but people were being polite). Eliot helped himself to a large portion, then complained at considerable length about it, while continuing to devour it.

There was an event tonight in Amy's wine bar: *The Midge*, a Wigtown version of the New York event *The Moth*, an informal storytelling evening. About three years ago I converted our warehouse into a sort of drawing room/club for the festival. I bought everything (furniture, pictures etc.) at auctions—including a huge Edwardian photo portrait of three boys in a gilt frame. *The Midge* event was called 'Lost and Found' and involved people telling stories about things they'd lost and found. One woman sat through until the very end, then put her hand up to speak. She pointed at the Edwardian portrait and said, 'I've come here from Cheshire for the festival. The boy in the middle of that picture is my uncle Frank. We accidentally put that picture into an auction about ten years ago and I've been looking for it ever since.'

Bed at 2.30 a.m. after reading *The New Confessions* for twenty minutes. Todd has now survived the war and is making films in Berlin. Plagued by ill-fortune, his magnum opus—an adaptation of Rousseau's *Confessions*—is completed as a silent movie, just as sound is introduced in film, and predictably flops.

Till Total £308.16
29 Customers

FRIDAY, 2 OCTOBER

Online orders: 3
Orders found: 3

Nicky arrived looking surprisingly smart, and with a hint of make-up, which means that she's seen something in the programme that she wants to go to, or that there's someone who'll be in the Retreat when she has her lunch up there that she wants to talk to. I looked through the programme, but couldn't work out who it was. The only names I recognised were Yannis Palaiologos, Don Paterson and Kirsty Logan, but I'm certain that it's not one of them.

Laurie and the girls set up the Retreat, which was the busiest it has been since Monday. Eliot tends to fit more events in on the second Friday, as people are more likely to come earlier for the weekend, and audiences are usually bigger then.

Ben and Beth insisted on going for a swim, so we went to Rigg Bay in the afternoon for a plunge into the sea.

At four o'clock a woman who's involved in a musical event this evening with the National Theatre of Scotland asked if we had somewhere that she could warm up, so I showed her to the snug. Beautiful strains of a violin emanated from there for the rest of the afternoon.

Overheard a couple in the Writers' Retreat:

Her: Can we drink as much of this wine as we like?
Him: Yes, let's drink as much as we can.

According to Twigger, this is the mentality of most writers to anything that's free, but particularly food and wine.

At 6 p.m. the two large polystyrene cool boxes full of lobsters were delivered to the Retreat by the man from the Galloway Smokehouse.

Stuart and Eliot disappeared at about 7 p.m. for an event in which they're both on the panel. It's a discussion of the books shortlisted for the Man Booker Prize, which is announced on 13 October. Stuart was one of the judges for this a few years ago, and will undoubtedly have read everything on this year's shortlist, and possibly even the longlist. I've never seen anyone devour a book as quickly as Stuart can: he has an eidetic memory and can literally flick through a 600-page book in a couple of hours and not only have actually 'read' it but be able to retrieve any detail from within it with pinpoint accuracy.

Closed the shop at 8 p.m.

The small German woman stayed the night again. She's very friendly and chatty, but—as yet—why she's here is a complete mystery.

Till Total £419.83
39 Customers

SATURDAY, 3 OCTOBER

Online orders: 2
Orders found: 2

Today was the penultimate day of the festival, and I am exhausted after so many late nights. I opened the shop at 9 a.m., and a fresh-faced Nicky wandered in shortly afterwards.

Granny asked if she could borrow a bike so that she could explore the area, since it was a beautiful day. She set off at 10 a.m. and told me that she'd be back late in the afternoon. Five minutes later she reappeared: the chain had come off. 'Oh sorry, I have breaked de bicycle.' I fixed it, and she set off again.

Finn's brother Rob and his wife, Sally, had an event this morning with local man Roy Walter about rural activism. All three of them have successfully fought campaigns against large organisations who wanted to force their land to different uses: Rob and Sally's farm in Australia was under threat from an open-cast coal mine, while Roy saw off an offshore wind farm that was proposed for Wigtown Bay. They all came to the Retreat afterwards for lobster and salad.

Alex Salmond was talking at the festival today. I spotted him in the Writers' Retreat, but didn't have an opportunity to say hello. As he was walking from the shop to the marquee for his event, a huge crowd gathered in his wake. Nicky looked out of the window and commented, 'Eh, you'd think it was Jay Z, looking at that, not that wee bampot.'

Tonight was the annual Festival Ceilidh. I wore my kilt, but because I've lost so much weight in the past three months, it kept falling down, much to the amusement of Siobhan, who's running WTF (Wigtown, The Festival, the part of the festival for younger people). At every opportunity she grabbed it and did her utmost to wrestle it down as far as she could. The event became a case of trying to keep as much distance between me and her as possible. Danced with Granny and Laurie, as well as (reluctantly) Siobhan.

Afterwards, everyone (including Siobhan and her parents) came back to the Retreat and continued late into the night.

Bed at 3 a.m.

Till Total £519.50
49 Customers

SUNDAY, 4 OCTOBER

Online orders: 2
Orders found: 2

Opened the shop at 9 a.m. to find that Monsoon had crashed.

Kirsty Wark was in the Retreat at lunchtime with her publisher, Lisa. They were heading to Loch Doon, the subject of Kirsty's new book. Loch Doon is a reservoir in Ayrshire, in the middle of which was a castle steeped in legend and history. Before they flooded the site, the hydro operators were forced to move the castle, stone by stone, to a new location on the banks of what was to become the loch, and rebuild it exactly as it had been.

Fiona, the woman who had spotted the portrait of her uncle at the event in Amy's wine bar, appeared at 2 p.m. to ask if she could buy it from me. I recall paying very little for it, and since she had far more right to it than I did, I told her she could have it for nothing. She was on the verge of tears when I handed it to her.

Visitors to the Writers' Retreat today included Janice Galloway and Matt Haig. Max Arthur dropped in at 4 p.m. to say goodbye before heading back to London.

As I was taking bin bags of waste from the Retreat downstairs to the bins, I passed a customer, a young woman who had been browsing in the craft section, who was gazing up at the top landing. She stopped me and asked if there was anyone up there. I assured her that there was nobody there. I'd been up there five minutes earlier and nobody had been up since. She was convinced that she'd seen a figure wearing black walk silently from one end of the landing to the other. It must have been either the cat or her imagination.

Closed the shop at 6 p.m. Festival over.

Laurie and I moved all the furniture in the big room while Eliot watched, casually sipping a glass of white wine. Afterwards we watched a Woody Allen film. About ten minutes in, I noticed that almost everyone had fallen asleep, and another ten minutes later so had I.

Till Total £457.78
40 Customers

MONDAY, 5 OCTOBER

Online orders: 0
Orders found: 0

Granny opened the shop, so I slept in until 10.30 a.m., then got up and said goodbye to Stuart, who left at eleven, then Twigger left at noon, and as I was saying goodbye to him outside the shop, I spotted my sofa on the pavement: Eliot had asked to borrow it for the duration of the festival for a venue called The Living Room. The men dismantling the marquees must have just dumped it there. Twigger gave me a hand getting it back upstairs.

After he'd gone, I drove to the dump with eighteen bin bags from the Retreat, as always—after the weekend—reeking of lobster and dribbling stinking juice all over the back of the van.

The big marquee in the square came down by 2 p.m., leaving the yellowed grass behind where it had stood. I spent much of the remainder of the day moving things back into the big room from the snug, where they'd been stored during the festival, like the television, footstool etc.

After the shop was closed, Granny cooked home-made pizzas for the interns and we set about getting the house back to relative normality. After supper Eliot and Yvonne, who also came over for pizza, had a massive argument in the kitchen, so the interns, Granny and I left them to it and retreated to the snug with a bottle of wine.

Bed at 2 a.m.

Till Total £76.30
5 Customers

TUESDAY, 6 OCTOBER

Online orders: 3
Orders found: 2

Callum came in to start work on building a roof over the new boiler before the winter sets in, now that he's finished the bothy. Carol-Ann seems to quite like the bothy and has asked if she can stay there for a bit longer.

After lunch a young couple brought in a box of books, mainly Just William, Jennings and Enid Blyton paperbacks—all good sellers—for which I gave them £20.

An Italian customer who had been here during the summer (and spotted a three-volume set of *Glasgow Geography*) telephoned to order it. Fortunately Granny answered the call, and he was able to order it in Italian.

Over supper, Granny and I discussed her returning to Italy following the summer's work experience. She's reluctant to return.

Till Total £106.98
5 Customers

WEDNESDAY, 7 OCTOBER

Online orders: 1
Orders found: 1

I opened the shop ten minutes late to find Mole-Man staring through the glass window of the front door, hand-shielding his eyes for a better view inside. He clearly didn't see me approaching and almost fell flat on his face when I opened the door and his weight was no longer supported by it. He raced past me and on into the cavernous depths of the shop.

Granny appeared at 10 a.m., so I went upstairs to continue the post-festival clear-up. So far, since the end of the festival, I've found nine cables from people's laptops and phones in various parts of the house, which will—in part—make up for the number that Eliot inadvertently wanders off with throughout the year.

When I came down to let Granny have a lunch break, Mole-Man was scuttling out of the front door, weighed down by armfuls of books. Granny asked me, 'Why he never say naffink, this man?'

Till Total £171.48
7 Customers

THURSDAY, 8 OCTOBER

Online orders: 3
Orders found: 3

Opened the shop at 9 a.m.

Callum in at 11 a.m. The sound of drilling, hammering and crashing about echoed through the shop for most of the day.

I left Granny in charge and went to the Steam Packet for lunch, then to Cruggleton and Rigg Bay for a walk.

Till Total £180
10 Customers

FRIDAY, 9 OCTOBER

Online orders: 2
Orders found: 0

Nicky was in today. When I opened the front door of the shop this morning, she was standing in the doorway brushing her teeth. Apparently she'd started brushing them in her van, assuming that she'd get to the bathroom in time to finish the job, then realised that I'd left my key in the door, so she couldn't get in. She'd been there for quite a while before I appeared.

Ben and Beth came round at eleven o'clock to say goodbye. They'd taken a holiday cottage in Ardwell (near Stranraer) to recover from the festival and appeared to have had a great time. While we were chatting in the kitchen over a cup of tea, Yvonne from the festival office came in to ask me about renting the bothy. Once Ben and Beth had left, she spent half an hour talking about her job, but I honestly have no idea what she was trying to say. She kept repeating herself and saying things like 'What I'm trying to say, I suppose is, well, you know, I'm not sure.' She doesn't seem particularly happy in Wigtown.

Till Total £330.60
17 Customers

SATURDAY, 10 OCTOBER

Online orders: 2
Orders found: 2

Nicky opened the shop today. Now that everyone's gone and the festival is behind us, the town seems deathly quiet once again. This time of year is not my favourite.

As I was putting the trestle tables back in the cellar, Nicky reminded me of the year I'd bought a huge elm table on eBay. A few years ago I'd decided that the Writers' Retreat needed something more elegant than the plastic trestles, and found a ten-foot-long Edwardian table for £100, which seemed like a bargain. At the start of the festival I was telling Philip Ardagh, one of the visiting speakers, all about it in the Retreat, and smugly boasting that it had only cost me £100. Unfortunately, he was the guest speaker at the Festival Dinner, and—right in the middle of the meal—the table collapsed. I was summoned from the pop-up wine bar by Laurie to repair it, and as I was screwing it back together, Philip sat on the sofa with his arms folded, smugly quoting me from our earlier conversation: '£100 on eBay. Bargain.'

Till Total £239.80
20 Customers

MONDAY, 12 OCTOBER

Online orders: 3
Orders found: 3

The swallows have set out on their migration to Africa for the winter.

Over supper Granny and I had a chat about her life. She told me that she'd hated school in Genoa because, with her thick glasses and intellect, she was quite introverted and didn't have many friends, so she was badly bullied and took refuge in books. When she went to university in Turin, she expected more of the same, but was surprised to discover that rather than being victimised for her differences she was fêted for them, and had a large and loyal circle of friends. We've agreed that she's going back to Italy next week. She was visibly upset at the prospect, but she can't stay here indefinitely, and I can't afford to pay her. She fitted in fine in Wigtown, probably because of the same eccentricities that worked against her at school. Everyone—from the butcher to the retired women who work in the charity shop—knows her, and her experience of the town is that 'everyone are so kind.'

Till Total £170.45
16 Customers

TUESDAY, 13 OCTOBER

Online orders: 1
Orders found: 1

Granny opened the shop; I slept in until 10 a.m. My post-festival recovery time gets longer every year. When I appeared downstairs, Granny told me that my 'snorking was very a-loud. I fink the loudest ever, like a fat pig.'

Sunny day. We've gone nearly a month with barely a drop of rain.

I came downstairs to find Granny in the doorway of the shop. She chain-smoked three cigarettes in a row—'Oh, there are no points in smoking less than three at one time.'

Back exercises in the evening with Granny and the usual G&T. I'm having to make them stronger and stronger, following her repeated complaints. They've now reached a 50:50 mix.

In today's news, Waterstones announced that they're no longer going to be selling Amazon Kindles in their shops. 'Douglas McCabe, analyst for Enders, said it was "no surprise" Waterstones was removing Kindle device sales from its shops. "The e-reader may turn out to be one of the shortest-lived consumer technology categories," he said.' I hope he's right.

Till Total £172.94
13 Customers

WEDNESDAY, 14 OCTOBER

Online orders: 1
Orders found: 1

Two customers brought books to the shop, loose in the boots of their cars, all rubbish, one in the morning and the other in the afternoon.

A customer came in at 2 p.m. and asked what had happened to the free coffees we used to have in the shop. I got rid of the coffee machine six years ago. When I bought the shop, John—the previous owner—had a filter coffee machine with a hot-plate from which customers could pour themselves free coffee. I continued with it for a few years until, tired of cleaning the machine every day, paying for decent ground coffee and Shearings coach trip visitors, who would devour it and complain if we ran out of milk, I eventually got rid of it. Not many people even noticed, and I felt guilty offering free coffee when other businesses in the town depend on selling tea and coffee for their livelihood.

Till Total £223.50
24 Customers

THURSDAY, 15 OCTOBER

Online orders: 1
Orders found: 0

Granny opened the shop again.

Jane, who works in the festival office, brought in the two volumes of the Christie's catalogue for the sale of the contents of Dumfries House. I offered her £75 for them. She told me that they belong to her mother, and she'll have to check with her.

The shop seems much busier than it usually is at this time of year, but that might be partly explained by the fact that it's a two-week school holiday in Scotland. This long break—longer than the English schools—was known as the 'Tattie Holiday' when I was a child, and was originally not really a holiday at all, but traditionally the time of the potato harvest when, pre-mechanisation, the potatoes were picked by hand, and everyone, including children, was co-opted into working the fields. It is now—in a triumph of pedestrian municipal nomenclature—just known as the 'October holiday.'

Till Total £281.99
22 Customers

FRIDAY, 16 OCTOBER

Online orders: 1
Orders found: 1

Nicky's Foodie Friday treat was an assortment of squashed Indian food. These seem to be her particular favourites when she's scavenging. There was, as usual, nothing appetising about it, other than the fact that she hadn't licked bits of it on the way in.

In the afternoon I drove to Dumfries with Granny to look at a book collection in a bungalow in a residential part of town. Granny had been complaining that she hadn't been on enough buying trips, and wanted to come along, so I left the shop in Nicky's hands and we headed off after lunch.

I'd bought books from this house before, and the man selling them was very friendly: he kindly brought us a cup of tea each and a tray of biscuits. The books were mainly about golf, and pretty run-of-the-mill, but I gave him £50 for two boxes. I dropped Granny off at the station and she took the bus back to Wigtown while I drove on to Edinburgh to stay with my sister Lulu for a wedding tomorrow.

Till Total £131
11 Customers

SATURDAY, 17 OCTOBER

Online orders: 1
Orders found: 1

Spent the day in Edinburgh.

Till Total £160.49
19 Customers

MONDAY, 19 OCTOBER

Online orders: 1
Orders found: 1

Arrived home from Edinburgh at 6 p.m. last night to find that Granny had spent yesterday tidying up the front of the shop. It hasn't looked so organised for years—in fact, probably since Nicky started working in the shop. Perhaps I've found a balance: Nicky can spend her time messing the place up, and Granny can spend hers tidying up after Nicky, neatly satisfying both of their compulsions.

Today's order was for the Dumfries House Christie's catalogues, which Nicky—unaware that I'm still waiting to hear whether Jane's mother has accepted my offer—listed online for £45 on Saturday. I emailed and explained the situation to the purchaser, and they were very understanding.

Till Total £136.48
12 Customers

TUESDAY, 20 OCTOBER

Online orders: 0
Orders found: 0

At 2 p.m. Donna, the wife of the late GP who was our family doctor for many years, popped into the shop to tell me that I had arranged to be at her house at 1.30 p.m. to look at his books. I'd completely forgotten, so I apologised, jumped in the van and drove round there. The collection consisted mainly of railway books, always a good selling subject in the shop, so I gave her £150 for them.

Granny spent the day packing up the books for this month's mail-out.

Till Total £84.48
9 Customers

WEDNESDAY, 21 OCTOBER

Online orders: 1
Orders found: 0

On her way down to open the shop Granny discovered a bat in the archaeology section. It was hanging from a book called *Digging for History*. I posted a photograph of it on Facebook, and Sheena, a friend who lives locally, messaged me and told me to put it in a shoe box, and that she'd come around later to collect it. I did as instructed, but failed to spot a tiny hole in the box, through which the bat escaped and flew up into the cornice in the drawing room. I thought it best just to leave it there until Sheena arrived.

Jeff the minister called in at ten o'clock looking slightly tired. His bike was parked outside the shop. He asked Granny if we had had any new theology books in. She looked blankly back at him, and a conversation ensued in which neither of them clearly had the slightest idea what the other was saying. It reminded me of the first month of Granny living here.

A woman from Castle Douglas came in with four boxes of books, mainly autobiographies, but there was a nicely illustrated copy of the *Arabian Nights*. Gave her £60. Shortly afterwards, a couple from Kirkcudbright brought in a collection of books, largely about the Loch Ness monster. She was quite overbearing and insisted on telling me where she'd bought each one of the books, along with a string of tedious anecdotes as I was going through them. Eventually I suggested that they go for a walk while I checked the values of the books I wasn't familiar with. Thankfully, they did. There was some interesting material among them, and on their return from their walk I offered her £130 for about twenty books, which she seemed quite happy with.

Sheena came around in the evening and extracted the bat from the cornice and took it home.

Stayed up late chatting to Granny. Today was her last day in the shop. Tomorrow I will drive her to the airport. She's been a fantastic help, and I'm sad to lose her, but staying here indefinitely isn't good for her, and I would appreciate my privacy back. As she was packing, I asked her if she'd remembered her passport, to which she replied 'Passport? I never owned a passport.' Further investigation revealed that her travelling—and she is well travelled—has all been within the EU, and just using her Italian ID card. Being born in 1970, I can barely comprehend that international travel is possible without a passport.

Bed at 2 a.m.

Till Total £131.99
14 Customers

THURSDAY, 22 OCTOBER

Online orders: 2
Orders found: 0

Awoke to discover that Captain had taken up residence in my laundry basket, from which his head was poking out.

Nicky was in today, so I asked her to go through the Loch Ness collection that I bought yesterday and list anything valuable online.

Drove to Edinburgh with Sally (the woman who's been running The Open Book for the past ten days) and Granny. As I said goodbye to a tearful Granny at the airport, she handed me a book as a leaving present. It was a copy of Mikhail Bulgakov's *The Master and Margarita*. The gaps in my knowledge of literature are vast and plentiful, but Russian literature is something of a chasm.

Home at 6.30 p.m.

Till Total £96.50
11 Customers

FRIDAY, 23 OCTOBER

Online orders: 3
Orders found: 3

Nicky arrived twenty minutes late: 'Sorry I'm late, a tractor clipped my wing mirror near my house and it took me twenty minutes to catch up with it.' It comes as no surprise that it took her twenty minutes to catch up with a tractor: she drives like a myopic nonogenarian.

One of the orders was for one of the Loch Ness monster books that Nicky listed yesterday. It sold for £70.

Till Total £173
8 Customers

SATURDAY, 24 OCTOBER

Online orders: 3
Orders found: 2

As I was tidying up the paperback fiction section and feeling fairly illiterate from looking at titles I hadn't read but felt I ought to have done, I started instead to notice the books that I had read: *The Wasp Factory*, by Iain Banks; several books by Gerald Durrell and Ian Fleming; *High Fidelity* by Nick Hornby; *A Prayer for Owen Meany* by John Irving; *The Mighty Walzer* by Howard Jacobson; *Love in a Time of Cholera* by Gabriel García Márquez; and others that I'd completely forgotten I had read.

There has been a brown trilby on the sofa in the big room since the festival. I assume that it is Nicky's Tyrolean yodelling hat, but keep forgetting to ask her about it.

Till Total £143.50
14 Customers

MONDAY, 26 OCTOBER

Online orders: 4
Orders found: 4

Surprise visit this morning from Daisy, the *Daily Telegraph* journalist who covered the festival two years ago, when they were our media sponsor. She brought her family along: they're here on holiday near Portpatrick. She's now working as a theatre critic.

A small child ducked under the barrier at the top of the stairs that lead up from the shop and used the toilet—I spotted him trying to sneak out unnoticed when I was coming out of the kitchen after I'd made a cup of tea. He slid under the barrier and ran off. I've no idea how he knew where it was.

Another small child found an unpriced book and told his sister that this is how we 'trap people into buying things,' so that they have to come to the counter and ask us what the price is. A man, who I assume was the children's father, asked 'Is it called The Bookshop because it's full of books?' How do these people feed themselves?

Sheena called to say that the bat was fine, and has been released back into the wild, probably to be devoured by Captain.

Till Total £333.99
30 Customers

TUESDAY, 27 OCTOBER

Online orders: 4
Orders found: 2

Callum in again. Managed to lose my glasses and spent most of the day feeling utterly helpless.

Till Total £247.99
22 Customers

WEDNESDAY, 28 OCTOBER

Online orders: 1
Orders found: 1

Telephone call this morning:

> Caller: Eh, I'm calling from Scunthorpe in England. I'm looking for a book which has a story about my grandfather in it. He was a famous poacher.

Me: OK, well can you tell me what the book is called?

Caller: Eh? No, I don't know what it's called. I know what he was called, though.

Me: Right, so you want me to read every book in the shop until I spot his name in one of them?

Caller: Eh, that's very kind of you.

An elderly woman and her daughter came in with three boxes of pretty average stock, but there was a mint copy of *Wigtownshire Agriculturalists and Breeders* among them. This is a very rare local book, and I have a buyer who snaps up every copy I can get hold of, so I gave her £65 for it.

Till Total £274.42

24 Customers

THURSDAY, 29 OCTOBER

Online orders: 0

Orders found: 0

I managed to get the 'Death to the Kindle' mug available for sale on Amazon. I wonder how long it will be before it is removed.

As I was pricing up books, I came across a copy of a book called *A Treasury of Bookplates*. Once, shortly after I'd bought the shop, I was looking at a photographer's library in Montrose. When I came across a book about the manufacturing process for Leica lenses, the photographer peered over the top of his glasses at me and said, 'Every industry has its porn.' For me, this book about bookplates is bookseller filth. It has now been squirrelled away into my collection.

Carol-Ann is still living in the bothy. This morning she told me that because I'd locked the garden door she couldn't get out to go to work yesterday morning and had to find a ladder, lean it against the wall, climb up and jump over.

Till Total £181.38

24 Customers

FRIDAY, 30 OCTOBER

Online orders: 1
Orders found: 1

Nicky was in today. Thankfully she didn't bring any gastronomic treats from the Morrisons skip.

A woman and her mother came to the shop because they had read Anna's book and wanted to see the town for themselves.

In the evening, after I'd locked up, I picked up Lindsey, one of this year's interns, from Barrhill railway station at 6.20 p.m. She's back for the weekend to catch up with people. Came back and met up with Margi (Open Book resident) in the pub, where she was happily chatting to Colin from the sawmill and a few other regulars. I spotted Callum and some friends sitting around a table, so we wandered over and sat down with them.

Till Total £168.49
15 Customers

SATURDAY, 31 OCTOBER

Online orders: 1
Orders found: 1

Nicky arrived in her customary good cheer and fashionably late, as ever.

Email on the shop's Facebook:

Dan

30 October 14:57

Good morning bookshop! My name is Dan I am a published author from Colorado I would love to meet you guys and potentially set up some events! I love your store! I have copies of my debut poetry collection which is titled 36 it would be an honor to be able to drop some copies off to you guys so your staff could check it out! And possibly pass some out to your customers! Also I would love to make a donation to you guys as well just to show support to you guys just a local artist trying to support a local business. Thank you for your time!

The Bookshop

31 October 12:43

Hi Dan, thanks for your email. Not sure what you mean by 'local'—we are in Scotland.

Dan

2 November 01:42

Hey! And I meant I'm a local artist from where I am!

My mother came in to drop off my belated birthday present: a picture of Captain painted by her octogenarian stoner friend Jean from Colorado. It's a bizarre sort of cubist affair. Jean and her husband used to come and stay in one of the holiday cottages on my parents' farm. They became good friends, and always kept in touch. A few years ago Jean began to suffer severely from arthritis. She would regularly email my mother complaining bitterly about the pain of it until one day she was prescribed medical marijuana. Since then she's never looked back and aside from the health benefits, has become a huge recreational user. Initially, this has confused my anti-drug mother considerably, but recently she's come to find Jean's correspondence highly entertaining. Last Christmas, Jean was going to put the fairy lights on the tree in her apartment in the sheltered housing community where she lives. She got them from the cupboard, then decided to test them before putting them on the tree (they were still in the cardboard box). She switched them on, then had a smoke and decided that they looked rather nice, glowing in the brown box, so she decided to just leave them there. As far as I'm aware, they're still there.

Till Total £104
12 Customers

NOVEMBER

Customers can be queer about prices. Some raise their eyebrows
when you tell them what a book will cost; others purse their lips.
Both are trying gently to convey that they would buy the book if it
were a shilling or two less. Some glance at you hopefully over their
spectacles; some just shake their heads. These are the let's-meet-
each-other-half-way clanjamfray. Others don't even go to that length.
When you say a book is seven and six, they bark at you 'Five bob.'
To them I reply that I am sorry I'm not permitted to lower the price
of a book. 'Keep it then,' he says. So I keep it. No chaffering, is Mr
Pumpherston's rule. 'This is a bookshop,' he says, 'not an Arabian
bazaar.' I have known him to reduce a book to an old customer, but
never if the customer himself has first tried to break down the price.
If a customer tries to haggle the book is snapped shut and replaced
on the shelf. Mr Pumpherston declares that if you're ready to break
down your prices, it'll soon go round that you charge too much in the
first place. There's a lot of sense in that dictum.

Augustus Muir, *The Intimate Thoughts of John Baxter, Bookseller*

If you're in a trade in which people feel entitled to haggle, no
amount of ink spent venting your frustration at people's eagerness
to beat your prices down is too much. It is a constant, grinding
feature of daily life in the second-hand trade, and many people, as
Mr Pumpherston implies, believe that you factor in a margin for
this kind of negotiation when you're fixing your prices. We don't,
and I don't imagine that many businesses do. You look at a book,
remember what you paid for it and price it accordingly. Customers
don't try to negotiate at the petrol pump, or the supermarket
whose owners and shareholders make millions, if not billions in
profits, but it seems that it is acceptable to try to screw the profit
out of struggling small businesses at a time when everybody is
fully aware that we're up against it thanks to, well, you know who

by now. Generally, like Mr Pumpherston, I'm considerably more inclined to discount if customers don't ask. If they do ask—and do so politely—I may reduce a large sale, but if they demand a discount they almost certainly will not get one. I'm tempted to start using his Arabian bazaar retort in such encounters, just as I'm tempted to use Dorothy Parker's 'What fresh hell is this?' when I answer the telephone.

It's strange that Scots have a reputation for meanness. In my experience the Scots are generous to a fault, and I honestly can't remember the last time anyone Scottish haggled with me over the price of a book. Americans, too, don't tend to argue about the prices we set. Before the days of online selling, there was an unspoken rule in the second-hand book trade that a 10 per cent trade discount was offered on all sales to other booksellers (although Irish dealers always demanded 20 per cent). This seems laughably small, now that even non-trade customers expect considerably more than that.

MONDAY, 2 NOVEMBER

Online orders: 3
Orders found: 3

I was on my own in the shop today, so I decided to read *Death at Intervals*, another book by José Saramago, author of *Blindness*, which Emanuela had given me. Sat by the fire and got stuck into it.

Went to make a cup of tea at about 2 p.m. and returned to find that Captain had stolen my seat by the fire.

Telephone call from BT about advertising in the phone book, which, like bookshops, has become a relic of the past as everyone now has their contacts in their mobile and can access information online anyway. For the past few years I've taken an advert in the phone book at a cost of £425. I told the rep today that I didn't want to do it any more, and he asked if he could call me back. He did so five minutes later and the price had dropped to £250. I reluctantly agreed to it. Now I'm starting to regret my decision.

Till Total £65.50
8 Customers

TUESDAY, 3 NOVEMBER

Online orders: 1
Orders found: 1

There was an email this morning from an Australian magazine asking for photos and anecdotes about the shop, so replied with both.

Drove to a book deal in Gelston again, at the same house. This time it included a good copy of *Edinburgh Revisited* by James Bone and a four-volume set of Burns. Less than one box, gave her £65.

Made Cullen Skink for supper.

Till Total £361.50
12 Customers

WEDNESDAY, 4 NOVEMBER

Online orders: 4
Orders found: 4

Nicky in.

Order from Kuala Lumpur, and another for a book from the erotica section to an address in Iran.

An old man came to the counter with four mint paperbacks from the humour section—one priced at £1, two others at £2 and the other one at £1.50—and said, 'You don't seriously expect me to pay that much for these, do you?' He left empty-handed.

Nicky found a book of French phrases (1960 reprint). Not sure quite what sort of holiday you'd have planned if you required the following:

You are requested not to wander about during the service.

Onions do not agree with me [*although Anna's father would find that one useful: he hates onions*].

The cooking is plain.

I have fallen in the sea.

The boy has drowned.

I am wanted by the police.

He has committed suicide.

The weather is dreadful.

Later on, Nicky told me that she's going to stop working here. She's applied for a job in an old folks' home—'Most of my pals live there anyway'—and had decided that she disapproves of my lifestyle. I think the fundamental problem is that she thinks I made a mistake ending things with Anna, of whom she is very fond.

Till Total £119

9 Customers

THURSDAY, 5 NOVEMBER

Online orders: 2

Orders found: 2

Opened the shop slightly late, on a cold, wet day.

Local farmer Sandy McCreath came in. He spent an hour telling me about his dyslexia. He wants to make a documentary about dyslexia within the farming community, and while he is clearly well informed about the condition, trying to get an idea of how the documentary would look is nearly impossible. I don't think he really knows. I suggested that he speak to Dyslexia Scotland—'Oh, I cannae do that. I've fallen out with them.'

Callum came in because he was worried about the rain running off the roof and down the flue of the new boiler, which the extension is designed to protect. We spent an hour, patching a repair together.

Isabel came in to do the accounts.

Till Total £40.50

5 Customers

FRIDAY, 6 NOVEMBER

Online orders: 2
Orders found: 2

Drove to Aberdeen for a book deal tomorrow. Text message from Granny: 'I'm sorry if I disturb you but this morning when I put in order my face, Zoe, my cat bite my ankle.'

Till Total £42.50
4 Customers

SATURDAY, 7 NOVEMBER

Online orders: 2
Orders found: 2

Drove home, via a house in Rosemount. Middle-aged woman whose late husband had an interest in history: several Spalding Club books among the collection. Gave her £300 for five boxes. Back home at 4.30 p.m.

The Spalding Club was founded in 1839, and named after seventeenth-century historian John Spalding. It produced books, mainly in the latter half of the nineteenth century, and largely relating to the history and archaeology of Aberdeenshire. They're easy to identify, being mostly the same size (large 8vo) and bound in olive green buckram. They're usually limited editions, and normally sell for between £20 and £60, depending on the title. They rarely sell quickly, but they are very well produced, and academic works of a high standard. These will probably sell online.

Finished reading *Death at Intervals*. I struggled with it, compared with *Blindness*. Although the concept of a country in which people stop dying is brilliant, the execution seemed more laboured and the pace much slower than that of *Blindness*.

Till Total £106.43
8 Customers

MONDAY, 9 NOVEMBER

Online orders: 6
Orders found: 6

At 11 a.m. a woman came to the counter with a book which she'd brought in and said, 'My grandfather gave me this book, see. He was a missionary in Africa, see. He left me this book. I can't remember who the woman is, but it's a story about this woman who was a missionary, and it's got a photograph of her on one of the pages, see. It's meant to be there, because there's an oblong bit for the photo, see. Is that the kind of thing you'd be interested in?'

No.

Wet and miserable day. After supper I lit the fire and started *The Master and Margarita*.

Till Total £20.50
3 Customers

TUESDAY, 10 NOVEMBER

Online orders: 5
Orders found: 5

I found all the orders this morning, which was windy and wet.

Two customers brought in a good collection of modern paperback fiction, for which I gave them £50. It's ideal material for the Random Book Club.

At eleven o'clock a woman came to the counter and explained that her boss, who had been in the Writers' Retreat during the festival, had left a brown trilby behind. It was the one that I thought was Nicky's Tyrolean yodelling hat, so I returned it to her.

After lunch I drove to a house in Glencaple, near Dumfries, to look at a book collection. It was another widow selling her late husband's library, and it is probably the best collection I've seen this year: everything in pristine condition, a mix of old and new, plenty of fishing and shooting (including about a dozen BBs) and more Ian Nialls than I've ever come across before, as well as an early printing of *Culpeper's Herbal* (volume II only—the anatomical volume). Her husband had been a surgeon, and there were a lot of curious medical biographies which (I hope) would have been small print runs, and consequently now scarce and valuable. I gave her £700 for ten boxes.

Eliot sent me a text message at four o'clock asking if he could come and stay tomorrow for an unspecified period.

Till Total £135.49
9 Customers

WEDNESDAY, 11 NOVEMBER

Online orders: 1
Orders found: 1

Opened the shop. Wet, miserable day, so I lit the fire in the shop.

Telephone call from Abe at 11 a.m. Apparently a customer isn't happy with the condition of a book we sent to them. It cost the customer £7, and we sent it to America, making a loss on the postage. I checked the emails and found one (to which I had failed to respond) from him:

Dear The Bookshop

You recently sent me a copy of *The Scottish Castle Restoration Debate*, your order number on the shipping note is xxxxxxx.

The advertisement on the Abe web site as far as I remember described the book as in very good condition and your shipping note repeats that assertion.

There are a couple of creases in the lower couple of inches of the back cover, the five or six pages behind these creases all appear to be water damaged to a lesser degree as one gets further into the book, but the damage to the last page immediately behind the back cover is especially bad with a small area of the coating of the inside face of the cover having been transferred to the preceding page.

The plasticized coating is beginning to peel away in places from the edges of both the front and the back covers and there is an approximately two inch stain on the edge on the pages opposite the spine of the book which fortunately has only traveled a minimal distance from the edge of the pages in to the book but is still easily noticeable.

None of this damage occurred in transit as the packaging was in perfect condition.

I realize that it has taken me a couple of weeks to get back to you but I only have intermittent access to the Internet and I have spent some time trying to find out if there was some way that I could leave negative feed back about this order on the Abe website, it appears there is not, something that I will be contacting Abe about in the not too distant future.

I would have described this book as in average condition at the very best, it is certainly not in 'very good' condition.

Yours,

Bryan

How depressing that his first instinct was to leave negative feedback, rather than try to resolve the problem with me.

Eliot turned up at three o'clock. His shoes were on the floor of the kitchen by seven.

AWB meeting at The Old Bank at 5.30. This time I remembered it, which is just as well since I'm secretary.

Till Total £77.50
6 Customers

THURSDAY, 12 NOVEMBER

Online orders: 5
Orders found: 4

Wild and stormy—apparently we're in the midst of an Atlantic storm.

I've decided that we ought to make a Christmas video for the shop, in the style of the John Lewis Christmas advert. I'm thinking of adapting ''Twas the night before Christmas.'

At four o'clock a Cockney man came in and bought three Bernard Cornwell books. He told me that once he'd finished them, he'll have read all of Cornwell's work. I suggested that he try Patrick O'Brian next.

Eliot fell asleep on the sofa at 7 p.m., so I read *The Master and Margarita*. Granny told me that I would love it, and if the first hundred pages are anything to go by, that's an understatement. I am transfixed.

Till Total £29.30
5 Customers

FRIDAY, 13 NOVEMBER

Online orders: 2
Orders found: 2

Nicky arrived on time at 9 a.m., but there were no treats from the Morrisons skip today. There has been a discernible chill in her approach to me since she announced that she's leaving.

Still stormy and cold. Eliot left at 7 a.m. amid a chorus of slamming doors and stomping feet.

Nicky (whispering and pointing at a customer): 'See that guy over there—he was in last week for two hours. He didn't buy anything, and asked me if he could photocopy some pages from a book.' This was a common occurrence in the early days after I'd bought the shop. People would just want a few pages from a book (usually relating to an ancestor), and we—very occasionally—obliged them, but it doesn't really happen these days. It's possible that now people surreptitiously photograph the relevant pages on their phones, or that the information is available online.

Nicky and I unloaded the boxes from the Glencaple deal, and she started going through them. I asked her to guess how much I'd paid for them. She said £100, then she started sorting through them and checking values online; one of the things she found was a Georgian ladies' blank notebook which had a lock and key, and had been partially illustrated and written in. It appears that they're not worth as much as I had anticipated, and her estimate was probably more accurate than mine.

Nicky and I were discussing what to do for The Bookshop's cheery Christmas video:

> Me: 'Why don't we base it on Byron's 'The Destruction of Sennacherib'?

Nicky read it aloud:

> The Assyrian came down like the wolf on the fold,
> And his cohorts were gleaming in purple and gold;
> And the sheen of their spears was like stars on the sea,
> When the blue wave rolls nightly on deep Galilee.
>
> Like the leaves of the forest when Summer is green,
> That host with their banners at sunset were seen:
> Like the leaves of the forest when Autumn hath blown,
> That host on the morrow lay withered and strown.
>
> For the Angel of Death spread his wings on the blast,
> And breathed in the face of the foe as he passed;
> And the eyes of the sleepers waxed deadly and chill,
> And their hearts but once heaved, and for ever grew still!
>
> And there lay the steed with his nostril all wide,
> But through it there rolled not the breath of his pride;
> And the foam of his gasping lay white on the turf,
> And cold as the spray of the rock-beating surf.
>
> And there lay the rider distorted and pale,
> With the dew on his brow, and the rust on his mail:
> And the tents were all silent, the banners alone,

The lances unlifted, the trumpet unblown.

> And the widows of Ashur are loud in their wail,
> And the idols are broke in the temple of Baal;
> And the might of the Gentile, unsmote by the sword,
> Hath melted like snow in the glance of the Lord!

Nicky decided that 'Captain could be the Angel of Death; we could glue wings onto him and throw him at the camera!'

This is not going to end well. We have each agreed to write a script, based on ''Twas the Night Before Christmas'/'The Destruction of Sennacherib' (the two poems have the same scansion).

While I was locking up the shop, I noticed piles of books all around the place which Nicky had deposited, rather than put on the shelves.

Till Total £73
7 Customers

SATURDAY, 14 NOVEMBER

Online orders: 2
Orders found: 1

Nicky in. I mentioned the piles of books all over the place to her and was (predictably) greeted with her usual 'Aye, there was a customer in the way so I couldn't put them on the shelves,' so I gave up and we moved on to one of her favourite topics: death.

> Nicky: If I die before Armageddon, my pal George is going to make me a coffin out of an old pallet, put me in the back of my van and dump me in the woods somewhere.
>
> Me: I want a Viking ship funeral.
>
> Nicky: Ye cannae do that. The only way around it is to have a Romany funeral. You'll have to build yourself a caravan and set fire to it. Oh, wait, you'll be dead. You'll have to get someone else to set fire to it.

I have developed what appears to be a foolproof system to deal with the incessant stream of cold callers trying to get me to switch electricity supplier.

> Caller: Could I speak with the person who deals with your
>   electricity supply?
> Me: He's not here.
> Caller: When will he be back?
> Me: In about a year.
> Caller [*long pause, every single time*]: A year?
> Me: That's right. A year.
> Caller hangs up.

Spent part of the afternoon filming Nicky reading her "Twas the Night Before Christmas' video.

Till Total £59.50
10 Customers

MONDAY, 16 NOVEMBER

Online orders: 4
Orders found: 4

Callum in at 10 a.m. to work on the boiler housing.

At two o'clock someone came to the counter and introduced himself as Jeff Shepherd. He brought in five boxes of books, mainly ex-library material, and I gave him £50 for what I took out. I couldn't help thinking that Jeff Shepherd would be a great name for a one-man Def Leppard tribute band, possibly with a sheepdog.

Farmer Sandy came in at 3 p.m. to tell me about how his dyslexia film idea is going. As usual, he was looking for help which I am not equipped to give him: 'Do you know any dyslexic celebrities we can get involved?' I don't know any celebrities, let alone dyslexic celebrities. As is also his usual manner, he didn't bother to ask if I was too busy to chat and just ploughed on. When I made it visibly obvious that I had work to do, he finally picked up on the signal and said, 'Right, you're busy. I'll let you get on.' Then proceeded to continue his monologue about dyslexic celebrities for another twenty minutes.

Till Total £26
3 Customers

TUESDAY, 17 NOVEMBER

Online orders: 2
Orders found: 2

Lashing wet day, and bitingly cold with it.

Typed up the minutes from AWB meeting.

By 1 p.m. Sandy the tattooed pagan was the only customer. He's after a copy of *The Hereditary Sheriffs of Galloway*. We normally have copies in stock, but today I couldn't find one.

Nicky appeared as Sandy and I were talking about business:

> Sandy: Nicky! Speak of the devil! Come here and give me a hug. I'm a lonely old man.
>
> Nicky [*leaping backwards in the opposite direction*]: 'No way! I'm not hugging you—I'm Scottish. Anyway, I didn't come in for this treatment. Shauny—did a bag of black feathers arrive for me? And can I work tomorrow?

She then went to the antiquarian section and located a copy of *Hereditary Sheriffs*, underpriced (by her) at £65, which she thrust into Sandy's hands. He bought it.

I still have no idea why she wanted the black feathers, but no doubt all will be revealed in good time.

Telephone call just before closing from someone near Castle Douglas who wants to sell twelve boxes of books, so I have arranged to view them on Friday.

Till Total £125
6 Customers

WEDNESDAY, 18 NOVEMBER

Online orders: 2
Orders found: 2

Nicky wandered in at 9.05 a.m.

Filthy wet day again, windy and cold. The radio in the shop never works properly when atmospheric conditions are like this, cutting in and out, so I switched it off.

Two women spent an hour in the shop, and eventually came to the counter with a relatively new book about tying fishing flies, in mint condition with a dust jacket. I'd priced it at £4.50. One of them asked Nicky if it was suitable for a beginner. Nicky pointed at me and said, 'Ask him,' so I had a look at it—it seemed pretty comprehensive, with patterns and materials all clearly shown so I told them it was ideal. They decided not to buy it and instead to go to the fishing shop in Newton Stewart instead, where they'll probably end up buying the same book for £20.

Nicky started packing the books for this month's Random Book Club mail-out. She managed to make the most phenomenal mess, with piles of books, both packaged and unpackaged, all over every surface, including the floor. When I asked her why she was incapable of keeping the place tidy, she called me a 'fussy old woman.' Carol-Ann appeared while she was busily making more mess and said, 'Nicky—why is there stuff everywhere? Look—even on the floor,' at which point Nicky accused us both of having OCD and said, 'Have you not heard of the saying "a tidy house is the sign of a dull woman"?' When I pointed out that this is a shop, not a house, and I'm not a woman, she shook her head and looked at the floor.

In the afternoon I filmed some material in the church graveyard and the shop for the 'Night Before Christmas' video.

Norrie brought in twelve boxes of books.

Till Total £22.50
4 Customers

THURSDAY, 19 NOVEMBER

Online orders: 1
Orders found: 1

This morning I finished packing and labelling books for the Random Book Club, then sorted the mail sacks and Royal Mail online postage. The total postal bill for this month's output came to £250.

The radio was working again because it was a clear, sunny day.

In today's post was a bag of black feathers, which (presumably) Nicky ordered for her Christmas video. It occurs to me now that perhaps she's thinking of attaching them to Captain somehow.

A group of eight students came in at three o'clock and wandered about taking photographs for half an hour. None of them bought anything.

The cockney Bernard Cornwell fan came back, and I sold him three Patrick O'Brians.

A customer bought one of the BB books from the Glencaple collection, so I'm slowly on the road to recouping my investment. Nicky was right, though. I overpaid for that lot.

Till Total £76.48
7 Customers

FRIDAY, 20 NOVEMBER

Online orders: 4
Orders found: 4

Nicky in. Callum turned up at 10 a.m. with an enormous pumpkin which he'd found in his garden. He hadn't even known it was there, so it must have germinated from one of last year's seeds. Nicky decided to paint a pair of glasses on it and put a wig (which we had for a window display) on it. She assured me that the likeness is uncanny.

Cold, sunny winter's day. Nicky spent it sorting through more of Norrie's books.

As I was coming down the spiral stairs after making a cup of tea, a middle-aged couple who were looking at local history books in the Scottish Room stopped me and asked me the price of a copy of *Scottish Ghost Stories*, a fairly common and cheap paperback. I told them that they could have it for £2.50, at which point the woman said, 'Of course, you know this house has a spirit.' I coughed to suppress my incredulity that a grown woman could believe in such a thing but was slightly taken aback when she continued, 'It's on the stairs. On the landing to be precise. I felt it there.'

For all my scepticism and conviction that this is no more than a coincidence (the landing was where Joyce told me that 'George' liked to conduct his ghoulish activities), this is now the third time that someone has mentioned the stairs as the site of supernatural activity. I remain unconvinced but slightly unsettled.

We filmed some more material for the 'Night Before Christmas' videos. Nicky has made a pair of wings for Captain—who she has decided will play the Angel of Death—using the black feathers.

Till Total £142.50
9 Customers

SATURDAY, 21 NOVEMBER

Online orders: 2
Orders found: 2

Nicky opened the shop this morning.

We spent most of the day ignoring customers and filming the necessary material for our respective videos, which we have decided to post on Facebook and let the people who follow the shop's page judge whose is best. Nicky is excellent in front of the camera—she doesn't need to make any effort, her natural comic timing is effortless.

By the end of the working day Nicky had piled so much junk ('props' for her video) onto the till that it was impossible to operate it.

I spent the evening editing the videos.

It's a month until the shortest day of the year. Most people I know dread January, but for me the worst time of year is between September and December: the fishing season is over, it becomes colder and wetter, and the days shorten until some days it feels like there has been no light at all. At least January is redeemed by the lengthening days.

Till Total £264.49
8 Customers

MONDAY, 23 NOVEMBER

Online orders: 4
Orders found: 1

Bitterly cold day.

Obligatory telephone call with The Pensions Regulator this morning in which they asked for my email address:

> Me: M A I L @ T H E - B O O K S H O P dot C O M.
> Her: So, that's nail@the-bookshop.com.
> Me: No, M A I L.
> Her: Right, so nail@the-bookshop.com.
> Me: Yes, just send it to nail@the-bookshop.com. I'm going
> to ignore it anyway.

Uploaded the 'Night Before Christmas' videos to Facebook with a post asking people to send a photo voting for their favourite.

Just a handful of customers today, but unusually they all bought books.

Till Total £204.50
9 Customers

TUESDAY, 24 NOVEMBER

Online orders: 2
Orders found: 1

It's very unusual to have a customer waiting outside the shop when I open at 9 a.m., but there was a man pacing about impatiently at the door this morning. He asked if we had any books on the Middle East. We have a reasonable selection—two or three hundred books, some antiquarian, some up-to-date. He spent two hours there and bought nothing.

Just before lunchtime an elderly Yorkshireman came to the counter with three books about fishing, all fairly scarce. The total came to £66 and on being told this he demanded my 'best price,' so I told him that the best price for me would be £100. His wife—clearly used to his haggling—burst out laughing and said, 'That'll teach you, George.' Finally let him have them for £60.

Telephone inquiry about a copy of *Dark Estuary* by BB. The customer wanted every detail about the condition, which is described online as 'mint.' It is tedious to have to explain that no, there are no tears to the dust jacket, there's no inscription, no folded pages, no creases, no foxing, no bumped corners etc. when 'mint' already means that. After five minutes he seemed satisfied with the condition and asked if he could have a discount if he bought directly from us, rather than through Abe. The book was £8. I said that no, he could not. He hung up.

My mother appeared at 4 p.m. with the couple who are running The Open Book this week. They're American: she is probably around fifty-five, he looks a bit older. He has a tattoo of a dolphin over his right eye. Went for a drink with them in The Ploughman after work.

The Christmas videos Nicky and I made are being shared a lot on Facebook.

Till Total £69.50
2 Customers

WEDNESDAY, 25 NOVEMBER

Online orders: 5
Orders found: 4

One of the shop's few regular local customers, Ian, dropped in and asked if we could order two Terry Pratchett novels for him. He told me that he could get them on Amazon but would rather give us the trade. I could have hugged him.

Emailed John, the builder, about the chimney. We need to repair it before the weather really turns wintery and causes further damage. No reply, so I phoned Wacek, the Polish builder.

Message from Granny on Facebook: 'Shaun, you shitty bastard, why you not write to the Granny? I miss Scotland, with the rain and the sheep.' Replied that I'll Skype her next week.

Isabel came in at two o'clock to do the accounts. She was raving about the 'Night Before Christmas' videos.

Telephone call at 2.30 from a man near Dumfries with 2,000 books to sell. I have arranged to visit him on Friday as he has Oxfam coming to collect them next Tuesday if I don't get there first.

Till Total £73.49
7 Customers

THURSDAY, 26 NOVEMBER

Online orders: 2
Orders found: 1

Today's missing order was for a book listed by Nicky last week. Hopefully she'll find it tomorrow.

Telephone call from a man in Dalry (about 25 miles away). He has been charged with the task of disposing of the library of Donald Watson, the wildlife artist, who died in 2005. I've arranged to meet him on Saturday.

There were no customers after two o'clock, so I closed half an hour early and started reading Nan Shepherd's *The Living*

Mountain. It's a short book, and comes recommended by Callum, whose taste in reading is quite similar to mine.

Till Total £144.50
4 Customers

FRIDAY, 27 NOVEMBER

Online orders: 3
Orders found: 2

Nicky was in with a bag of squashed welshcakes. She spent the first ten minutes of the working day scarfing them.

Wacek, the Polish builder, appeared at 10 a.m. and had a look at the problem with the chimney. He told me that he could fix it for £3,000 and could start in a week.

After lunch I drove to Dalswinton, near Dumfries, to look at the books the caller on Wednesday had told me were going to Oxfam if I didn't get there first. The man selling them is a retired academic, and he and his wife live in a beautiful mill which they converted twenty years ago. They're moving to a two-bedroom flat in the west end of Glasgow and have to dispose of most of the contents of the mill, including (so far) about two thousand of his books. They were charming, and I had a cup of tea and a chat with them before looking at the books, most of which were in agricultural feed sacks, with the more valuable books on the table in the sitting room, including a book signed by Bertrand Russell. I went through about five of the forty sacks to ascertain an average value (hoping that the rest were similar) and wrote them a cheque for £1,300, which was probably considerably more than I ought to have offered. It's going to take a long time to break even. They helped me load the sacks into the van. Left at 4 p.m., home at 5.30.

Till Total £56.28
7 Customers

SATURDAY, 28 NOVEMBER

Online orders: 4
Orders found: 4

Nicky was in. She's back to wearing the black ski suit again, now that the colder weather has set in, and the temperature in the shop drops below the legal requirement for working conditions.

We unloaded the sacks from the van and dumped them in the corner of the front room of the shop. It's getting seriously cluttered now, with a dozen boxes of fresh stock to process, thirty-seven boxes of reject stock to take to the recycling plant in Glasgow, and now forty bags of God-knows-what.

I asked Nicky to prioritise the books in the boxes, as the more valuable material was in those, rather than the fertiliser sacks, whose contents were more modest in value. She gloatingly told me that she's discovered that she is entitled to eleven days' paid holiday a year. One of her friends told her. Neither of us had any idea that there was holiday entitlement for part-time workers, but it appears that there is. She's backdating her claim for the past four years.

I left the shop at 2 p.m. and drove through torrential rain to Dalry to look at Donald Watson's library. Donald Watson was a wildlife (predominantly birds) artist, and highly regarded. He wrote and illustrated a number of books, and as a young man was encouraged to follow this career by Archibald Thorburn, one of the most famous wildlife illustrators of the twentieth century. He lived in Galloway for most of his life, and died in 2005. I met the executor of the estate at his house on Dalry's main street, and we drove up to the house: an attractive cottage in the town, but very run down, damp and dirty. The best of the book collection had been removed and given to a public library. What remained consisted of seventeen cardboard boxes full of a wide range of subjects, mostly of little value and in poor condition. I left with five boxes of the best of it, including a first edition *Peter Pan*.

Home at 4 p.m. to find that Nicky—contrary to instructions—had started raking her way through the fertiliser sacks and not bothered with the boxes.

I listed the signed Bertrand Russell book on eBay after work, and read a bit more of *The Living Mountain*. It's a truly beautiful book; Nan Shepherd's powers of description are pure poetry, and her passion—obsession even—for the Cairngorms is plainly evident. Her description of the texture of light describes Galloway exactly: 'Light in Scotland has a quality I have not met elsewhere. It is luminous without being fierce, penetrating to immense distances with an effortless intensity.'

Till Total £212.40
19 Customers

MONDAY, 30 NOVEMBER

Online orders: 3
Orders found: 3

It was a wet morning, and cold, but it brightened up around lunchtime. This seems to have been the pattern for much of November.

At 10 a.m. a man with an enormous beard came in, dripping all over the floor, and said, 'I'm from Devon, I'm working up here for a month. The woman who lives next door to me has written a children's book. She published it herself. It's not very good. Would you like to stock it?'

Later on, a customer accosted me as I was tidying up the topography section and said, 'I was here six months ago and you had a book on RAF bases. Do you still have it?' We have around 600 books in the aviation section. He then dropped a book while standing on the top of the stepladder, said 'Oops,' then just left it on the ground. He found the book he wanted, which was £28.50, and demanded a discount, then, as the credit card machine was processing his payment he said, 'Well, you obviously won't have fibre optic in a backwater like this.' We've had superfast broadband for six months.

We have several stepladders throughout the shop, and customers usually help themselves when they need them, occasionally asking if it is OK. Once, when I was clearing books from a house near Kirkcudbright (about 30 miles away), I spotted a set of very small spiral library steps. I asked the woman whose books I was buying if it was for children (thinking that I might ask if I could buy it for the children's section of the shop), to which she replied that it had been custom-made for Jimmy Clitheroe, the diminutive star of radio and television during the 1960s. She and her husband had helped clear the contents of his mother's house after they had both died (he had lived with her, and he died of an accidental overdose of sleeping pills on the day of her funeral). Apparently, they found hundreds of empty whisky bottles in the loft when they were clearing it out. I bought Jimmy Clitheroe's library steps from her for £20.

Till Total £88.50
5 Customers

DECEMBER

A well-known Edinburgh residenter sent round a crate of books to sell a month or two ago. He had been clearing out part of his library. We were glad to buy, and offered a good price. He rang up on the phone a few days later to acknowledge the cheque. 'I make only one stipulation,' he said. 'Every one of those books has my personal bookplate. I want them all steamed off before you offer them for sale.' There were between eighty and ninety volumes.

'I'm sorry, sir,' replied Mr Pumpherston. 'We are not a public laundry.'

'Then you can scrape them off with a sharp instrument,' said the man

'Nor a barber's shop either,' added Mr Pumpherston. 'You should have thought of that, sir, before you plaistered on the bookplates.'

Augustus Muir, *The Intimate Thoughts of John Baxter, Bookseller*

Bookplates are one of the many reasons that the second-hand book trade is endlessly fascinating. They are usually unique to the book owner, but there are the generic things that you can buy in card shops and the like, which have a picture of Garfield or Snoopy and just say 'Ex Libris' and leave a blank space for you to fill in your name before you peel off the adhesive tape and stick it on the endpaper, immediately reducing the value of the book. Custom-made bookplates, though, are a different matter altogether. Generally these would have been commissioned by the wealthy or the aristocracy, and more often than not they are heraldic, and come from country house libraries. Occasionally, though, book lovers commission something different, and you can sometimes recognise the hand of a well-known artist. I had one by Jessie M. King a few years ago. It was in a copy of Thorburn's *British Birds*, and had been custom-made for the owner of the library. It was a beautiful thing, and worth considerably more than the book. In aristocratic libraries, or where the owner has a coat of arms, this is usually what the bookplate shows, more often than not from a copperplate engraving, with the name of the current incumbent of whatever title it may be. The purpose of bookplates, rather like writing your name on the endpaper, was originally to ensure the book's return to its rightful owner when lent out, but they have become *objets d'art* in their own right.

Bookplates don't generally devalue books and frequently add value, depending on the owner or the artist involved. Removing them, however, does significantly devalue the book. Even a well-executed bookplate's removal will leave some damage. It used to happen that customers bringing in books to sell would have removed the front free endpaper in the mistaken belief that their name, written on the page, would devalue the book more than ripping the page out. Someone's name in ink on a blank page does very little, if anything, to reduce the value of a book, and, like endpapers, depending whose name it is, it can significantly increase the book's value. There are numerous books about bookplates, and even a Bookplate Society. Perhaps my favourite was from a collection I bought from the daughter of a man called Robin Hodge in Glasgow. It pictured a caveman wielding a club, and underneath were the words 'Gonna geezit back, eh?,' perfectly encapsulating the original purpose of the bookplate.

TUESDAY, 1 DECEMBER

Online orders: 1
Orders found: 1

Driving rain all day.

Hamish, a retired actor and regular customer who lives in nearby Bladnoch, came in this morning, presumably waiting for his prescription from the chemist, three doors up. He bought a book about Lancaster bombers. He has a keen interest in military history.

Another telephone call from The Pensions Regulator.

Pensions Regulator: Hello, is that Shaun Bythell?

Me: Yes.

Pensions Regulator: And your business address is 17 North Main Street, Wigtown?

Me: Yes.

Pensions Regulator: It's Anne from the Pensions Regulator here. We need to go through your declaration of compliance.

Me: Really? Do we have to do it now? When is it due?

Pensions Regulator: Seven months ago, so yes, we have to do it now.

Me: OK. What do you need to know?

Pensions Regulator: Firstly, your name.

Me: You've just called me by my name. You know what it is. You even pronounced it correctly.

Pensions Regulator: Yes, but you need to tell me what it is.

Me: Shaun Bythell.

Pensions Regulator: And your business name and address?

Me: You already know that too. You've just asked me if my business is at 17 North Main Street, Wigtown.

When the interminable conversation finally reached its conclusion, a customer came to the counter, holding a book open at the first page, on which were two different prices: 'I don't actually want to buy this book, but it has two prices in it. Which one is the correct price?'

At 3 p.m. there was a delivery of four boxes of books from Samye Ling.

Sandy the tattooed pagan turned up with his friend Lizzy. The last time he was here he bought her a copy of *The Hereditary Sheriffs of Galloway* for her Christmas present. Today she sneaked up to the counter and asked me if I could make a voucher for him for credit in the shop as his Christmas present. This will probably be the only Christmas trade I get this year.

I took thirty-seven boxes of rejected stock over to The Open Book after I'd closed the shop. I was going to take them to the recycling, but Finn asked me if they could have them.

Till Total £40.55

7 Customers

WEDNESDAY, 2 DECEMBER

Online orders: 3
Orders found: 2

One of today's orders was for a book in the theology section, but I couldn't get to it because of the agricultural feed bags from the Dalswinton deal.

The first customer of the day bought a £60 book on the history of driving horses.

Isabel was in to do the accounts all afternoon.

A wild-looking man with a huge beard brought in a box of books as a donation. Among them were *The Book of Grass: An Anthology of Indian Hemp*, *LSD: The Problem-Solving Psychedelic* and *Drugs of Hallucination*.

Reading *The Living Mountain* after work, I came across a passage that neatly summarises an element of the personality of the native Gallovidian:

> I remembered an old shepherd in Galloway, whom I had asked which spur of the hill I should take to go up Merrick. When he had told me, he looked at me and said, 'You've not been up before? Do you know what you're undertaking?' 'I've not been up before, but I've been all over the Cairngorms.' 'The Cairngorms, have you?' His gesture dismissed me.

This is a perfect example of the capacity of the people who live in this area to bring you crashing back down to earth if they suspect that you're getting above yourself. In many ways it's grounding and prevents one's ego from becoming too inflated, but equally I've seen it used to belittle people's genuine achievements.

Perhaps Nan Shepherd's desire to climb what is now prefixed with a definite article as 'The' Merrick—the highest of the hills in the south of Scotland—is because it shares with her beloved Cairngorms a granite rock base. The hard, igneous mineralogy that forms the Galloway Hills—once sharp edges, rounded by the unrelenting power of the retreating glaciers of the Ice Age—is not too dissimilar to that of the rugged mountains of her familiar Deeside range, and the mountain's familiarity may well have appealed to her more than the sharp lunar landscape of the Lewisian gneiss of the north-west of Scotland, so iconic in the popular perception of Scotland: Suilven, Torridon, Assynt—those exceptional, stunning, dramatic hills that form so small a part of the country, but which appear to have captured the imagination of those who have visited them so overwhelmingly that they have become the chocolate-box images of how the entire country is perceived. The flora and fauna of the Galloway Hills would have been more home to Nan Shepherd than the spiky inverted canines of the craggy Atlantic top-left quadrant of Scotland.

Once, when Callum and I were climbing in the Cairngorms, we took a route up Fiacaill Ridge in the depths of winter with a group of his friends. I genuinely thought I was going to die that day, as we picked our way up the icy, exposed face towards the summit, tethered together in what seemed like a suicide pact, but, put in the situation of 'returning were more tedious than go o'er,' we found our way to the top in spite of the terrifying drop to certain death if we failed, and after the ice climb I found a part of myself that I had not known before.

Till Total £179.49
7 Customers

THURSDAY, 3 DECEMBER

Online orders: 5
Orders found: 5

Among today's orders I found *A Pictorial History of Dumfries and Galloway Fire Brigade*. It was in the natural history section, and Nicky had listed it and put it there. As always, there will be an irrational explanation, although I'm not sure when I'll see her again. She has twenty-two weeks off—we agreed to compromise on this year's holiday entitlement and one year backdated—and she's said she plans to take them all back to back.

Wacek appeared at 9 a.m. with his builders and they set to work on scaffolding the chimney.

At about 4 p.m., as darkness was falling, a customer asked, 'Where did you get your lights from? They're really good.'

> Me: Which lights do you mean?
> Customer: The emotionally sensitive ones out the back.
> They come on really quickly.

I'm not sure if incredulity can be considered an emotion, but if it can, those lights should be blazing right now.

Skyped Granny. She talked for over an hour, barely letting me get a word in edgeways, and complaining that I never message her. She's clearly missing Scotland and threatening to come back.

Till Total £15
2 Customers

FRIDAY, 4 DECEMBER

Online orders: 3
Orders found: 3

Norrie in.

As we were sorting through the endless boxes of books, I found a book called *The English Tourist in Italy*, which contains the following extremely useful phrases:

> Your niece has very beautiful arms, how old is she?
>
> Whose trunks are these?
>
> You have eaten too many oranges.
>
> You have a cat which is very ugly.
>
> Mrs Folli is a beautiful woman, but her daughter is very ugly.
>
> You are as studious as my son, but you are not so intelligent as he is.
>
> I am angry with you.

I left the shop at eleven o'clock and drove to a house near Hawick (three hours away) whose owners wished to sell some of their books. It was a beautiful Georgian stately home, and from its appearance I was expecting an antiquarian library, but it was largely modern books, and not particularly interesting, but just about enough to make the trip worthwhile. I wrote the (relatively young) couple a cheque for £310. They were moving house and wanted to divest themselves of all the books that they hadn't already packed up, so I ended up taking all the books I didn't want, as well as those I did.

As I handed the cheque over, the man said, 'This must be the most profitable day of the year for you.' I assume that he was implying that I had just ripped them off—a bit much, considering they'd just sold their house, which, I imagine, must be worth over £1m.

Till Total £2.50
1 Customer

SATURDAY, 5 DECEMBER

Online orders: 3
Orders found: 2

Wild and wet again today.

No Internet connection when I opened the shop this morning, so I spent the first hour and a half working out how to repair it.

In our Amazon inbox this morning (when I eventually worked out how to get us back online) was a lengthy inquiry into the condition of a book, *The Paradox Men*, which is priced at 60p. Ian, my book dealer friend from Grimsby, is right. Years ago he predicted that with the relentless rise of Amazon and their prioritisation of customers at the expense of sellers, the day would come when people expect fine copies of books for almost nothing. This would have been a £10 book ten years ago.

Bum-Bag Dave came in at lunchtime. I made the mistake of letting him engage me in conversation. He rambled on endlessly about South America and how beautiful the women there are. He bought two books and managed to cover the counter with various revolting-looking things, including several tissues and a few crumpled receipts as he dug through his principal bum-bag in search of his wallet.

Till Total £159.55
8 Customers

MONDAY, 7 DECEMBER

Online orders: 4
Orders found: 1

Callum in at 10.30.

Very quiet day. Nicky and her friend Morag turned up to taunt me at about two o'clock. They're off metal-detecting tomorrow and wanted to borrow Anna's metal-detector, which is in the cellar.

I found a Victorian photograph album among some boxes of books, complete with photographs. Normally, when I come across these, the photographs have been removed, but these were mostly studio portraits, which may add a little to the value of the album.

At three o'clock Wacek appeared and told me that he'd finished repairing my neighbour's roof, and had fixed the chimney. When I asked him how they'd got the huge lump of granite up there, he told me that they'd cut it into three bits and lifted them and mortared them back in. It's a huge relief that it's fixed before the rest of the winter rains and frosts can cause further damage.

Till Total £161.99
7 Customers

TUESDAY, 8 DECEMBER

Online orders: 5
Orders found: 4

Calm, sunny day after what feels like weeks of storms.

All today's orders were from Amazon. I suspect that we may have been suspended from Abe again.

A man from the RSPB called Chris came to tell me about a book that he's producing. He was here for three hours. The book sounded quite interesting: it's a naturalist's notes on birds he'd seen in Wigtownshire between 1890 and 1935. The original naturalist was Jack McHaffie Gordon, whose grandfather owned (in the 1830s) the building that is now the shop.

My father dropped in after having his hair cut, and we discussed next year's fishing plans again.

After lunch I unloaded the boxes of books from the Hawick deal. Later, as I was thumbing through *The English Tourist in Italy* again I came across some even more useful phrases:

I have never known so avaricious a man as you.

Your ill-bred friends gathered all the ripe peaches in my garden, and took them away.

I cannot eat this bread, it is too stale.

You are a rude and selfish man, and this is the reason why they cannot endure you.

That Scotchman is very young.

Our King is better than your President.

Only one customer through the door all day.

Wacek and the boys finished taking down the scaffolding and headed off to their next job.

Till Total £25
1 Customer

WEDNESDAY, 9 DECEMBER

Online orders: 2
Orders found: 2

As I was looking for the orders this morning, one of which was for *William Maxwell to Robert Burns* (located in the Scottish poetry section), I spotted copies of Milton and Shelley's works in among the Scottish poetry. I sense the hand of Nicky, from whom, coincidentally, there was an email this morning: 'Here are a couple of helpful "festive" shots—hope you appreciate the robin! We did it especially for you—the robin was lying in the playpark where we went metal-detecting and found £6.76! Cool eh!' The 'festive' shots she was referring to consisted of photographs of a pile of empty bottles, on top of which was perched the stiffened corpse of a robin which she and Morag had clearly found when they were out yesterday.

There's something slightly unsavoury about metal-detecting in a children's playground, when you consider that the loose change they gathered probably fell from the pockets of children.

The lorry arrived with a delivery of pellets for the new boiler at 11 a.m., just as my mother dropped in to say hello. When I tried to explain to her that I needed to give the delivery men a hand unloading them, she replied, 'Yes, of course dear. You get on with that,' then continued to talk for the next ten minutes while the driver and his assistant wrestled with the sacks of pellets.

Email from someone called Ian Kitt with a list of books he wants to sell, so I emailed him back and asked him if he could bring them in.

Till Total £24.50
1 Customer

THURSDAY, 10 DECEMBER

Online orders: 1
Orders found: 1

The shop computer—which needs to be on twenty-four hours a day in order to receive orders—was locked in a 'restart' mode when I opened up this morning, so I spent the first hour working out how to get it running again.

The depressed elderly Welsh woman telephoned and surprised me by asking if we had any Wainwright guides, as opposed to her usual request for antiquarian theology. I responded by surprising her in return and telling her that yes, we have almost all of Wainwright's guides to the Lake District. 'Oh, can I have the cheapest one?' I found one priced at £4.50, she gave me her card details and I took her name and address.

There was an email from Anna at Wenlock Books when I checked this morning, suggesting that we run the Readers' Retreat again next year, this time in March. I replied that I would be very happy to do so.

The book signed by Bertrand Russell sold for £103 on eBay.

Seven customers through the door all day, and two of those commented, as they left the shop, that they wished they'd brought their glasses. It seems like a singular oversight to neglect to bring your glasses to a bookshop.

After closing, I set up the big room for the festival volunteers' dinner tomorrow night. Every year, once the hangover of the festival has worn off, the paid staff in the festival office organise a thank-you meal for the volunteers. This year we're having it here, in the Writers' Retreat.

Till Total £47.50
5 Customers

FRIDAY, 11 DECEMBER

Online orders: 0
Orders found: 0

Beautiful sunny day.

Maria arrived at 9.30 with all of her catering gear for tonight's meal, then headed off home.

No orders today, but I posted out the book signed by Bertrand Russell which sold on eBay yesterday for £103.

At lunchtime a white-haired man came to the counter and asked if we had a book about Mochrum, a nearby town, written by a local farmer. I showed the customer to a copy of it and left him sitting there for an hour, after which he left, saying, 'Thank you, but it's not quite what I'm looking for.'

Shortly before closing, a customer stopped me by the biography section and said, 'This might sound like a crazy question, but

[*pregnant pause, then whispering*] do you have any books in Dutch?'
I have to admit that I've heard crazier questions. Perhaps it was
code for something.

Shona and Maria arrived at 6 p.m. to set up for the Christmas
dinner. As they were doing so, Eliot arrived with his suitcase and
asked if he could stay the night. As always, he immediately kicked
off his shoes.

I went to Emily's Christmas opening gallery night at 6.30 and
bought a picture of a pig for my sister. On the way back about
a hundred people were gathered in the square singing carols for
the switching on of the Christmas lights. The volunteers' dinner
began at 7 p.m. and went on until about 1 a.m., with twenty-two
people being catered for by Maria. We ran out of wine and I had
to raid the cellar for more. Spent much of the evening being wine
waiter.

Till Total £54.49
4 Customers

SATURDAY, 12 DECEMBER

Online orders: 2
Orders found: 2

I got up early and cooked breakfast. Eliot left at eleven.

An elderly customer came to the counter with twelve books, all
relatively new. The total came to £65, and I told him that he could
have them for £60. Rather than show any kind of appreciation, he
said, 'Is that all the discount I'm getting? £5?'

No customers between 11.30 a.m. and 3.45 p.m., then nine
appeared within five minutes. None of them bought anything.

Spent the day sorting through boxes and bags of books. I've
barely made a dent in the massive pile of things to do.

After work I lit the fire and finished *The Living Mountain*. Sad
that it was published posthumously, as it is a brilliant, moving
book. Her description of the risks and joys of mountaineering,
skewed with hindsight, is particularly familiar and resonant:

But there is a phenomenon associated with this *feyness* of which I must confess a knowledge. Often, in my bed at home, I have remembered the places I have run lightly over with no sense of fear, and have gone cold to think of them. It seems to me that I could never go back; my fear unmans me, horror is in my mouth. Yet when I go back, the same leap of the spirit carries me up. God or no god, I am *fey* again.

The *feyness* of which she speaks will be something common to many who have tramped and climbed in Scottish hills and mountains; there's a sense of being in a disconnected world, at once familiar and unfamiliar.

Till Total £158.99
8 Customers

MONDAY, 14 DECEMBER

Online orders: 5
Orders found: 5

At 9.30 a.m. Maria came round to collect the plates and cutlery left here following the volunteers' dinner on Friday, and the fridge which has been in the kitchen since the festival. Just after she left, Petra dropped in to kill time while she was waiting for something or someone (I forget who). I'm not sure whether people who come in to kill time realise that they are killing my time too.

A customer looking for a Christmas present for a dyslexic nephew bought two Asterix books.

A Northern Irish customer came to the counter with three books and mauled them for a while, before pointing to a price sticker in one of them and asking 'Is that really £20?' When I confirmed that it was, he said 'No, that's too expensive' and replaced it on the shelf. There's a difference between a book being too expensive and a customer being too cheap.

Till Total £110.50
8 Customers

TUESDAY, 15 DECEMBER

Online orders: 2
Orders found: 1

My parents appeared at 11 a.m. for a chat. We covered my mother's usual favourite subjects: who's died, who's dying and who's got dementia.

A woman called to sign up her friend for the RBC as a Christmas present. Hopefully membership will prove to be a popular gift.

Later, as I was making a cup of tea, I heard a shout from downstairs. It was Ian Kitt, the man who had been emailing regarding the list of books he sent last week. He'd brought six boxes of them to the shop. Shortly afterwards a woman who had moved here from France with her husband and brought five boxes in a few weeks ago appeared. I pointed to the boxes she'd brought in last time and told her that I didn't want most of them. She told me that she had no room in her car because she'd brought me another seven boxes. I had to turn her away because the shop is now full of boxes.

I sorted through Ian Kitt's boxes of books. All in mint condition, checked a few prices online and gave him a cheque for £300. I feel like I'm drowning in books.

Till Total £76
3 Customers

WEDNESDAY, 16 DECEMBER

Online orders: 5
Orders found: 3

Chris Mills appeared at 9.15 to valet the van, which was in an embarrassing state. I've known Chris since 2000, when I worked on a documentary about the loss of the *Solway Harvester*, a scallop dredger that sank near the Isle of Man on 11 January of that year. His brother David was one of the crew.

In the morning I started going through the books that came in yesterday. Among them was a box of photography books in excellent condition, so I have emailed photographs of them to my friend Aíne, who is a collector of modern portrait photography books.

At 5 p.m. I went to lock up the shop and discovered that Chris had gone off with my van key after he'd finished cleaning the van. The shop key is attached to the van key, so I slid the curling stone we use as a doorstop behind the unlocked door and went for a pint with Callum.

Till Total £49
4 Customers

THURSDAY, 17 DECEMBER

Online orders: 7
Orders found: 7

At 9 a.m. a woman blasted the door open and stormed into the shop, laden down with bags, clearly full of books she wanted to sell. She headed at considerable speed through the shop shouting 'Hello' and completely ignoring my replies. Eventually she reappeared in the front of the shop, the obvious place for the counter, till and staff to be positioned, and said with some surprise, 'Oh, there you are.' She then asked me if I was interested in buying books. Every surface and space in the shop is now covered with books and boxes which I have yet to process and which have arrived in the past two weeks, so I told her that unless they're pretty special, I'm not interested. She began flinging the books from her bags all over the floor, and told me that they were very special hardbacks 'John Grisham, Dan Brown, James Patterson.' When I told her that I wasn't interested, she looked genuinely astonished.

After work I picked up my copy of *The Master and Margarita*, which I had interrupted to read *The Living Mountain,* and carried on with it. Granny was right: it's an extraordinary, brilliant book.

Till Total £70.50
6 Customers

FRIDAY, 18 DECEMBER

Online orders: 3
Orders found: 1

One of today's orders was for the two-volume *Lands and Their Owners in Galloway*, which Nicky had listed for £40, about £100 less than it is worth.

Dropped off the orders for the last few days at the post office. On the way in, I noticed that the part of the window where they post the notices of impending funerals was completely covered. Carol-Ann's mother, Alison, always used to say that as December crept on the number each week would always increase until, by Christmas, there was no more space for notices of the dead.

For today's blackboard I wrote a haiku:

> Christmas is hellish.
> Lose yourself in a bookshop;
> All will be well (ish).

Till Total £85.48
8 Customers

SATURDAY, 19 DECEMBER

Online orders: 7
Orders found: 7

I was looking for a book that I listed yesterday and for which we had an order this morning, and found that Nicky had put four books in a series called *Rivers of America* in the philosophy section.

Two of the books in today's orders were from the £300 lot that came in earlier in the week. So far, from the few that I've listed online, £210 worth have sold. Knock off the Amazon cut and that's about £150, which is a good, fast return. If only it was always like this.

In the afternoon I did the Christmas window for the shop: a pile of books in the shape of a Christmas tree, with some fairy lights around it. It's the most effort I've ever put into a Christmas window.

Till Total £236
8 Customers

MONDAY, 21 DECEMBER

Online orders: 14
Orders found: 12

Foul, wet and windy day, but it's the shortest day of the year, so once that is past there is—at least psychologically for me—a renewed sense of optimism. This would prove to be short-lived: Nicky appeared with a chest of drawers and four bags of books. She told me, with some glee, that she's not coming back to work for me again. I don't know what made me more sad, the news that she's not coming back or the fact that she seemed so delighted to be leaving a job that she so obviously once adored. It will be the end of a golden era in the shop.

Just the one customer by lunchtime, huffing and puffing his way around the shop. He managed to redeem himself by spending £50 and telling me—with no apparent sense of irony—about a bookshop in Cornwall that has a huge sign at the counter which reads 'NO ANECDOTES.'

As I was putting the labels on the parcels for the Random Book Club, a man with a German accent asked if we had a copy of *Mein Kampf*.

Till Total £174.98
11 Customers

TUESDAY, 22 DECEMBER

Online orders: 3
Orders found: 3

There was a parcel in today's post from Italy. I opened it to discover all manner of delicious treats—speck, pecorino, salami and a bottle of Barolo—along with a message from Granny: 'Eat this at Christmas, you shitty fucking bastard.'

I took the mail over to Wilma at the post office just before they closed for lunch, and asked her if she could give me £100 in pound coins. She whispered that William, who owns the post office, would be furious if he found out. Then, the moment he left the room, she shoved them through under the glass and told me to come back later with the notes to pay for them.

I was putting more books out from the £300 buy last week when I noticed that—by pure coincidence—all our Scottish mountaineering books are located on shelf K2 in the Scottish room.

Till Total £135.99
14 Customers

WEDNESDAY, 23 DECEMBER

Online orders: 3
Orders found: 3

Jeff the minister called in at 10.30. He's back to travelling by bus again, now that we're into the depths of winter. He spent a while looking for something in the theology section to inspire his Christmas sermon. It seems that the Kirk is keen to move him out from the manse, where he's lived since his appointment here several decades ago. When I asked him where he was moving to, he replied 'I have no idea. I'm like Abraham, standing on a hill and shouting "Ur".' I had no idea what he was talking about, but I have no doubt whatsoever that it would mean something to someone.

In the post this morning were two Christmas cards, one addressed to 'King Prawn' and the other to 'Masterful Shaun Bythell.'

At 11 a.m. I went upstairs to make myself a cup of tea and briefly warm myself in the relative heat of the kitchen. On my way back downstairs I was surprised to find Mole-Man working his way through the art section on the first landing. He didn't even look up at me as I passed him, so engrossed was he in a book of Dürer's woodcuts. I suspect he's buying himself Christmas presents.

I spent the afternoon pricing up books and putting them on the shelves, returning from a lengthy spell in the Railway Room to see the familiar site of Mole-Man at the counter, although this time from a different angle. I worked my way through his pile of books, which included two on climbing (he doesn't strike me as an outdoorsman, but I may be wrong), a book on timber preservation, a history of Portugal, the Dürer woodcut book and one on the geology of West Yorkshire. The last title caused me to question an assumption that I've made since his first appearance: that Mole-Man is Scottish. Since I've never heard him speak, I have no idea whether or not this is the case. If he is indeed from Yorkshire, then he's one of a very rare line of that breed who never ask for a discount. Perhaps I've subconsciously picked up that he always pays with Scottish notes, or something that leads me to believe he is a Scot.

As he left the shop I almost thought that I'd seen him smile, but it may have been trapped wind.

Till Total £40
5 Customers

THURSDAY, 24 DECEMBER

Online orders: 0
Orders found: 0

In today's post was a card addressed to 'Shaun Bythell, Belligerent Bookseller.'

Email in the Amazon inbox:

> I regret to say I am very disappointed with this order. The
> book was described as 'Used—very good' condition. No

mention was made of the fact that it was an ex-library book. The frontispiece was cut out, 'cancelled' was stamped on the next page and the page edges, and the book was extremely grubby and smelt fusty. The book was intended as a Christmas gift and the recipient will probably just be pleased to have a copy of this out of print book. However I do feel your description of the condition of the book was inaccurate.

I look forward to receiving your reply.

The book in question was £2, so I have given her a full refund. Ah, the spirit of Christmas washes over everyone.

Often the shop is busy on Christmas Eve, as frantic farmers panic to make sure there's something under the tree for their wives, and often people come up early to visit family for the festive period, but the latter depends entirely on what day of the week Christmas falls: taking a couple of extra days off can mean a week off if Christmas Day is a Monday or a Thursday. This year I suspect that the working population who descend on relations in Galloway will be driving up or down today. Perhaps the period between Christmas and New Year will be better.

Till Total £86.94
10 Customers

FRIDAY, 25 DECEMBER

Online orders:
Orders found:

Closed.

Woke up to discover that the door to the spare bedroom in which the cat has taken to sleeping lately, and which I always leave open for the fat fiend, was firmly closed. It's the bedroom on the top landing next to my bedroom, and isn't vulnerable to the vagaries of the draughts that whistle through the shop. I'm quite certain that it was open last night when I went to bed. This morning, when I opened it, Captain shot out like an Olympic sprinter on laxatives with an eye on the loo.

At lunchtime, I cycled the 5 miles to my parents' house for lunch with their friends Bill and Tess. Bill is in his nineties and one of my favourite people, and Tess is wickedly entertaining too, so the bike ride back in the half-light was fuelled by wine and laughter.

Home and read most of the rest of *The New Confessions*. It is starting to read like a practice run for *Any Human Heart*. Extremely good, and thoroughly researched and informed, but slightly lacking the warmth of the later book.

SATURDAY, 26 DECEMBER

Online orders: 5
Orders found: 5

Opened the shop at 10 a.m. The first customer appeared at 2.45, to return a £3 copy of a Simenon novel, green Penguin, which I'd sold to a nervous farmer on Christmas Eve for his wife. It turned out that she had—as he was worried—already read it. Not the most auspicious of starts to what is normally the busiest week of the winter.

I picked and packed the orders and took them to the post office. I opened the door to be met by William, so I asked him if it was open. He just grunted 'No' at me, then turned around and carried on with whatever it was he had been doing, without the slightest pleasantry.

I wrote another haiku for the blackboard:

> Boxing day is here.
> Run away to a bookshop:
> Escape the fake cheer.

Only one other customer appeared and she told me that she was only here 'to get out of the rain.'

In all, it wasn't worth bothering opening the shop. Although there are people around, they probably assumed we'd be closed.

Till Total £44.30
6 Customers

MONDAY, 28 DECEMBER

Online orders: 7

Orders found: 5

Packed up the orders and took them over to the post office, which was shut again.

Telephone call at 10 a.m. from a customer looking for a local history book:

> Customer: I'm looking for a book called *Borgue Academy*, written by Adam Gray.
>
> Me: Yes, we've got three copies of that.
>
> Customer: Let me tell you why I'm looking for it. We're off to New Zealand next week, and we're visiting someone whose father was from this area and we thought it would be nice etc ...

I have no idea why people feel the need to offer lengthy explanations as to why they're looking for particular titles—it's not as though it makes any difference to whether or not we've got the book in stock, but it never seems to stop them.

The shop was completely dead until 11.30, at which point twenty-two people came in, an extended Jewish family. Most of them bought something, including copies of *Three Things You Need to Know About Rockets*.

Four former employees ganged up on me and decided that we should have had a Christmas party in the shop, so I invited my sister and her husband too. Catherine, who was in the Readers' Retreat back in February, arrived with her son Miles, on their way back south from Christmas in the Highlands, and the Spanish couple who are running The Open Book came too. Christmas is normally a time of year when everyone else has time off but I don't. In fact, I usually end up working more hours than usual and generally on my own, so to be forced by former employees to have a party in the house, and for other people to turn up out of the blue, lent the place a convivial atmosphere and for the first time in years I felt a bit of Christmas spirit. But not much.

Bed at 3.30 a.m.

Till Total £101.48
9 Customers

TUESDAY, 29 DECEMBER

Online orders: 3
Orders found: 2

I opened the shop at 10 a.m. with a hangover, but to my delight everyone else had tidied up the house after last night's celebrations. I have no idea when they did it, but it was an enormous relief to come down to a clean kitchen.

In the post today was a letter from the planning department telling me that they've approved planning permission for the concrete book spirals. The sense of relief was almost physical: I had to sit down after I'd absorbed the news. A customer came in at eleven o'clock and asked for 'religious books,' so I pointed him at the theology section. After about a minute he returned to the counter and asked, 'Do you have a list of your books, or do I just have to stare at them?'

Catherine and Miles left at about noon.

A young woman bought a copy of the Kama Sutra and offered to do a reading from it for Facebook. I thought it best to decline.

There's more wintery weather coming; Storm Frank is forecast to bring heavy rain and high winds tonight and tomorrow.

Finished *The Master and Margarita* at midnight, as the howling wind and lashing rain beat at the front of the house. It was nothing like I'd expected, or anything I'd read before. It's an extraordinary book, the cleverest and most wonderfully evocative use of the supernatural of any book I've read, although Hogg's *Justified Sinner* might pip it at the post, now that I think about it.

Till Total £132.99
13 Customers

318

WEDNESDAY, 30 DECEMBER

Online orders: 5
Orders found: 4

Torrential rain all night and this morning thanks to Storm Frank. Apparently Newton Stewart (7 miles away) is badly flooded, with hundreds of people evacuated from their homes and put up in the Macmillan hall.

Callum came in to tile the kitchen and the bathroom in the bothy.

Maya Tolstoy called in to say hello at lunchtime. Her mother, Margie, lives in the Old Station House in Wigtown and is a wonderful woman, generous to a fault, and with a towering intellect. I met Maya a few years ago at Margie's and we became friends. She—like her mother—is enormously intelligent and charming. She lives in New York but comes back to Scotland as often as she can to visit her parents. At the same time Jess Pym, whose parents live locally, also popped in to say hello, then Tom and Willeke appeared too, to discuss Hogmanay plans. The shop can very easily become a bit of a social hub for estranged Gallovidians at this time of year. I was hoping to have a night in on my own, but they're insisting that we all get together. Christmas holidays are a strange time when you have a shop whose income is almost totally dependent on footfall. Everyone is on holiday and wants to have a good time, but for me it's essential that the shop is open, so I can't really join in. I suppose it suits my misanthropic nature to have an excuse to avoid being sociable, the party a few nights ago being the exception.

Paula (one of the two Spanish women running The Open Book) came to ask me if I could scan and print copies of a poster that she's made inviting everyone in the town to come to the shop at 4 p.m. tomorrow to share the Spanish new year tradition of eating grapes.

At 1.01 p.m. the Internet and the mobile phone networks went down across the whole peninsula, so I went to the post office to get an update on what was going on. They've shut down the electricity sub-station in Newton Stewart because of the floods.

At three o'clock I spotted a butterfly on the lamp in the shop. It flew around for a while, to the wonder of the customers until it disappeared. The bloody cat probably ate it. He has a penchant for butterflies. When I went to the co-op to pick up a loaf of bread after I'd closed the shop, I discovered that people had been panic buying because of the floods (we are officially cut off) and the shelves were completely bare, so I scratched around in the cupboards at home and found flour and yeast, and had a go at making my own. The result was a substance so dense that I suspect I may have created a new element. Periodic table, make space for Bythellium.

Finished *The New Confessions* after work. Adored it. In another example of injustice beyond his control, Todd falls victim to the McCarthy witch hunts. I won't ruin the ending, although I've probably ruined the rest of it. Doomed relationships, moving in exalted cultural circles, disasters—it really is a template for *Any Human Heart*.

Till Total £185.50
11 Customers

THURSDAY, 31 DECEMBER

Online orders:
Orders found:

Awoke at 6.30 to the news that Newton Stewart's flooding is so bad that it's made the national news. The River Cree burst its banks, and the whole of Princes Street was flooded.

The Internet was still down because of the flooding, so I couldn't check the online orders.

Jeff the minister dropped in at ten o'clock to kill fifteen minutes while he waited for the bus. He spotted my copy of *Any Human Heart* on the counter and told me how much he'd enjoyed *A Good Man in Africa*. We had a very interesting chat about contemporary fiction. He's into Jonathan Franzen at the moment, an author I've never read.

Dropped off a parcel at the post office. Wilma has modified the Christmas opening hours notice. Perhaps a judicious insertion of the word 'not' between 'We're' and 'here' might have been more accurate:

The mobile phone signal came back at 11 a.m., but still no Internet connection. What little frustration this is causing me is significantly outweighed by the fact that, since I can't deal with the orders or list books online, I have the luxury of having little option but to read a book, so I started reading another spoof autobiography, *Augustus Carp, Esq., by Himself*, a book I'd never heard of, but which Anna found in a bookshop in Edinburgh and thought I'd enjoy. This is more like the old days, before the tyranny of the Internet, and it was an enormous pleasure to spend the entire day reading, with a few interruptions, *Augustus Carp*, which so far has proved to be one of the funniest books I've read in a long time. Augustus, the narrator of his own life as he sees it, is magnificently pompous, self-righteous and completely hypocritical. He has much in common with Ignatius Reilly in *A Confederacy of Dunces*, and I wonder if John Kennedy Toole had read it before he put pen to paper.

Sophie Dixon, a friend I first met ten years ago, dropped in for a cup of coffee and a chat on her way to stay with mutual friends for Hogmanay. They very kindly invited me too, but I had already agreed to spend the evening with Tom and Willeke, Callum and the Spanish women from The Open Book.

An old woman came in with a middle-aged, considerably over-weight man. She introduced him (with a broad Geordie accent) as her son. 'He's come up from London. He always comes to this shop when he's here. He loves it.' Two hours later, as they left, she said, 'This is the first time he's left here empty-handed'—words guaranteed to make you question the quality of your stock.

We were back online at 5.30, too late to pick and pack the orders and get them to the post office in time for collection, so now they'll have to wait until Tuesday.

After I closed the shop, I went to the pub with Tom, Willeke, Callum, Sigrid and the Spanish women. The atmosphere was dismal so we all came back here after about an hour and cooked up a load of pizzas and drank until about 1 a.m. They all stayed the night, apart from the Spanish women, who went back to The Open Book. For several years I celebrated Hogmanay with twenty or so friends in the Loch Maree Hotel, which we booked for a week (it closes for the winter, but we managed to convince the owner to give us the key). It was always a highlight of the year, and often the highland landscape was dusted with snow for it. Recently, though, Hogmanay has become a more sedate, often solitary, affair, so it was a pleasure to see out the old year and bring in the new one in the company of friends.

Till Total £202.49
17 Customers

EPILOGUE

The shop is now busier than it was when I wrote this year of the diary, in part—I think—because people have begun to realise that online trade has an impact on the high street. Now that more than 50 per cent of retail purchases are made online, it is unlikely that the trend will reverse, but nobody wants to live in a place where shops are closing all around them and nothing is moving in to fill the void. Even governments have finally begun to recognise that the demise of the high street and the questionable tax affairs of online giants are having a deleterious effect on people's lives.

Nicky, as far as I know, is happily managing a woodland about 12 miles away.

Granny has moved back and forth between Wigtown and Italy but seems determined to settle in Galloway, where her eccentricities are appreciated in a way that they might not be in a more conventional place. Her eyesight has deteriorated at the same rate that her confidence has appreciated, and her sophisticated Italian appearance—once so alien to the townscape—has now been absorbed into the place to the point that she is part of the fabric. Her absence would now be as noted as her appearance once was.

Anna and I remain friends, and I hope we always will.

Captain has continued to increase in weight, but not intelligence, although he still charms customers on a daily basis.

A NOTE ON THE TYPE

Confessions of a Bookseller has been set in Granjon LT Standard, a typeface designed in 1928 by George Jones for Linotype and named for the sixteenth-century French printer, publisher, and lettercutter Robert Granjon. The display has been set in various styles of Gill Sans, a typeface based on the sans-serif lettering originally designed for the London Underground.